Some English Dictators

HENRY VIII

From the painting by Hans Holbein

Some English Dictators

BY

MILTON WALDMAN

KENNIKAT PRESS
Port Washington, N. Y./London

SOME ENGLISH DICTATORS

First published in 1940
Reissued in 1970 by Kennikat Press
Library of Congress Catalog Card No: 77-112820
ISBN 0-8046-1087-8

Manufactured by Taylor Publishing Company   Dallas, Texas

PREFACE

THIS book has a twofold purpose: to tell the story of the dictatorship which ruled in England almost continuously for 150 years; and to portray in their dictatorial capacity the characters of its three most successful exponents, Henry VIII, Elizabeth and Oliver Cromwell.

In practice the two are, of course, inseparable. Events and personality constitute a dynamic equation, a system of action and reaction so exact that neither can affect the other without being affected in equal degree. Yet in strict reason they are curiously irreconcilable. For events taken by themselves strongly suggest a principle of design in history which personality flatly contradicts. Personality may modify events, but it is scarcely deniable that they remain in general subject to the great prevailing tendencies of their time, which themselves appear to be subject to some mysterious and inexorable law of repetition. Of this the phenomenon of dictatorship is a conspicuous example. Over and over again the same or very similar conditions, the same familiar desires, fears and passions, have brought it about that the power previously distributed amongst the many or the few has been concentrated absolutely in the hands of the one. The circumstances may be widely dissimilar but the symptoms are recognizably akin. Repetition denotes pattern and pattern signifies design.

But there is also the incalculable force of accident, subject to no principle and insubordinate to any discernible pattern: the sudden cataclysm of nature, the unlooked for and seemingly irrelevant discovery, the missing horseshoe nail for want of which the battle and kingdom

are lost. And of all the manifestations of accident the most
unaccountable, fascinating and potent is surely human
personality.

Accompanying this book are four portraits. The story
they tell would seem to mock any pretended obedience of
events to design. Substitute the fine, proud, sensitive
countenance of Charles I for the brutal, arrogant, domineer-
ing features of Henry VIII; both men believed with the
same unshakable conviction in the same autocratic principle; yet is it conceivable that Charles in Henry's place
would have made so consummate a success of favouring
though stormy circumstances or that Henry in Charles's would
have succumbed so utterly to adverse ones? Could Cromwell,
on the face of him Charles's foredoomed master, have been
Elizabeth's, whether in her time or his? Somehow, looking
at her, one doubts it. And if one compares Elizabeth's
handling of Parliament in 1566 with Charles's in 1628, it
becomes doubtful whether he would even have had the
chance to be: whether he would, in fact, ever have been
heard of at all. And *then* to what issue would the decay of
the dictatorship, sooner or later inevitable, have led in his
absence?

Perhaps what appears to be design is mere coincidence.
Perhaps what appears to be accident is really an unas-
sorted fragment in an inscrutable design. We cannot know:
the first hypothesis offends instinct and the second tran-
scends reason. Between the impossible assumption of
eternal chaos implied in the one and the uncapturable
certainty of ultimate perfection inherent in the other, we
can but pursue understanding along the narrow and elastic
frontier where the two overlap in the dictum that no historical experience ever entirely repeats itself and none ever
entirely fails to repeat itself. And if that be true, it must
follow that to stress events at the expense of personality is
to disparage the element of variation without which history

would not exist, while to stress personality at the expense of events is to slight the element of repetition, without which it would be meaningless.

The first chapter is outside the temporal scheme of the book, just as its subject, John, is a sport, a freak in relation to its general theme. Henry VIII, Elizabeth and Cromwell represent the fortunate conjunction of personal character and current trend; they swam with and at the same time harnessed the tide, so to speak. Charles I, though apparently swimming with it but lacking their ability to harness it, was overborne by it. John, with all their energy and genius, nevertheless failed as dismally as did Charles because he insisted on swimming against it. He was a turbulent accident striving vainly with a hostile contemporary pattern: the pattern majestically traced in Magna Carta and again in the Bill of Rights on its next emergence after four hundred years.

CONTENTS

LIST OF PLATES

CHAPTER I

John, the Spoiled Child

LIBERTY is the rule of the majority. Liberty is the protection of the minority against the tyranny of the majority. It is the bulwark of the weak against the strong; the illusion with which the strong dupe the weak. In its name men have overthrown despotisms; to guard it they have set up despots. It is a paradox, since the only logical form of it is anarchy and the only practical form is order. It is a series of self-evident propositions all of which can be honourably disputed. " Taxation without representation is tyranny." Is taxation by the representatives of those who have nothing to tax then liberty? And if so, for whom? Is an able-bodied unemployable man who faints from hunger in the act of registering his sovereign will at the polls in enjoyment of liberty? Is the Englishman's melodious conviction that " Britons never shall be slaves " on another scale of truth from the Italian's that

> " *Noi saremo la mitraglia*
> *Della santa libertà* "?

What *is* liberty?

Its dilemmas arise from the fact that it is an end which must also serve as a means, a commodity as well as an ideal. An ideal for the adjustment of human relations, a commodity employed to further other ideals. The French Revolution set out to establish the principle of free institutions because they seemed likely to favour the general welfare, safety, and dignity. When they seemed likely not to, another

1

system of adjustment was tried. The history of liberty seems to show that those communities do best out of it which know just how far to treat it as an ideal, " a value beyond inestimable treasure ", and how far as a commodity which, like other human commodities, is worth approximately what can be got or has to be given for it.

None has done better out of it than England, who gave an empire for it in the thirteenth century, got unity and riches for it in the sixteenth, and in the end managed to have the lot. The choice in each case was as straightforward as such choices can be. Two kings, John and Henry VIII, held their own will to be the supreme law. So far as character, conduct, and power of giving offence went there was not a great deal to choose between them. Neither stuck at killing an inconvenient rival, marrying a lady he had no business to marry, warring against Holy Church, or annexing his subjects' rights and other valuables. In fact Henry VIII, the successful one, considerably outdid John, the unsuccessful, in all these respects. No doubt the Dark Ages took murder, marriage, and religion more seriously than did the Age of Enlightenment, but it was not the reform of John's morals that his subjects primarily demanded—it was the liberty of which England is no less proud than of the price she later obtained for it from Henry and Henry's daughter.

The nature of that liberty was defined by the operation of the unwritten contract known as feudalism. Its subject matter was the relations between men rising out of the land which they occupied. The owner for the time being of any parcel of it was simultaneously landlord to tenants of smaller parcels under him and tenant to the landlord of a larger parcel over him, until one reached the landless labourer at the bottom, who virtually belonged to the land, and the king at the top, to whom the whole land vaguely belonged as tenant-in-chief on earth of God who created it.

As landlord each man owned certain obligations from the man below him and owed them to the man above him: rentals in money or kind, service in arms or household, special payments or "reliefs" on various specified occasions, such as the marriage of the superior's eldest daughter, the knighting of his eldest son, ransom to release him from captivity in war. As tenant each man owed security and justice to the man below and was owed them by the man above.

If the length of time a system endures is any measure of the amount of satisfaction it gives, then the feudal system was about as satisfactory as any ever evolved, since it lasted over most of Europe for the better part of a thousand years —perhaps because it recognized no antithesis between the economic and the moral basis of society. It rested solidly upon the land, in an age when all men lived by the land and most men by the labour they devoted to the land; and its fundamental tenet held that the land belonged to everybody and to nobody. To everybody to the extent needed to support existence, to nobody to the extent of depriving others of the means of existence. For every obligation a right, for every right a corresponding obligation, and liberty consisted of an honest balance between them. Like all systems, it favoured the few, but, unlike most, not to the disinheritance of the many. Even the serf had rights, even the king obligations.

It was an exceedingly loose system. That was its virtue, as well as the disease of which it was ultimately to die. The principle of authority, instead of being concentrated in a central government, was dispersed downwards and outwards until it became next to impossible to find it. A man's first loyalty was to the lord from whom he held his parcel of land, his public duty virtually nil outside the mutual understanding on which he held it. To his lord's manorial court he brought his disputes with his neighbours, answered for his trespasses, protested against overcharges on his produce or violation of his rights to pasture on the manor's common lands, kill game or cut timber in its common forests, fish in its common streams. For his lord he performed the various duties of citizenship, such as paying taxes, bearing arms, assisting justice, and the like. The lords of the manor went through the same process with regard to their baronial overlords. Thus, then, in the affairs of everyday life the king's sovereignty made itself directly felt only upon the superior vassals who owed him personal allegiance, paid him his revenues, and stood between his will and its effect on the great body of his subjects.

But there were also affairs, some of them of the highest importance, not of everyday life; loose ends of the feudal contract growing out of the fact that England was already something more than a geographical term for a shaggy area of farm-, pasture-, and wood-land divided and subdivided by invisible lines amongst some two million individuals. It had interests independent of any manor's, larger than all of their interests put together—internal peace, for instance, without which other activities could only be carried on precariously or not at all. A lord might keep the peace in his own domains, but who was to keep the peace between the lords? Or to enforce justice in a dispute referred to a local court in which the judge, or the judge's master, might be one of the parties? Moreover, few manors produced all that they consumed or consumed all that they produced. Exchange of goods meant markets and markets meant cities, corporate bodies exceedingly difficult to fit into a social scheme based upon persons. Beyond its primitive state trade demanded a uniform currency, fostering tariffs at home and a protection at sea which the lords of the land were in no position to supply. And beyond that lay the problems of diplomacy and war, involving at times the stark choice between a surrender of individual will or submission to collective disaster.

Who was to grasp those loose ends? If they were joined to the general downward and outward pull, the whole structure might collapse at the bottom. But if they were seized by an inward and upward force, they might concentrate too much strength at the top. It was the old dilemma of liberty and authority again. In England, owing to certain special circumstances, the answer had been given tentatively in favour of the second solution. John's great-great-grandfather, William the Conqueror, had brought over with him from Normandy a theory of kingship that was the awe of contemporary Europe. His nominal suzerain, the King of France, had had nothing to say in the duchy, and even in his own domains nothing like the say to his barons that William had to his. Fortified by the very fact of being the Conqueror, he had been able to transplant his prerogative to the more laxly organized England of the Saxons. Under his rule and that of such capable successors as his son, Henry I, and John's father, Henry II, the great territorial magnates had had taken from them the more showy attributes of sovereignty which they enjoyed elsewhere. They might not make war on one another or alliances with foreign princes against their own. They were forbidden to dispense high justice or strike their own coins. Instead of commanding office by privilege of rank, they were called to it by royal invitation. Along with felons and other disturbers of the peace, they could in certain instances be cited before the king's courts in London or the shires to answer for abuses of justice in their own. At times of grave national emergency the king's sheriffs had successfully cut across the horizontal feudal boundaries to raise levies for the king's service. The towns had their charters from him, commerce looked to him for security at home and abroad. He had even exercised, though he had far from established, the right to tax his subjects directly when in need of money beyond what custom allotted him. Dimly upon the living stone of the feudal pyramid had already been sketched at John's accession, on 6th April, 1199, the outline of the Eiffel Tower-like national state.

The process was still far from irreversible. In façt those who hated it, in particular the great and powerful who suffered most from it, fully expected to reverse it under John. It had been largely a personal process, like nearly everything else in that age, gathering or losing momentum according to the character of the reigning king; gathering it rapidly of late through the skill and experience of Henry II and the determination and enormous popularity of his elder son, Richard I. But Henry had had the misfortune to kill a saint—an evil omen, men thought, for the monarchy as well aṣ the monarch—and the Lion-Hearted to be killed at forty-one by a cross-bolt in the neck during a quarrel over a treasure-trove with one of his French vassals. His successor was neither experienced nor popular, and nothing in his record gave reason to suppose that he would prove either skilful or determined.

He loved power, like any Plantagenet, but he loved his stomach more and he hated work. Energy he had in plenty but, as with his money and his sense of humour, rarely chose the right place to spend it. He had brains, too, and enough charm to make people's heads spin, but a thoroughly good spoiling by his parents, whose adored Benjamin he was, had somewhat perverted these gifts into a cunning and petulance not uncommon with spoiled children. It had been one of Henry II's great regrets that after satisfying his elder sons he had nothing to bestow on his youngest—whom in consequence he apologetically nicknamed Lackland—and a good part of his life he devoted to making the deficiency good. When the lad was seventeen he gave him an army to go and carve himself an estate out of his brother Richard's duchy of Aquitaine, but Richard showed himself so well able to look after his own that the project miscarried. Two years later Henry sent him with another army to become King of Ireland: the style he kept in Dublin on their pay while they starved in the bogs did not recommend him to his soldiers, however, nor did the Irish chieftains who had come to render him obedience appreciate his quips at their clothes and manners and his playful tweaks of their long pointed beards. In the end he was forced to return to his father with an exhaustive report on why Ireland could not be governed.

Moreover, he succeeded Richard under the handicap of a doubt that he was rightfully king at all. Strictly speaking, his nephew Arthur, posthumous son of his elder brother Geoffrey, had a better claim, but the law of succession was still somewhat elastic. It became a matter of who could get there first, and John, a man of thirty-two, had all the advantage of mobility over Arthur, who was only twelve and unable to move without his mother. Within seven weeks he had got himself acknowledged over nearly all of his family's vast dominions, including the northern and western half of France, and had been crowned in Westminster Abbey. But for all that he got so readily he had to give something: the usual pledges to the Church and to his French vassals, an even more solemn pledge to his English vassals and chartered towns that he would sustain them in their old privileges even as against the new power of the Crown. In short, having no absolute title to rule from God, he had to obtain an elective title subject to the limitations imposed upon his rule by the feudal contract.

If election promises are not to be kept, they had better be evaded with grace or broken with apology. John, the spoiled child, took the trouble to do neither. At his installation as Duke of Normandy, he turned to the giddy young gentlemen of his train, with whom he was carrying on a running repartee, and flung them a particularly good one at the moment of receiving the lance, with the result that the sacred symbol eluded his hand and clattered ominously to the floor. A month later, in England, after his coronation, at which the Archbishop of Canterbury pointedly alluded to the elective nature of his office, he published a resounding proclamation giving his claim by blood the maximum and his subjects' consent the minimum of credit for his elevation. To treat the ceremony of investiture, regarded as the solemn consecration of the mutual pledges between ruler and ruled, in a spirit of comedy and then make a bonfire of his election platform was an almost unnecessarily fair warning of his real sentiments and intentions.

Nor did he wait long to translate them into action. He had been married for nearly ten years to Isabel of Gloucester, by whom he had no children. Now wanting some for good dynastic reasons, he divorced his wife in the episcopal courts on the ground of a blood-relationship for which no proper dispensation had been obtained. No one seems to have objected, particularly since he proposed to contract a useful alliance with a Portuguese princess. But in the course of a tour of his French possessions he came to the castle of the Count de la Marche, in Poitou, where he saw and promptly fell in love with another Isabel, the very lovely twelve-year-old daughter of the Count of Angoulême, who was staying at the castle as the affianced bride of the heir. By every law of God and man as then understood he should have let the girl alone. But he wanted her, he was in a position to get her, and by doing so made it plain that he did not care a rap about the law.

Other people did. The la Marche's neighbours appealed to the King of France, Philip Augustus, John's suzerain outside England. Philip, implacable enemy of English power in France, was only too glad to entertain the cause.

He ordered John to Paris. John haughtily denied that a King of England could be haled before any tribunal whatever—the plea to be made effective by Henry VIII in similar circumstances three hundred years later. Philip answered relevantly that he stood accused not as King of England but as Count of Poitou. When he still failed to appear, the court declared his possessions in France forfeit for neglect of feudal duty. Laying aside the robe of judge, Philip put on his armour to execute the verdict.

If he succeeded, the forfeited estates would revert to Arthur, whom he immediately invested with them (save Normandy, the largest) and affianced to his daughter. But John in a dashing raid swooped down on his nephew and imprisoned him at Falaise. So far so good: and had John done no worse his energy might yet have got him out of the scrape his morals had got him into. By inviolable custom Arthur, as Count of Brittany, was entitled to be ransomed by his vassals, to whom John had, moreover, in order to win their support against Philip, sworn an oath in writing to deal with Arthur according to their judgment if he fell into his hands. They duly appeared to claim him, John duly broke his word, and Arthur disappeared for ever. What probably happened to him, what his contemporaries suspected to have happened to him, is that John tried to have him maimed, by blinding or otherwise, so as to unfit him for rule, but that his jailer proving too soft-hearted, John either found a ruffian to kill him or did the job himself.

No crime could have been more useless. Arthur's claims, instead of dying with him, passed into the abler and greedier grasp of his overlord Philip. The nobles of Brittany, of course, went into rebellion. Of John's other vassals many did the same or held aloof in disgust, even the English, despite the danger to their own extensive holdings in France. Within two years of Arthur's death Philip had overrun all but the south-western corner of John's overseas inheritance.

Neither John nor England was inclined to let it go at that. For one thing, he could not have afforded to; no ruler that ever lived could have. He had cost his people dear in pride as well as in pocket, and unless he made good the consequences of his folly, they would sooner or later see to it that he had no power to commit more follies. But in order to regain what he had lost he had once and for all to make up his mind to a momentous choice: whether to invite their support in the enterprise as responsible partners in the commonwealth, or to browbeat them into such subjection as to be independent of their support. No one could say for certain which method was the better in the circumstances—only character could determine which would be tried. And character did. Nearly everything that happened in the first six years of John's reign led up to this decision, and a very large part of what Englishmen understand by liberty followed from it.

To do what he wanted he had to have money, the first need of all governments. So much so, in fact, that the history of liberty in any country is largely the history of its finances. In theory the king was supposed to " live of his own ", that is, meet the ordinary expenses of the Crown out of his private income. But this was no longer possible, even apart from John's personal extravagance. Long ago his predecessors had been compelled, in order to run their new machinery of centralization—courts, a spreading administrative system, and the like—to impose various special taxes as occasion arose; and John had already stretched the expedient a good deal further. Still he was short, owing in part to the wide discrepancy that then existed between the invention of revenues and their collection. The reconquest of France would cost incalculable sums, which the lost provinces themselves could obviously not be expected for the present to pay. To compel them from his English subjects—since he was not minded to solicit their voluntary co-operation—was only feasible with a force of mercenaries at his back. Mercenaries, as their name implied, did not fight for nothing. In this extremity he thought of the Church.

It was a natural but risky thing to do. Natural because the Church had the money to endow any despotism, risky because she also had the resources to break any despot, as she had shown a century before when Pope Gregory VII kept the Holy Roman Emperor standing three days barefoot in the snow to await his pleasure. She was stronger now than she had been then, and her present head, Innocent III, even less to be trifled with. No king could altogether rule without her. Her priests guided the minds of his people, thus establishing a platform from which her prelates could in many cases direct the policy of his kingdom. Everywhere she owned her own lands, collected her own revenues, made her own laws. Even in England, where her political pretensions had so far been on the whole most successfully resisted, she had been able to put up a better fight against the monarchy than the barons had done.

It had not been an easy fight. The Conqueror, while otherwise granting her independence of the state, had forced her into dependence upon the king. He chose her high officers and approved the laws she made for her own government; without his consent she might not receive or obey any papal decree. From Henry I she gained after a furious struggle a voice in the election of her own Bishops and their right to spiritual investiture with ring and staff by the Pope—an apparently trivial victory in that the king still nominated them to their sees and invested them with the episcopal property in their capacity of vassal, but of profound significance in establishing for the future the Church's fundamental principle of her priesthood as a sacred class apart. Between Henry II and his Archbishop of Canterbury it was fought literally to the death. Was a member of the priestly class who had committed a crime, even the ultimate crime of murder, accountable like other men to the king?   In the case at issue, Becket not only refused to hand the murderer over to the royal courts, on the ground that " laymen cannot be judges of the clergy ", but loftily summoned the king, if he felt himself aggrieved, to appear like any other petitioner before the Archbishop's court at Canterbury.   Henry finally conceded that the criminal had first to be tried and unfrocked by his own order before he could be sentenced in the lay courts, but that was for Becket only a beginning . . . until the king in impotent wrath let slip the wish that someone would rid him of the priest grown too great to be a subject. Someone obliged, but the hacking to death of the Archbishop in his own Cathedral failed to exorcise his spirit.   Three years later Henry did in fact obey the summons to Canterbury, a humble petitioner for forgiveness before the tomb of his victim.

Bit by bit the Church exempted her servants and their belongings from lay interference. Bit by bit, as sole guardian of literacy, she extended the " benefit of clergy " to all who could read. Bit by bit her precincts became even for the illiterate who had broken the law a sanctuary where the king's writ did not run. Slowly but irresistibly the Conqueror's idea of the Church *of* England evolved into that of the Church *in* England, local branch of a mighty universal monarchy claiming a direct authority over the national monarchy and a joint authority with it over their common subjects.

Into the midst of this evolution stepped John with his necessities. Nothing was further from his mind than to provoke the Holy See. All that he desired was enough money from his English clergy to make him independent, in a particular emergency, of his English nobility, and he began by the orthodox method of convoking them in

assembly and asking for it. They refused, twice, though
voting their assent to his getting it if he could from the
laity. In a rage he ordered them to be assessed individually
and sent out his minions to collect. There were cries,
opposition, threats, but the heavens did not fall in flames
nor the people rise in wrath. Observing the Church's
command of these two phenomena not to be so effective as
was popularly supposed, John began to have a vision, an
extraordinarily prophetic vision—a State in which everybody's will, purse, and notion of the good life lay at the
unhampered disposal of the ruler. An incident swiftly
following gave him the chance to try whether the vision
might not be enfleshed.

The see of Canterbury fell vacant.· According to precedent, it would have been filled by a nominee of the king's,
formally elected by the monks of the cathedral chapter and
the bishops of the province. But the monks, to forestall the
interference of king and bishops alike, elected one of their
own number and sent him secretly to Rome to be invested.
The man babbled, however, to the fright of his colleagues,
who dropped him and turned to the king for permission to
elect in the usual way. As a result John de Grey, Bishop of
Norwich, one of his intimate counsellors, was duly installed
as Archbishop in December, 1205, and an embassy sent to
the Pope for his confirmation. Instead of granting it,
however, Innocent III exploited the situation to attempt an
immense new gain for the Church. He threw out the
election and transferred the proceedings to Rome, where
at his orders a delegation of the monks elected the English
cardinal Stephen Langton, whom, after a fierce dispute with
John, he consecrated. Not even Becket had dreamed of a
day when St. Augustine's successor at Canterbury would
reign as deputy for the successor of St. Peter over every
soul in England.

John's answer was to outlaw the monks and confiscate

the whole archiepiscopal property. Innocent retorted by
laying an interdict on the kingdom. It was the next thing
to shutting the gates of heaven upon it. In the darkened
churches no mass might be said, no body buried in the
consecrated earth surrounding them. Of the holy sacra-
ments only baptism and extreme unction could be administered, and marriages celebrated only at the church
door—that is, if a priest could be found, for many fled
abroad with all but two of the bishops. At a word the
familiar pageant of Christianity, with its precious wares of
comfort in this world and hope for the next, faded from the
sight of a terrified people. John, quite unterrified, merely
scooped up the estates of the clergy who obeyed the interdict and used them to defray his expenses against any who
might care to criticize his ecclesiastical policy.

The Pope threatened him with excommunication—the
last and awful penalty that cut a man off like a rotten limb
from the body of Christ, consigning his soul to eternal
torment after death and isolating him in life from his own
kind by threat of a similar fate to all who had any sort of
dealing with him. John warded off the blow with glib
offers of accommodation and went on. Money not only
gave power but brought in more money. His well-paid
mercenaries garrisoned every stronghold and strategic point,
ready to deal with the first least symptom of discontent or
disobedience. A word from the king, and the most exalted
of his subjects might be pressed to death or driven into
exile, leaving his lands to be seized and his wife and children
deliberately starved to death in prison. The terror did not
stop at the borders. It spread into the mountain fastnesses
of Wales, hitherto immune to English craft and force alike.
A strong military display induced the King of Scotland to
hand over a lump sum of money in order to secure John's
good-will.

The Church hurled her bolt—and John laughed. With

practically the whole of the higher clergy abroad and the ports of the kingdom almost hermetically sealed, there was no one even to publish the sentence. When it began to trickle through in devious ways, he countered by a demand upon all the freemen of the kingdom for a renewal of their allegiance; and though many knew that he stood before them excommunicated, none dared refuse. Nor did they dare refuse the tangible performance of their oath when he demanded their assistance for the conquest of Ireland—his first direct tax since the windfalls from the Church. The clergy paid again, more heavily than before but without protest. Next, as if to prove that although lawless he was not altogether godless, he applied even severer measures to the Jews; though since they were not allowed to own land various novel devices had to be employed, such as the famous extraction of a tooth a day, to make them divulge the whereabouts of their wealth. Thus endowed, John again crossed to Ireland, and this time there successfully instituted the blessings of government as enjoyed in England.

It was a test case. No one rebelled in his absence. No one questioned his supremacy on his return. He had become absolute: the law had ceased to operate except in his favour. All that remained now was to work out his plans for the recovery of France. With patience and forethought, with his prestige and his money, he gathered together a coalition of Philip's hostile neighbours, England at its head, to surround, invade and destroy him—leaving the master of Great Britain and Ireland autocrat of Europe.

And then Holy Church rose and struck. Composing her secular quarrel with the Ghibelline Hohenstaufens, she hurled the young Frederick II of that house upon John's nephew and chief ally the Guelfic Holy Roman Emperor, Otto IV. John's ally on France's southern border, Count Raymond of Toulouse, she smashed as a protector of heretics. John himself she declared deposed, released his subjects from their oaths of allegiance, and authorized Philip to possess himself of the kingdom in her name. This was in January, 1213; three months later Philip's vassals had collected and manned for him fifteen hundred ships which lay waiting in the Channel ports to carry his army across.

John called out his own vassals. Some refused outright to obey. The rest assembled at his order on Barham Downs to the south of Canterbury. The forces at his disposal were amply sufficient to repel the invasion—if they chose to fight. But as he scanned their faces he knew they would not fight for him. He even knew that many in fact had already made their deals with his enemy. For John no choice remained but to call off Philip or to lose England. He sent for the Pope's emissary, upon whose word the French fleet waited, to cross from Calais to Dover, and there agreed to everything . . . Langton to be Archbishop, all fugitives, whether priests or laymen, to be restored with suitable indemnities as might be arranged. Indeed, he agreed to more than everything, for in order to discourage invasion or rebellion in the future he made the kingdom over to the Pope and received it back as his vassal on the basis of an annual tribute in commutation of feudal service.

The French fleet dispersed and John, absolved from excommunication, was apparently as invincible as ever. But only apparently. Whatever the gloss put upon it, the dictator had been dictated to. More, the Church now had a new dominion. It was of paramount importance to her that peace should prevail in that dominion. Therefore in lifting the excommunication she required the barons to stand sponsor for the good conduct of the king. She also required the king to take his oath that " he would renew all the good laws of his predecessors . . . and annul all the bad ones, and that he would judge all men according to just judgments of his courts ". His hearers took note of that oath; it bound him to honour not only the Church of Rome but also the law of England.

So that when John, at long last ready to set out in earnest for France, ordered his vassals to report for duty, a number refused on the ground that " the good laws of his predecessors " in no way bound them to spill their blood and treasure on his projects without being first consulted. Breathing fire and slaughter, he set out to punish them, but the new Archbishop bobbed up in his path to remind him of his promise to commit no violence against a subject " without just judgment of his courts ". John told him to go to the devil, but in the end had to remit to a jury of their peers the question of whether they were bound to follow him or not.

Few did follow him. The expedition to France ended in failure. Even his French barons would only agree to fight for him on terms, one of which apparently exempted them from exposure to the hazards of battle unless protected by fortified walls. Beaten, his allies crushed at Bouvines, John returned to England determined once and for all to have it out with the barons who had let him down.

They were ready for him. They had learned his weakness, and he, by forcing them to see that their only safety lay in unity, had finally taught them their strength. To his assessment of a punitive tax against those who had failed to accompany him to France, they responded with a petition containing a schedule of the law as they conceived it. When he refused even to consider it—" Why do they not go on," he raved, " and demand the kingdom itself?"—they took up arms to compel him to.

With glittering promises he enlisted more mercenaries from the Continent. He appealed to the Pope for aid, meantime lavishing concessions on the priesthood. But neither paid troops nor papal edicts could confront the spirit he had aroused. Even the clergy were divided, for their leaders

the bishops were also barons and the Primate himself went
over to the insurgents after a vain effort to arbitrate. Eight
months after John's return from France the victorious
barons lay encamped at Runnymede to receive his seal on
Magna Carta.

There was really nothing very new in the document.
There scarcely could be, seeing that it was a declaration of
liberties, which in general appear to men as rights of which
they have been deprived rather than as fresh privileges they
are wresting—at least, they always have so appeared to
Englishmen. The clauses against cruel and unusual punishments, the capricious seizure of private property, and the
corruption or sale of justice were already platitudes of the
feudal contract that appeared to need the emphasis of
written restatement; but taxation on the basis of representation and an independent judiciary armed with the powers of
bail and *habeas corpus* were not mentioned, for the good
reason that they were as yet untried. In its specific pro-
visions Magna Carta is, therefore, merely a solemn anti-
quarian record of a certain critical stage in the development of mediæval society. But its importance to the history
of liberty is not in what it introduced but in what it preserved.
Four centuries later Englishmen were still affirming what
they had affirmed four centuries before Magna Carta—that
even the king was subject to the law and that they had a
perfect right to resist him if he broke the law.

That was one point of view. There is another, equally
tenacious, held no more strongly by John than by various
of his successors centuries after him. That the Charter was
an out-an-out breach of the sacred covenant between sovereign and subject as underwritten by God and handed
down from father to son since time out of mind; an outrageous usurpation by selfish men in their own interests to
the detriment of the kingdom's; at best an empirical compromise imposed by force, properly to be annulled by force

when available. It was to anticipate just that reading of
the transaction that the operative clause of the Charter
empowered a committee of twenty-five from amongst the
barons to organize—a characteristically practical English
device—a legal rebellion should the king fail to keep it.

Of course he did fail, being what he was and believing
what he believed. Nor did the barons fail to provoke him
to it once they thought they had him where they wanted
him. Once again he called up his mercenaries. The Pope
denounced the Charter as an impudent infringement of his
suzerain rights over England. With heaven now indubitably
on his side and the distinct earthly advantage of a single
command united in his own capable person, John was
within three months hunting down his enemies in every
direction. To save themselves they had to call in the young
Dauphin Louis of France and swear allegiance to him (only
to crawl out of it later when he had served their turn).
And in the end John, reduced to the position of outlaw in
his own realm, tracked across it killing and burning, fighting
all the while like the madman of genius that he was, until,
spent with frustration and rage, he swamped his army in
the Wash, succumbed to a fever, and died confessed after
one last orgy of eating and drinking.

Liberty survived, enshrined in Magna Carta . . . though at
times more like embalmed in it. Some fifteen generations later,
in England's greatest age, her greatest poet dramatized *The
Life and Death of King John* without once mentioning Magna
Carta. In fact, in the whole of his considerable writings
Shakespeare never even mentioned liberty. He would
almost certainly have got into trouble if he had.

CHAPTER II

Henry VIII—The Halcyon Years

THE feudal system ran its course. So far as those living under it were concerned, it seemed destined to run on for ever. They took it for granted that it was part of the divine order of things, an earthly version of the system by which God timelessly regulated in heaven the hierarchy of angels, saints and all the community of the blessed, just as everything on earth was but an imperfect copy of an ideal reality in heaven. Much happened, nothing really changed.

Yet under the surface change was preparing. The new middle class of merchants, lawyers, and the like, recruited largely from ambitious younger sons of the landed classes, made money, acquired a political sense, used both to obtain a share of political power. The clergy, derived from all classes, steadily diminished temporal activity in their own sphere while enlarging theirs in the temporal sphere. When, by the end of the thirteenth century, the king's search for allies against the barons expanded the Council of his tenants-in-chief into a High Court of Parliament, the lords spiritual sat as of right in its upper chamber and representative burghers in the lower: from which positions they could make their wishes audible to government by expressing them in terms of supplies. By the fourteenth century the new assembly had grown so great that it twice assumed to lay down the law on the supreme question of the throne's ownership. For when the barons, in their endless quarrel with the monarchy, deposed Edward II and Richard II, it

was Parliament that seated Edward III and set up the
Lancastrian dynasty with Henry IV.

For a while the experiment worked well. Burgher paid
and priest blessed the army of nobles and yeomen whose
victories at Crécy and Poitiers raised the England of Edward
III to the rank of first power in Europe. The House of
Lancaster, creature largely of the Commons, renewed and
even outdid Edward's achievements.

Then weaknesses developed. Henry V, the second
Lancaster, died young and was succeeded after a long
regency by a feeble-minded boy, Henry VI. Parliament,
considering the royal house its own creation, attempted to
bully the king and succeeded in dragging him and itself
alike into contempt. The barons, washing their hands of
both, did more and more as they pleased. Meanwhile the
war in France still dragged on at an ever-increasing expense,
until the French pulled themselves together after a hundred
years and won it. Cheated, misgoverned, and desperate,
the country went right off its head. York threw out Lancaster and Lancaster York in a twenty-five years' civil war
fought for no other purpose than the brute desire of rival
gangs to rule by exterminating each other. Both very
nearly succeeded: so nearly, that after four kings in a row
and most of the nobility had been butchered one way or
another, an outsider coming in late was able to carry off the
prize and set it on his own head as Henry VII.

For over four hundred years, from the landing of the
Normans in 1066 to Bosworth Field in 1485, no decisive
alteration had occurred in the structure of English life. In
all that time none but direct descendants of the Conqueror
had worn the Crown for even a single day. During practically
the whole of it their struggle for mastery with a small
privileged caste had regulated the country's political and
social balance. Now the Crown had passed to a stranger
whose natural adversaries were either dead, in hiding, or

anxious to come to terms with him. There being no other material with which to construct a fresh balance, the stranger was not only able, he was virtually compelled, to knock together a radically different form of structure. The result was the New or middle-class Monarchy. Its founder was the great-grandson of a bishop's steward, a Welshman by the name of Tudor. His grandfather, the steward's son, had started the family on the way to fortune by seducing a royal widow, the relict of Henry V; his father had contrived to graft it on to the Plantagenet-Lancaster stock by more honourable though equally successful overtures to a princess of the blood. A similar adventurous strain carried Henry himself to the throne at twenty-eight, but there it stopped. From first to last he ruled in a middle-class way. Glory never tempted him, nor the show of power, only power itself measured quantitatively in terms of money. The ministers he selected were middle-class men, lawyers preferably, who knew how to get it for him; and preferably they got it by manipulating the screws of the law to squeeze it out of the demoralized aristocracy.

His purpose was undisguised. The more of his enemies' resources he transferred to his own coffers, the smaller their chances of revolt, the greater his facilities for suppressing it when it broke out, as it occasionally did. With peace secure, there was no need for him to keep a standing army, a showy extravagance which always annoyed the people and not infrequently bit the hand that paid it. With financial independence he could increasingly afford to treat Parliament as if it had exhausted its usefulness with the formal acknowledgment of his title. Nor did Parliament, chastened by unpopularity, the Lords thinned by death and the Commons only too glad to stay away to mind their private affairs, enter any sustained objection. Against all possible rivals the Crown at last exercised the undivided authority of the State.

It was what the mood of the time demanded. The values of a military society were in full retreat before those of a commercial; the struggle for privilege was yielding to the struggle for wealth. In Henry Tudor the new lords òf business found their man. He was cautious, prudent, hard, like themselves. He represented their prime need, stability, without which he could no more hope to survive than they to prosper. That was his trump card. All whose business was not disorder wanted him strong because the stronger he was the safer they were, whether from another upper-class outbreak like the Wars of the Roses or an eruption from below such as had occurred in the past when disorder had ignited misery.

Yet he never sought to be absolute. For one thing, there was the Law to which he must render obedience, if he was to command it. For another, the Church, mighty and apart but by no means aloof, held a place in his people's affections far older than his, maintained a contact with their daily lives profounder and more intimate. She took them at their birth, instructed them, married them, buried them; punished their commoner failings, ruled their domestic arrangements, probated their wills, brought employment to many and their chief taste of beauty to most, tended them when they were ill, fed them when they were hungry; all in addition to interceding for them against the terrors of the life to come. The riches and influence she acquired through these services excellently equipped her to defend herself against whatever royal temptation they excited. Henry, pious as well as prudent, was content to compound with her for a larger share of the profits—fees on the appointments to bishoprics, the sale of patronage, sees left vacant while he collected their incomes, benefices withheld for the payment of political debts. Some of this plunder he redistributed amongst the abler churchmen as a reward for working for him, and since the Church remained free to recoup herself from the people, everybody was satisfied.

Even the people cursed his extortions but thanked God for him on balance all the same. For if he twisted the law in his own favour he revived it, after a generation of lawlessness, in theirs. And to abuse it was, after all, a form of conceding it respect. Statute, replacing desecrated custom where necessary, endeavoured to bring into play again the old and treasured equity between rights and obligations. Abetted by vigorous administration, the law still entailed as a first charge upon the community a livelihood for all who were willing to work for one, with the right to punish those who would not and the duty of providing for those who could not. Through the workers' own guilds acting as judges, it continued to exact from every man good quality, good workmanship, and honest measure in whatever he supplied. On the theory—direct survival of the Middle Ages—that no man ought to suffer from having too little nor the community from any man grabbing too much, it fixed prices, discouraged cut-throat competition, regulated wages and conditions of labour. In comparison with all this the changes above and around him seemed to the average man of little moment. The king had taken over from the barons, disconcerting new forces were drawing or driving many of his acquaintance from country to town; otherwise the feudal system appeared by the test of daily experience to be carrying on pretty much as before.

What the average man failed to realize was that it was carrying on by habit only, as systems often do. Its spirit was all but dead, though men could not yet perceive the fact since it was dying invisibly inside themselves. War had enfeebled it, and disillusion, and impatience in a rising class to be quit of its restrictions; but mostly the New Learning, by undermining its very foundations. For the New Learning, whose classical model held men to be the measure of all things, taught that a thing was right only in so far as it worked, whereas the feudal spirit, to which all things were

unreal save as reflections of the divine, stood committed to
the outworn doctrine that a thing worked only in so far as
it was right.

It would no longer serve. It failed to square with Reasons
of State, a handy recent invention which enabled nations to
extend their possessions under cover of defending their
honour or the strong to exploit the weak for the public
welfare. It sorted too awkwardly with the current growth
of enclosures, the fencing-in of the common lands when it
was found that they yielded a bigger return if used by the
rich to graze sheep for wool than if left to be tilled by the
poor for food. To king and people alike, however, these
were but blots or improvements, as the case might be, upon
the fair face of the old rather than incurable symptoms of
the new. Only seers, and not many of them, may read
correctly the signs of their passage through a great transition.
It took a hundred years and the vision of a Francis Bacon to
observe that the late fifteenth century had already " bowed
the ancient policy of this realm from consideration of plenty
to consideration of power ".

To Henry VII succeeded his son and namesake in 1509.
The new monarchy was less than twenty-four years old, the
new monarch less than eighteen—a mathematical conjunction against which history proffered the most dismal
warnings. In England the feat of holding on to an inherited throne had only once been achieved since the death
of Edward III in 1377; and the first Tudor, however much
feared and respected, had never been loved. The harsh
lines of his sunken cheeks and the sombre distrust in his
shrewd grey eyes told only too plainly what life had made of
him and what he made of men. The dynasty sorely needed
a popular king to ensure its continuance; three million
individual energies rushing they knew not whither needed
an able king to head them in a suitable direction, or at

least keep them from exploding in all directions. In the circumstances Henry VIII seemed no less than an answer to prayer.

Simply to look at him gave pleasure. " He is the handsomest potentate," wrote a travelled observer, " I have ever set eyes on; above the usual height with an extremely fine calf to his leg, his complexion fair and bright, with auburn hair combed straight and short in the French fashion, and a round face so very beautiful that it would become a pretty woman. . . ." [1] But to watch him break in a fractious stallion or handle a boat in a storm; or neatly topple an opponent out of the saddle in the tiltyard or beat his own professionals at tennis, " at which game it is the prettiest thing in the world to see him play, his fair skin glowing through a shirt of finest texture "; or at military exercises shoot " as strong (a bow) and as great a length as any of his guard ", and on public holidays take on the crowd's own champions each at his particular feat of skill or strength . . . in short, as the best athlete in the kingdom, he could count upon the very special consideration of a sports-mad race.

Art and nature, Henry VII's diligence lavished upon originally first-class material, had done their best for him. Even the defects of his ancestry had been remedied so far as possible by his father's choice of a daughter of Edward IV, one of the most gifted and personally attractive of English kings, to be his mother. From infancy the best masters to be found in Europe had collaborated to turn him out the very pattern of a Renaissance scholar and gentleman. He was at home in at least four languages and literatures—French, Spanish, Latin, and his own, which he wrote with the same easy simplicity that he spoke it. The

---

[1] The familiar portraits of him, painted after he had raised a scraggly red beard in hopeless emulation of Francis I's luxuriant dark one, and after fat and hard experience had contracted the lines of his mouth, give no idea of how he appeared at eighteen to an age in whose eyes fairness of colouring was in itself a claim to beauty. And which observed him, moreover, not as a portrait, but alive with strength and grace.

universal sciences of mathematics and philosophy he had
at his fingers' ends—particularly the branch of philosophy
known as theology, for which he showed an aptitude which
in a layman would have been regarded as positively alarming
had it not been combined with a piety which led him to
hear " three masses a day when he hunts and sometimes
five on other days ". While for music, whether as listener,
patron, performer, or composer, he displayed not only a
passion but a really serious talent of which evidence still
survives in various religious pieces and some swinging
ballads better than all but the very best of their time.

Nothing seemed to have been left out. " Courteous and
benign in gesture unto all persons, and especially unto
strangers, seldom or never offended with anything ", so
" liberal, so humane and kind that the poorest person can
easily approach him ", he had the rare gift of mingling
with ordinary men as if he were one of them without for an
instant tempting them to forget that he was not. His affa-
bility was a charm, his knack of saying the right thing in the
right place a proverb. Nor did it at all injure him in the
esteem of an insular people that he carried insularity at
times to the point of outright insolence: as when he laughed
off a French ambassador's compliment on a prize bit of
marksmanship with " Oh, it's good enough for a French-
man ". Pride in his breed as well as in himself, together
with magnificence and generosity, made just the difference
between his own personal and the specifically royal distinction needed to catch the imagination of men in the
mass.

" Love for the king is universal with all who see him,"
reported a foreign diplomat after several years' residence,
" for his Highness does not seem a person of this world but
one descended from heaven." Love of that sort was very
precious, alike to a dynasty seeking to endure and to a
nation for whom the throne had come to represent the only

possible focus of unity. But it was also very dangerous. If forfeited through incompetence it would end by destroying peace, while if justified by success it might end in extinguishing liberty. To steer between the two would require other, less amiable traits than any the young man had yet had occasion to exhibit. Industry, thrift, a knowledge of how much trust to give to facts and how little to men if he was to govern well; a disciplined control over his own pampered headstrong self lest he be tempted to govern too much. Whether these, or the ability to develop them, had also been included in his endowment circumstances would sooner or later urgently demand to know, unless he were inconceivably lucky.

For eighteen years he was lucky—or perhaps not. At any rate, the first half of his reign passed off too smoothly to afford a proper schooling for the fierce tests of the second. Occasionally a group of dispossessed peasants broke into revolt against the enclosures, or a mob of artisans broke a few heads amongst the foreigners flocking over in droves to exploit the boom in trade; less vehemently but no less unmistakably the merchant community now and then made known to Henry that his distinctly florid diplomacy, with its wars which nobody ever quite won and its treaties which nobody ever quite kept, might be good for his prestige but was bad for their business. But these seldom rose to more than ripples on the general surface of content, and even they as often as not flattened out before his genuine dislike of suffering and injustice and his obvious desire to remedy them within the limits of his power. For he still acknowledged limits to his power.

The fact was that, just as things had been made easy for him all his life until his accession, they continued to be made easy for him till he reached middle age. He got along, as it were, on inherited capital. Capable servants trained by his father relieved him of the details which

normally comprise the work of government, his father's
bulging treasury spared him the need to choose—com-
monest cause of a ruler's troubles—between an undignified
economy and unpleasant expedients for raising revenue.
Even through the tangle of unforeseen events he had but to
follow the general lines of policy marked out by the same
useful parent.

In foreign affairs these directed him to co-operation
with Spain and distrust of France, though not to the point
of tolerating such injury to the hostile power as would
leave him alone at the mercy of the friendly one. Indeed
the House of Tudor's whole family architecture had been
reared on this diplomatic ground-plan. Early in his reign
Henry VII had engaged his infant son Arthur, at that time
his heir, to Catherine, daughter of Ferdinand and Isabella
of Spain. Scarcely had the nuptials been celebrated than
he threw out a counter-prop in the form of a marriage
between his eldest daughter Margaret and James IV of
Scotland, a country historically allied to France. That
same year, 1502, Arthur died: whereupon Henry at once
joined with Ferdinand in a prayer to the Pope, Julius II,
for a dispensation authorizing his second son, the future
Henry VIII, to marry his deceased brother's widow. After
some hesitation Julius complied; but owing to acrid differences of opinion between the two fathers over the bride's
dowry, the union did not take place until after the groom
had been three months king.

It worked out well nevertheless: even better, so far as
general harmony went, in its domestic than in its political
aspect. Catherine was six years older than her husband,
but handsome and intelligent, with a high spirit combined
with a wifely obedience that exactly suited him. If he did
not exactly return her devotion, he remained astonishingly
faithful to her almost to the very end; so far as the evidence
goes, he indulged in only two extra-marital adventures,

from one of which, with the Lady Elizabeth Blount, he had
his first male child, Henry Duke of Richmond. Unluckily
for Catherine, the boy painfully emphasized the greater of
her only two faults. She could not produce sons; out of
many pregnancies and many miscarriages there survived
only a sickly daughter, Mary, on whom to build the future
of the dynasty. Her other fault, though equally exasperating,
had less irremediable consequences. She was too much her
father's daughter. In all innocence but with obstinate
Spanish self-righteousness she loyally assisted the most
fertile liar in Europe to delude, cheat, swindle her young
husband's inexperience. Here, however, Henry was not
altogether helpless. He could learn, and in time he did
learn, tricks quite as good as his father-in-law's—as when,
after a particularly outrageous abuse of his confidence, he
coolly left Ferdinand out on a limb by a secret negotiation
for the marriage of his younger sister Mary in 1515 with
their common enemy, the valetudinarian Louis XII of
France.

That is to say, he saw through Ferdinand and so agreed
to the negotiation being carried out in his name. The
idea of it almost certainly originated in the head of the
statesman who from 1511 on relieved him largely of the
effort of thinking up ideas and entirely of the responsibility
for carrying them out. In that year there entered the royal
household as almoner a forty-year-old priest named Thomas
Wolsey, son of an Ipswich wool-trader, who swiftly proved
himself to be just the man that Henry could not do without. For high thinking and higher living could not in
themselves take the place of hard work, which Henry hated
and Wolsey loved—almost any kind of work, so long as it
brought him nearer to the fulfilment of his two other
obsessions, power and magnificence. In startling measure
he gratified all three; " so fast as the other councillors
advised the king to leave his pleasure and to attend to the

affairs of the realm, so busily did the almoner persuade him to the contrary ".   Henry took the more agreeable advice—according to Catherine their early years together were one round of " continual feasting "—while Wolsey, a " second king ", buried up to his glittering pig-like little eyes in reports, instructions, accounts, looked after England for him.   And looked after it well, on the whole, almost as well as he looked after himself. He amassed abbeys, bishoprics —including the Archbishopric of York—a Cardinal's hat, the offices of Lord Chancellor and of Papal Legate, and the riches of a sultan.   He also developed the tastes and manners of a sultan.   His palaces, his horses, his entertainments, and his women were a tale out of the Arabian Nights;   his arrogance was a prime and universal incitement to homicide. Even in the hatred he provoked, however, he did Henry service: every atom of irritation against government for something done or not done that might otherwise have been blamed on the king found lodgment on the burly, loftily indifferent shoulders of the minister.

On the other hand, he also served as an incessant and brutal reminder of the time's gravest preoccupation.   The Church was under attack, and he, her most conspicuous representative, provided a living example of the worst that could be said against her.   Like him, she was too rich, too greedy.   She mixed too much into politics.   Like her Legate in England, who seldom said mass, never visited his bishop-rics, and appointed his satellites and bastards to the more lucrative cures of souls at his disposal, she neglected her spiritual concerns and allowed her priesthood to fall into decay.   These criticisms, long accumulating in men's minds, received a violent and terrible articulation in 1517 from a German monk named Martin Luther.   Portions of her ancient unity split away in a roar of fear, exultation, and battle.   But the English, never the most dutiful, still remained amongst the most devoted of the Church's children.

None but the rabid yet clamoured to disown her, though even the conservative prayed for her own sake to see her reformed. The king and Wolsey both granted the need, but for reasons peculiar to each never did anything about it. Wolsey dared not lest he jeopardize the supreme ambition of his life, which was to be Pope. And Henry revered her, not only for religion's sake, but also because all his instincts ranged him—as so often happens with the newly risen—on the side of tradition. Whatever the shifts of his continental alliances, he entered upon no quarrel save as her ally. Pen as well as sword he took up in her cause. When Luther attacked her he burst into print with a spirited, exhaustive, and almost incoherent defence of the whole catalogue of orthodoxy. For his military aid he received a golden rose from one Pope, a cap and sword from another. For his literary exploit he was awarded in 1521 the proud title of Defender of the Faith. To ally himself openly with her critics would not only seem ungrateful, it would make him look ridiculous. Besides, the movement for reform on the Continent had degenerated into revolution; and it scarcely befitted a king to become a revolutionary.

So Wolsey piloted the ship of state in his own way, while Henry, a princely captain, made the voyage almost as agreeable to the passengers as to himself. Every man enjoys doing what he knows he can do superlatively well, and in one art Henry had nothing to learn from the beginning— the art of pleasing public opinion. At his accession it had been hot against the legal extortioners who had enriched themselves while enriching—much more abundantly—his father: as almost the first act of his reign he twisted their own law into a noose for the two most hated of them, to the public's delirious satisfaction. He amused it by his competition in personal vanity with young Francis I. He awed it by his vigorous repression of a bloody May Day riot against London's foreign colony in 1517, indulged it by pardoning the rioters when the ropes were already round their necks, and moved it to grateful tears by the scene he staged and the language he used in communicating the pardon. By the splendour of his going to war he quickened its appetite, long dormant, for glory, and by the gorgeous mummery of the Field of the Cloth of Gold dazzled it into forgetting the futility of the war and the fatuity of the peace.

Then, after eighteen halcyon years, things began to happen to Henry. No longer slim and rosy but paunchy and red, he discovered that he was getting on for middle age—the dangerous age. He found that he was tired of Catherine and in love with a younger woman. Brooding over the lack of a son to succeed him, he began to wonder whether he had not offended Heaven, despite Pope Julius's dispensation, in taking to his bed a wife who had already shared his brother's. He resolved to look into the matter . . . and called down the hurricane through which he was to drive an England straining, heaving, almost foundering, by the sole chart of submission to his will.

CHAPTER III

Henry Defies the Church

THE exact process by which Henry arrived at his resolution is unknown. That in itself casts a most interesting and important light upon him. For he was one of the not uncommon sort of men who, when they want something, must believe that they are right in wanting it; the one uncommon thing about him was that his position and temperament gave his wants and his need to be right a size and an urgency quite beyond other men's. He was King, a being in whom millions believed, and to whom those he most trusted daily explained that he could do no wrong; even—or especially—when he did nothing. He was wilful and subtle, an extravert and an egotist, as nature and the world had made him. Having decided what he wanted, why be plagued to go back and determine in what order and with what weight his motives had carried him to a conclusion which by the very fact of his having come to it must necessarily be right?

It was not the first time he had thought of divorcing Catherine.[1] His exasperation against her father, which had provoked him in 1514 to marry his sister Mary to the King of France, had also burst out in a threat " to repudiate his present wife, daughter of the King of Spain and his brother's

---

[1] The word "divorce" is merely used for convenience' sake. The Catholic Church recognized, of course, no such thing as the dissolution of marriage for causes arising after it had taken place; the ecclesiastical courts merely granted annulments on the hypothesis that there never had been any lawful marriage owing to some prior impediment.

widow, because he is unable to have children by her " and
to replace her with a Frenchwoman.   Perhaps he then
thought divorce wrong, perhaps the Spanish alliance was
still too valuable; at any rate Catherine, whom the threat
had caused to miscarry of her fourth son in five years, not
long afterward entered another period of pregnancy which
in February, 1516, successfully terminated in the birth of
the Princess Mary.   " We are both young," exulted Henry,
" if it was a daughter this time, by the grace of God sons
will follow."   But only more miscarriages or still-births
followed; presently even they stopped.   By the time he was
thirty-four and Catherine forty he knew that they would
have no more children.   The future of the dynasty, the
peace of the realm, hung on the life of a sickly girl.   Even
if she survived him, which seemed doubtful, she would
have to marry in order to carry on the line: and whom
was she to marry?   A husband from abroad would mean
the subordination, possibly the annexation, of England to a
foreign power, and that the English would never tolerate.
A subject as partner of her throne would fatally drive all
those envious of him into faction and civil war.   Any way,
every way, loomed disruption.

No man could have been less disposed than Henry to
await it with resignation.   Matters could not have gone so
awry unless there had been a fault somewhere.   The first
thing to do was to find it, the next to look for the cure.
Plainly the fault could not be with him, the lustiest male in
his kingdom; there was the sturdy little Duke of Richmond
to testify for him.   Directly it could not be with Catherine
either, since she had conceived several sons.   But why had
God, Who did nothing without good reason, removed all
of hers and left only the other who was not hers?   There
must be some fault common to both of them. . . . Anxiously
Henry scanned Holy Writ for a clue—and found it.   " For
some years past," he reported in 1527, " he had noticed in

reading the Bible the severe penalties inflicted on those who marry the relicts of their brothers." The prohibition in the eighteenth chapter of Leviticus was explicit to the point of baldness. On the other hand, the Pope had a right to dispense . . . but might not there have been something wrong in the particular dispensation of Pope Julius? " The more he studied the matter, the more clearly it appeared to him that he had broken the divine law."

His doubt suddenly received practical crystallization. That same year, owing to a tilt in the continental balance, negotiations were under way for a marriage between the Princess Mary and Francis I. In the course of the bargaining, the English delegates raised the question of whether the King of France, by reason of a previous engagement, was really free to marry. Back came the suave retort of the Bishop of Tarbes, one of the French delegates: what assurance was there that the bride's parents had ever been married at all? that she was the legitimate heiress of England, as represented? That was a shock—one of the rudest of his life, confessed Henry—to find the doubt over which he had been darkly brooding flung in his face by strangers in its most ominous form.

Yet there were powerful arguments bidding conscience be quiet. Deuteronomy, xxv, 5, in answer to Leviticus, xviii, 16 . . . Henry's deep respect for the marital sacrament and papal decrees . . . his daughter's birthright . . . the inconvenience of offending Catherine's nephew, young Charles V, new ruler of Spain as well as of the Holy Roman Empire, most of Italy, the Indies, and England's best customer the Netherlands. All these might have prevailed and Henry, who hated to give pain, have decided in favour of the wife aged and sorrowed by much futile childbearing, if at about this time Anne Boleyn had not come along.

She was then within a year either way of twenty, swarthy

and buxom, with full red lips and large active dark eyes. In 1519 she had gone to the French court as maid of honour to the Queen; in 1525 she had returned from that brilliantly depraved finishing school thoroughly versed in all the accomplishments to which she was receptive. She could talk, dress, arouse expectation in men, and keep them indefinitely suspended in it. With Henry her triumph was swift and utter. He abased himself at her feet. All his pride, all the elaborate artificiality of contemporary language alike vanished from the letters in which he poured out his longing for her " from the knees of his heart ". Other people—with the exception of her other victims—wondered what he saw in her. Their wonder was even more pointless than such wonder usually is. All that part of him which was not kingly discovered itself in her; just as Catherine, so regal, so honest, so almost too fine, matched only what *was* kingly. Under the French veneer Anne's tastes, her respectabilities, her instincts, were as English as Catherine's were through and through Spanish—and English of Henry's own hereditary class, clever newcomers risen through marrying well. Her paternal grandfather had been a prominent merchant who had served a term as Lord Mayor of London, her maternal uncle was no less than the Duke of Norfolk. That some attraction existed for Henry in the Boleyns had already appeared in favours shown her father and brother and favours received from her elder sister Mary, one of his two known mistresses. Why he did not simply make Anne a third can only be surmised. Perhaps she played her cards too well, perhaps he loved her too much or saw in her robust vitality the promise of healthy sons. Very likely all three.

Having made up his mind, he called in Wolsey to start things going. It was a significant moment. He did not ask the Cardinal if he could or ought to have what he wanted; he told him to get it for him. Nor did he tell him everything. Of Anne he said not a word, but merely instructed Wolsey to obtain from the present Pope, Clement VII, an annulment of Julius II's dispensation. For he no longer felt implicit confidence in his grand vizier. If the annulment went through, Wolsey would want for his own purposes to marry his king to a lady of high political consequence. Anne was not only a diplomatic cipher, but of a family than whom the Cardinal numbered no more deadly enemies. Wherefore Henry, an apter pupil than the Cardinal had realized, did not put it past him to hinder the divorce from Catherine rather than assist in the advancement of Anne. Moreover, he had other reasons for distrust. Rumours had come to him of Wolsey's taking bribes to let individuals off their debts to the Crown; of actually earning the pensions Henry graciously permitted him to accept from foreign princes by rendering services to them incompatible with his own prince's interests; and more than rumours, evidence, only too convincing, of such general dissatisfaction with his management of affairs as at last to touch Henry himself. In these circumstances it behove Wolsey to carry out the task assigned him as expeditiously as possible. Else a long farewell indeed to greatness.

On the face of it the annulment would have presented little difficulty to so adroit a canonist as the Cardinal Archbishop of York. Royalty and sub-royalty were constantly getting dispensations to marry forbidden persons, fresh dispensations to cancel the first, and still other dispensations to contract second equally forbidden marriages. If precedent alone had been able to free Henry, Wolsey would have had him a bachelor again in little more time than it took a man to ride to Rome and back. Unfortunately precedent was not to be counted on in this case; nor law—or for that matter justice—either. For this Wolsey had himself in part to blame. Two years earlier, in disregard of Henry VII's precepts, he had inclined too far to the side of Spain, with the result that the Spanish armies had been able to annihilate French military power in Italy. The Pope lived in Italy; for the time being, therefore, he took his orders from the King of Spain, and the King of Spain was the nephew and avowed protector of the lady whom it was Wolsey's business to turn out of her place like a superannuated courtesan.

It seemed an impasse from which even the most resourceful brain in Europe could find no way out, when an earthshaking catastrophe unexpectedly opened one. On 6th May, 1527, a polyglot horde of Charles V's unpaid veterans broke into Rome, drove out the Pope, and burned, killed, raped, desecrated, and pillaged until there was nothing left on which to expend those respective activities. Wolsey at once grasped the possibilities. With the Holy Father a fugitive, the Holy Office virtually suspended, all might yet be arranged for the best. If he could persuade the French —on whom his diplomatic strategy had now in any event to be centred—to join forces with him, together they might agree to repudiate Clement, perhaps even set up a new Pope, English by preference, in his place . . . or, if that proved unfeasible, offer to restore him under such conditions as in his present plight he could scarcely resist. As an inducement to the French and to seal the bargain, Wolsey proposed to offer his master's hand in marriage to a cousin of their king. On 17th May he opened an inquiry in his Legatine Court into a complaint that Henry was unlawfully cohabiting with his brother's widow. A few weeks later he left in vice - regal magnificence for France.

Soon after, Henry sent off on the quiet a more modest embassy of his own. It consisted of his secretary, Dr. William Knight; it headed for Rome, where the Pope was again to be found; and it bore a request to him from Henry for a dispensation to marry Anne once he had disposed of Catherine. For as Mary Boleyn's ex-lover he stood to her sister in the same prohibited degree of relationship as his brother's ex-wife had once stood to him—an impediment only to be removed by a dispensation of exactly the same kind as the old one whose annulment he had determined he was entitled to. Clement granted Knight's petition easily, almost eagerly. He was even ready to consider a very much more unusual petition that Knight brought with him, for a licence enabling Henry to marry Anne without the formality of divorcing Catherine, the children of both to be equally legitimate. But this second idea Henry abandoned before it could be acted upon. If he was right in believing that he had never been married to Catherine—and by now " an angel descending from heaven would not be able to persuade him otherwise "—he had no need, on second thought, for any " licence to commit bigamy ". He did not deny the Pope's right to dispense; on the contrary, had he not admitted it in asking the Pope to unbar the way to matrimony with Anne? He merely asked the Pope in return to examine with an open mind the flaw, so glaringly visible to himself, in the dispensation which had bound him in the innocence of his youth to Catherine. With gentle candour Dr. Knight intimated that it would be better for the Pope to look at this simple matter as every right-thinking man must.

Unhappily it did not look so simple to Clement amidst his wrong-thinking Spanish jailers. Nor did it to Wolsey, labouring to woo the French into an arrangement which his master had not the slightest intention of carrying out. The Cardinal, frightened at what he had already promised to Francis I, even more frightened at what Henry might be up to behind his back, decided to return to England. There at least he could keep an eye on the king and the threads in his own hands. Deftly taking hold of the thread he found already connecting Henry with the Vatican, he caused Knight to demand that the case be referred back to the Legatine Court in England for final judgment, as the only means by which Clement might avoid disobliging his master while enabling Wolsey to oblige his: otherwise, explained the Cardinal, converting Henry's hint into an open threat, the English king and people would most likely renounce their obedience to the Holy See. The Pope dreaded that calamity as much as did the prelate who aspired above all things on earth to be his successor. He wrung his hands, wrote out orders for the transfer, revised them, tore them up. The dodge was so transparent . . . if only something could be done about Charles V to make him stand a little farther off. Something was done. In the spring of 1528 a rejuvenated French army pushed its way south into Italy, passed Rome, pressed on to Naples. Early in June Clement dispatched Cardinal Campeggio to England with a commission empowering him and Cardinal Wolsey to decide, finally and for ever, whether Henry was lawfully married to Catherine.

Campeggio sailed. The Spaniards met the French before they reached Naples and drove them north again. Clement sped a courier after Campeggio ordering him to delay the trial in every way possible . . . to reason with the parties . . . in no event to give sentence, whatever his commission said, without further word from Rome. Campeggio did his best. Arrived in England, he pled with Catherine to cut the knot by retiring to a nunnery. Catherine agreed on condition that Henry also took the vow of chastity. Henry said he would if the Pope would absolve him of his vow beforehand. Meantime someone discovered a brief of Julius II which entirely eliminated any flaw that could be alleged against the original Bull of dispensation. Someone else pronounced it a forgery. Wolsey demanded to see the original, which was in Spain. Charles V refused on the ground that he might steal it—a suspicion not altogether unwarranted in view of the mysterious disappearance of important documents from Campeggio's luggage. Bull and brief alike momentarily lost relevance when Catherine swore on examination that her marriage with Arthur had never been consummated. But there was no one to bear her out —naturally. Wolsey swiftly reconstituted the case on the theory that a public wedding was as good as a consummation. He also rounded up witnesses to prove that Catherine lied.

This went on for nearly a year, but it could not go on for ever. With a sinking feeling that the ground was not yet adequately prepared for a satisfactory verdict, yet dreading to have the matter at any moment snatched out of his hands, Wolsey at length chivvied his colleague into opening the trial. On 31st May, 1529, the proceedings began in Black Friars Hall. Three weeks passed before the King and Queen appeared in person. In an impassioned speech Catherine appealed against the court's jurisdiction . . . on her knees made her wonderful plea to Henry to have pity on her, a friendless stranger in his realm, and on their child . . . wrung from him the admission that she was " as true . . . a wife as I could in my fantasy wish or desire " . . . and when both court and husband had denied her appeals, with quiet majesty left the courtroom for good. They pronounced her contumacious and went on without her. With the unlovely testimony to her relations with the fifteen-year-old Arthur, the trial reached its lowest point; with the Bishop of Rochester, the great John Fisher's defence of her, its highest. On 23rd July the moment for sentence arrived.

It was never to be pronounced, at least not from that place. The previous year Wolsey, in his efforts to win over the French, had all but let England in for a war with Spain. War with Spain meant exclusion from the Netherlands, which meant ruin to England's commercial classes. They reacted with such vigour as to compel the government to back down. The French, going on alone in the spring of 1529, had sustained another defeat so severe as to reconcile them to peace. That left the Emperor, at the very moment his aunt's cause seemed most desperate, free at last to deal with the Pope. Clement knew when he was beaten. Meekly he sent word to Campeggio; and Campeggio, rising to utter the expected verdict, instead adjourned the court till autumn. No one had to be told that autumn signified the Greek Kalends. No one was surprised to learn in the next few days that the case had been revoked to Rome, where Henry had at present as much chance of winning it as of becoming Pope himself.

And now? Fight or submit? John had fought and been compelled to climb down; so in effect had his father, Henry II. No king had yet carried a controversy with the Church to the breaking-point and won; the stoutest of them had preferred to compromise rather than force decisive issues. But for Henry the issue admitted of no compromise. Either Catherine was his wife or she was not. Either he must surrender his will in the matter to the Pope or the Pope must surrender his will to him. There was no middle way: anything less than aggressive attack leading to unconditional victory amounted to total defeat, since he remained married to Catherine unless and until he made the Pope agree that he never had been. And though the papacy seemed less formidable than of yore, its arsenal still stocked the tried if slightly antiquated weapons of interdict, excommunication, deposition—backed, in this instance, by the secular might of Spain. Whereas Henry's resources numbered no more than those of the chief second-rate power in Europe.

If indeed that much. The accumulated loathing of Wolsey had at last mounted to the level of Wolsey's employer. The people hated the divorce, admired Catherine,

detested the upstart Anne—feelings in no way mitigated by
the latter's ostentatious callousness to the sufferings of her
queenly rival. Priests in general they might dislike, but
they loved the ancient forms of their religion; and though
they regarded the Pope rather as a petty Italian princeling
too prone to mind other people's business, they dreaded any
injury to the friendship with Spain which had become the
cornerstone of their worldly well-being. Out of this confused
welter of sentiments was certain, if Henry proceeded, to
emerge one clear, sharp emotion, and no one could foretell
what it would be . . . whether disgust with the man
whose private appetite had dragged his people into an
unholy mess, or truculent loyalty towards the Majesty
of England whom the Italian princeling had had the insolence to cite into a foreign tribunal to give an account
of himself.

Henry proceeded. Haughtily declining the summons to
Rome, he convoked Parliament, which had met but twice in
fourteen years, to arm him for the conflict. He had defied
the Church, thrown himself upon his people. The die was
cast, the stake double or quits. If he won, there would no
longer be a Pope in England; if he lost, he would no longer
be King of England.

Afar off, in York, Wolsey watched the beginning of the
contest. The revocation of the case to Rome had, of course,
been the end of him. Stripped of the Great Seal and much
of his property (including his more than royal palace of
Hampton Court) but not otherwise unkindly treated by the
sovereign whose reign he had so magnificently graced and
disgraced, he had been packed off to look after his spiritual
duties for the first time in his life. And for the first time in
his life won love by the way in which he performed them.
But he had left hatred behind; and perhaps brought old
habit along. His enemies unfolded to the King tales of new
treasons, and Henry—now swiftly disburdening himself of

all such useless appurtenances as gratitude—ordered the block to be made ready. But Wolsey was too old and cunning a hand to be caught like that. On the way south to the Tower he simply laid himself down one night and died.

CHAPTER IV

The Divorce

ON 3rd November, 1529, there packed into Black Friars Hall, where four months earlier two Cardinals had judicially entertained the griefs of a King and a Queen, a crowd of several hundred " serving-men, parasites and flatterers lightly apparelled in short cloaks and swords ". At least, so one of the Pope's partisans later described Henry's new House of Commons elected the previous month and now meeting for the first time. Serving-men most of them were, in the sense that they enjoyed posts of profit or honour under the Crown; flatterers many of them had to be in order to stand in well with the great local magnates by whom the Court's notice might be attracted and appointments procured; but parasites they were not, unless to be a squire holding county office or a lawyer or merchant risen to be recorder or alderman of his town affixed the stigma of parasitism to otherwise typical members of the well-to-do classes.

Certainly so far as the members went, few of them regarded their election to Parliament as anything but bad luck. The salary offered by their constituents was small and more often than not in arrears, the respect paid them in London was painfully inconsistent with their importance at home. Hence no doubt the " short cloaks and swords ", sartorial evidence of equality with the swells of the capital. Only the strenuous pressure of the magnates, abetted by the neighbours' opinion and occasionally the outright command of the Crown, succeeded in filling the House at all; only the arbitrary vigilance of the government kept it from being emptied by artful excuses for leave of absence.

But though they felt no call to govern the country, they had strong and definite ideas as to how it ought to be governed. Laws should help and not injure trade, a subject on which the reluctant lawmakers shared intimate knowledge and a collective enthusiasm. In this they fully and without need of specific pledges represented the class of eligible voters in the country. In this consisted the primary bond between that class and the Tudor dynasty, whose policy it was to cherish trade and whose fall would instantly bring about a trade-destroying anarchy. But in this also lurked a most serious complication for Henry. He had called Parliament together to help him get his divorce, and Parliament hated the divorce—not so much by reason of chivalrous sympathy for Catherine, like less responsible persons, as because it might endanger trade with the Spanish Netherlands. He had therefore to invent, and to obtain Parliament's co-operation in forging, legislative instruments capable of striking the Pope while sparing his close protector the King of Spain.

Such discriminating weapons were not easy to design. They were rendered no easier by the nature of the material out of which they would in large part have to be fabricated —money. For without armaments and well-subsidized friends abroad it would be useless to expect the Pope to take a high tone on Henry's part seriously. And Henry had no money. He was in fact deeply in debt. Even his father's millions had proved insufficient to support Wolsey's dream of making England arbiter of Europe; and when they were gone, the Cardinal, rather than face Parliament, had preferred to pursue the dream on forced loans from the mercantile community. So it was now up to Henry not only to ask to be forgiven his debts by those to whom he owed them, but for fresh supplies to carry out a scheme as unpopular as any of Wolsey's. For that he would have to give something in return. What? The scheme necessarily involved measures against the Church with whose head he was joining battle. So far so good. The Commons, who resented the Church's opulence and believed that her priests would be much the better for some salutary discipline, could be counted on to approve with pleasure any number of laws to restrict ecclesiastical privileges and redistribute ecclesiastical wealth. But could they be counted on to know where to stop? A too drastic assault on the established religion might well end in splitting England asunder and bringing down on her the united wrath of Catholic Christendom . . . a programme as far as possible from Henry's, who wanted no more from the Church than his divorce, and from Parliament such discreet collaboration as would just induce the Pope to grant it. To master his adversary would be of no earthly good unless he could at the same time master his ally.

That was where Thomas Cromwell came in. Henry needed someone in his close confidence to manage the House of Commons for him. Cromwell, a veteran parliamentarian, was member for Taunton. He was also Henry's secretary, a discovery of Wolsey's who had had the decency to stand up for the fallen Cardinal to the limit of prudence. He was now about forty-five, with the figure, the gait, and the face—apart from a too-long upper lip and eyes too close together—of a bulldog down to the very dewlaps. Descended of parents seemingly neither poor nor respectable—contemporary report fathered him on a Putney brewer or ironfounder who got into trouble over a stabbing affray, dabbled in forgery, and died young—Thomas on his mother's remarriage set off for Italy to make his fortune. The line he chose, that of cloth-shearer, failing to gain it for him, he came home again on sixteen ducats and a horse borrowed from a friendly Florentine banker. Back in England his luck turned. He met the daughter of a prosperous wool-dealer, married the one, became partner of the other, studied law, set up as a solicitor, made money, lent it out. Then he attracted Wolsey's notice and was made. Like his patron, he revelled in work. Like him also, he never let scruple or pity stand in the way of getting things done. But unlike the late prince of the Universal Church who longed to be pope, he was the perfect New Monarchy man. As solicitor and money-lender to the economic middle classes, he not only had his hands in their pockets but his fingers on their souls. As statesman it was his avowed belief that the good of England demanded the concentration of all power in the king, his expressed intention to make Henry the richest prince in Christendom and an autocrat on the style of the Grand Turk.

Henry and Cromwell consulted, Henry decided, Cromwell went off to arrange. Though whenever the members of either House grew too difficult Henry came in his own royal person or sent for them to come to him. And almost invariably they grew less difficult. For Henry suddenly displayed an unexpected genius for dealing with such folk. How he acquired it heaven only knows; certainly not from Wolsey, whose bullying of his rare Parliaments into exasperated obstinacy had hardly been an object-lesson. The talent must simply have lain latent in him until need brought it forth. He never bullied, never lost his temper, never stifled criticism. One member in 1527 fumed against making the King a present of his debts, another later dared to suggest that if the King would take back his wife there would be no need of spending their substance on armaments: to both he communicated his pleasure at their frankness and his hope that further discussion would bring them to his side. Before that air of sweet reasonableness, of flattering anxiety to hear the opinion of the humblest backbencher, opposition seldom found its grievances as unbearable after entering the Presence as before. And though some might resist his reasoning, few found it possible to doubt the sincerity imprinted by nature on the round, rosy, open countenance of a sovereign whose bluffness had become a favourite national legend. Men saw, as usual, what habit had accustomed them to see—a merry monarch: not yet suspecting that the grey matter behind the smiling blue eyes was in process of incubating an intelligence shrewd, supple, and secretive enough to meet any crisis its owner's imperious will might henceforth pro-voke. "One may keep counsel," ran the motto of the new Henry, enunciated this same year, " and if I thought my cap knew my counsel, I would cast it into the fire and burn it." Even Cromwell never guessed until it was too late how little his master's looks gave clue to his thoughts.

In mingled disappointment and dismay the two Houses heard the reading of the first three measures they had been summoned to consider. They contained so much less than many had hoped for, so much more than many had feared. In that lay their exquisite rightness for Henry's purpose. They simply invited Parliament to eliminate certain clerical abuses the objections to which were common ground between them—common even to the majority of the devout. It could scarcely be denied that the clergy made too good a thing out of death: instances were notorious of exorbitant probate fees exacted from the prosperous, of the very clothes they died in being stripped from the bodies of the poor before granting them burial. No one could seriously urge that a priest holding half a dozen or more benefices at once was able to perform his spiritual duties properly in them all. Certainly no one with a solid interest in land or commerce would be likely to approve of ecclesiastical competition in farming or trading for profit. In introducing his three bills to limit mortuaries, pluralities, and the clergy's engagement in business, Henry could truthfully allege that far from seeking to injure the fabric of the Church he was merely restoring it for its own good in accordance with the wishes of the people. And in so doing he flattered Parliament into believing that he acknowledged its right to regulate the spiritual as well as the temporal estate of England. It would be time enough to disillusion it when it had squeezed enough perquisites out of the Church to extract a divorce from the Pope.

Nevertheless the debate on the three bills was bitter, often threatening. Without waiting for it to conclude, Henry hurried to carry out an independent operation against Rome, suggested to him by a young Cambridge theologian named Thomas Cranmer, which if successful would render Parliament's further collaboration unnecessary. For several hundred years the universities of Europe had been considered the final repositories of wisdom in matters of canon law; [1] and though their authority was not quite what it had been, it still stood very high. High enough, at least, that if they could be got to say that Henry was right and Clement wrong in their dispute, it would be exceedingly awkward for the Pope to render a verdict contrary to their opinion. To each principal university, therefore, Henry sent a delegation, or rather two delegations, one equipped with arguments and the other with money. So too did the papal-Imperialist party. Dialectically and financially the year 1530 was a treat for the professors of divinity; in fact for the whole brotherhood of sacred learning. Upon dazed Talmudic scholars in their ghettoes descended Henry's agents flourishing silver for Mosaic support; into the hand of an accomplished bibliographical forger Charles V's intermediaries pressed a recompense for a library catalogue which threw the enemy off the track of an adverse commentary by an early Christian Father. When the returns were

---

[1] It was only after an appeal to the University of Paris that Joan of Arc's judges deemed their legal case against her strong enough to proceed to condemnation.

in, it appeared that Henry's thesis had prevailed at Oxford and Cambridge (though not without difficulty), and at five French and four Italian universities, Clement's in most of Italy, all of Spain, and, owing chiefly to Lutheran indifference to orthodox matrimonial niceties, all of Germany.

Meanwhile the Pope had not been idle. First he had tried to block Henry's appeal to the scholars by forbidding anyone to uphold it. Failing in that, and fearing lest Henry's partial success should encourage him to seek a schismatic divorce and remarriage in England, he pronounced a threat of excommunication against " all women in general " who might be tempted to marry him and any court or legislative body, ecclesiastical or lay, which should assume to divorce him. They were strong measures, a showing of the papal teeth. They were also, however, just the sort of measures most likely to irritate insular pride. At the best of times the English laity had resented anything in the nature of orders from the Vatican, and these particular orders not only affronted the national King but dared to tell the national Parliament what it might or might not do. Henry took full advantage of his opportunity. In a resounding proclamation he invoked the ancient laws of the kingdom with their dire penalties for whoever ventured to introduce papal decrees without the King's consent. Then he turned upon the clergy and indicted the lot as willing accomplices of foreign impertinence.

It was not a very pretty trick. The accusation filed by the attorney-general charged them with having criminally accepted a Legate from the Pope in the person of Thomas Wolsey, contrary to the old statute of *præmunire* designed to prevent the subject from giving any part of his allegiance outside of the kingdom. If, as seems improbable, it was ever intended to cover the question of Legatine authority, then the worst offender was clearly the King, who had not only for years allowed his subjects to recognize the Legate, but had also brought his own suit into Wolsey's Legatine court. But the clergy were unpopular, and treatment of them that at any other time might have been criticized as unfair was now applauded as hugely clever; the helpless priests had no option but to offer to buy themselves off. Henry assessed the damages at £100,044, 8s. 4d., which the Convocation of Canterbury duly voted . . . and which Henry, after brief thought, announced that he could not accept. His conscience had discovered another scruple: to take their money would simply be compounding a felony unless they granted it to him in his right of " Supreme Head of the Church and clergy of England ".[1]

The priests gasped. They knew of only one head of their Church since its Founder transmitted the keys to Saint Peter. But what could they do? They were not of the temper to accept jail and deprivation, and they knew it. Old Archbishop Warham proposed that they insert " as far as the law of Christ allows ". No one even troubled to dissent from the meaningless evasion. " Whoever is silent seems to consent," wearily suggested the Archbishop as a salve for conscience. " Then are we all silent," mocked one, and that was that. For their compliance Henry handsomely let them off the £44, 8s. 4d.

Further than that he did not dare go at the moment. He had put himself dangerously out of tune with the concert of Europe as it was. Pope and Emperor were openly considering an excommunication to be followed by an Imperial crusade against him; France seemed more likely than not in that event to stand aside in disgust. Henry talked big;

[1] It was Henry's theory, presently to be articulated by law, that the Church of England was a national and independent offshoot of the Primitive Church as established by Christ, the Gospels, and the early Christian Fathers; that a Donation of the Emperor Constantine (generally considered apocryphal) had affirmed the King to be its Supreme Head on earth; and that the Popes—" the Bishops of Rome "—had later usurped his authority and corrupted its teachings. The Reformation in Henry's view was therefore an act of liberation with a view to returning the Church of England to its pristine purity.

if the Pope started trouble, he loudly informed the papal
ambassador, he would finish it with an armed invasion of
Italy—heart-stirring words, greatly relished by the mass of
his subjects. How he proposed to invade Italy on the clergy's
£100,000, which at the moment constituted the bulk of his
war-chest, they did not perhaps pause to reflect. Henry
knew better; that was why he preferred to await the effects
of his subtle blackmail rather than challenge the papacy
to outright war. Also, things were not going altogether
smoothly at home. His high-handed methods were beginning
to frighten even those who approved of his aims; in order
to reassure the laity he had to promise that he would not
have them all up for *præmunire* like the clergy. Riots broke
out against the assessment of the £100,000. As a means of
soothing orthodox opinion he thought it wise to begin a
persecution of heretics which drove hundreds of them to
cover in Holland and Germany.

Nearly all of 1531 he waited. Still the Pope resisted.
So did Catherine, despite honeyed appeals and brutal
insults. So in another way did Anne, apparently. There
was nothing to do but strike again. Henry did, both hard
and with cunning, when Parliament met again in January,
1532. He warned the papal nuncio that the Commons,
fresh from contact with the people, would demand further
severities against the clergy—and sure enough the Commons
brought in a supplication for a drastic reduction of the
Church's millennial rights of self-government. The author
of the document was, by an odd coincidence, the member
for Taunton, Mr. Secretary Cromwell. What could Henry
do but agree? Loudly protesting his loyalty to the Faith of
which he had been appointed official Defender, he rammed
the demands contained in the petition down the throat of
the Church in Convocation assembled. Under his frown the
terrified English priesthood gave up the right to make or
enforce its own laws, agreed to the overhaul of its existing

laws by a royal commission, abolished the oath of allegiance to the Pope. Though not yet severed from Rome, the Church in England had by these articles made absolute submission to the State represented in this connection solely by the King.

Nor was that all. Parliament, still on the scent of ecclesiastical money, set to work on a bill for depriving the Pope of his valuable income from the annates or first-fruits paid him by bishops on their consecration. It had an extremely close passage; so close that it is difficult to imagine that it could have passed without the King's connivance. But anyone watching Henry must have concluded that his attitude was one of helpless distress: " you shall instil into their ears," he instructed his emissary at Rome, " how incessant have been our efforts to resist the importunity of our people for passing the statute." When it was clear that it would pass, he suggested a compromise. Let it go on the books but not into effect until he had had further opportunity to bring the Holy Father to reason. So amended, the bill staved off immediate reprisals. It also gave him a club to hold over the Pope's head.

He soon needed it. The Pope's resistance continued; so did Catherine's; but Anne's toward the end of this year, 1532, apparently broke down. Some time early in the New Year she knew she was with child. That considerably altered matters. The child would, of course, be a son, and if he were born out of wedlock, all Henry's labours of these past years would have gone for nothing. But how to avoid that misfortune? The Church was still, despite everything, final judge in matrimonial causes. If he erected his own machinery *ad hoc* to give him his divorce, it was extremely doubtful whether the English people would stand for it, and absolutely certain that they would never accept the offspring of his remarriage as his lawful heir.

Quietly—for he had been expressly forbidden to do so

under pain of excommunication—he went through a biga-
mous ceremony with Anne some time in January, 1533.
Round about the same time he applied to Rome for the
necessary Bulls of investiture for a new Archbishop of
Canterbury in place of the old one, who had (luckily) died
the previous August. As successor to the post he named the
clever young Cambridge theologian, Thomas Cranmer. The
Roman authorities naturally hesitated; though unaware of
what had passed with Anne, they distrusted Cranmer on
his record. But with his request Henry had sent the intimation that unless it was granted, the Act for the suppression
of the annates would come into immediate force. Tensely
the papal advisers debated. He might not dare; on the
other hand he might, and the loss of revenue would be
serious; especially now, with many of the English bishops
so old that a large harvest of first-fruits impended. They
took a chance on Henry's intentions and sent the Bulls.

Whereupon the new Primate at once instituted a court
for determining the cause of Henry v. Catherine—a procedure
which the Pope himself had privately recommended to
Wolsey, before the controversy became embittered, in order
to disengage himself from the whole affair. Simultaneously
Henry, by a masterly application of histrionics, bluff, and
bamboozlement to a now thoroughly worried House of
Commons, obtained a bill for the restraint of appeals to
Rome, thus blocking the way for Cranmer's decision to be
tested in the supreme court of Christendom. On 23rd April,
after a hole-and-corner trial, the Archbishop pronounced
as unsensationally as possible sentence of divorce against
Catherine. On 1st June Anne's coronation proclaimed to
the world Henry's successful *fait accompli*. On 7th September
her child was born—a daughter, disappointingly; named,
after Henry's mother, Elizabeth.

There could be no going back after that—at least for
Henry. Either he dragged England forward with him willy-

nilly, or England trampled him into the earth in her rush
back to the arms of the Universal Church. Over his head
hung excommunication, under his feet trembled revolt. In
October Clement concluded a marriage between his niece
Catherine de Medici and the heir of France, which threatened
to leave Henry friendless on the Continent. The great jugger-
naut of Imperial Spain slowly clanked into motion. Distracted and aghast, squire, lawyer, and merchant, the
whole band of once eager skirmishers against the local
regiment of the Church Militant, huddled together and
looked to the King. Throughout he had assured them that
this business of reform was a purely domestic affair, easily
managed at home, of no really genuine concern abroad.
Apparently he had been wrong. . . . At the first sign of
fear on his part, they would almost certainly have dived for
safety, every man for himself.

But he showed no fear. Instead, he showed the stuff of
which, for better and for worse, he was made. Mounting
the high horse of patriotism, never again so long as he lived
to be unsaddled, he broke off diplomatic relations with the
impertinent Italian princeling " who calls himself Pope ".
As for " the Spaniards . . . he did not fear them. They
might come, but they would not find it so easy to return."
Fifty-odd years later Anne's new daughter would declaim
similar words on Tilbury Plain with even greater effect.
But Henry could not, and did not, trust only to patriotism.
His agents sounded the Lutheran princes of the north for
alliances. His guns, manned by his absurdly few troops,
pointed at turbulent London from the Tower. He suppressed the annates and whipped a Parliament, cold with
dread of a reaction, into finishing what it had begun. A
series of swift legislative strokes cut the last ties with Rome.
An Act of Supremacy installed him as Head of the Church
with greater powers than any he yet claimed in the State
or than the Pope exercised over the Church of Rome. An

Act of Succession ratified all that he had done by entailing the Crown upon his issue with Anne.

But it was not enough for him to have the power to do what he wanted. The people over whom he wielded the power had to believe that what he wanted was right. Shortly before the end of the parliamentary session, in March, 1534, the Pope finally handed down his decision in favour of Catherine, amidst fireworks and the joyous clamour of the Roman mob for an immediate crusade against the disturber of the peace of Christendom. Here was the test. Whoever held that the Pope had acted within his competence, or acted justly, thereby held Henry to be wrong. Outside England he could not prevent people thinking what they liked, but inside they must all be made to believe what he believed, even if it killed them.

CHAPTER V

The Terror

THE killing had, in fact, already begun.

Some seven or eight years previously, a servant girl
on one of the outlying farms of Canterbury Cathedral had,
probably as the result of an illness, fallen into a trance,
in the course of which she correctly foretold the death of
her master's child. The trances continued, the village
church where she uttered her prophecies became a shrine
for pilgrims and Elizabeth Barton herself the Holy Maid of
Kent. A committee of monks sent by the Cathedral Chapter
to investigate brought back a report so favourable that she
was officially adopted and received as a nun into a convent
in the town of Canterbury itself. From then on, however,
a group of priests (including several of the investigating
committee) took charge of her hallucinations, her fame, and
her income, all of which inflated to fantastic size. She
spoke with the angels, who performed miracles at her
bidding. She received in audience the greatest and the
wisest, most of whom accredited, few of whom altogether
dismissed, her pretensions. She dispensed advice, sought and
unsought, to statesmen, kings, popes.

The general hysteria over the divorce elevated her into
a national oracle or a public nuisance, according to the side
one took. Under the guidance of her priestly directors,
who of course took Catherine's, she raved that if Henry
married Anne he would die within a month, and when he
failed to, that God would move his subjects to depose him

within seven. . . . Considering the state of the popular mind and her influence over it, this came uncomfortably near incitement to sedition; and Henry, though convinced after a personal interview that she was not all there, handed her over in the autumn of 1533, together with five of her associates, to the ungentle rigours of a Star Chamber examination. On 23rd November all six were publicly exhibited to a huge crowd before Saint Paul's Cathedral as impostors by their own confession.

That disposed of their capacity for harm but not of them, and Henry had determined to demonstrate by the thoroughness of their punishment the hideousness of their error. In the present state of popular feeling against the nun an ordinary trial by jury would have suited him best, but it proved impossible to attain. There was as yet no law making opinions displeasing to the King a crime, and though he pressed the judges to lay it down that whoever accepted the nun's views on his marriage was guilty of heresy and whoever overhearing them failed to report them was guilty of treason, they respectfully declined to prostitute themselves by manufacturing such a law for him. He tried another way. He laid before Parliament the confession of fraud obtained in Star Chamber—a court composed almost entirely of himself and his councillors; Parliament obliged with a bill of attainder; and so on the strength of a secret executive inquiry and a special legislative sentence for a crime that did not yet exist, the nun and her accomplices were delivered over to the executioner's rope and carving-knife.

Having thus assembled the machinery for dealing with the felons who disagreed with him, Henry proceeded to create the felony. The Act of Succession, as finally amended, fell into three parts. The first recited the reason for the breach with Rome, the divorce, the remarriage. The second transferred the Crown from Catherine's descendants

to Anne's. The third made opposition to the Act by word or
deed treason, and required every subject to subscribe on
oath his approval of the whole of its contents. Not only was
it a crime to break the law, it was a crime, the gravest of
crimes, to doubt any of the propositions on which the law
was based. The Act of Supremacy, enacted in the same
session, took the same line, with the difference that Henry's
ecclesiastical prerogative constituted the essence instead of
being implied in the preamble.

The majority of the English people did doubt profoundly
the propositions on which these laws were based. That was
the reason for Henry's putting his arguments in a form which
ordinary flesh and blood would scarcely presume to resist.
At the same time he had to be careful. The notion of men
and women being punished for what they thought, as distinct from what they did, was comparatively new in England.
The right of the Church over belief, though absolute in
theory, had always been limited in practice by the power of
the State, and that in turn by the vague but none the less
real liberty of the subject. It was now up to Henry, by grace
of God head of the State and by the law of man head of
the Church, to exercise both the right and the power in
such a manner as to convince a race the very opposite of
supine that to echo his will was the equivalent of liberty;
or if not, something very much better.

For that he needed time, and he took it. The cold
efficiency with which he conducted his Terror was no less
impressive to the timid and the uncertain than the burning
righteousness that inspired it. As in his dealings with the
papacy, he struck, recoiled to await the reaction, struck
again when his almost animal instinct for the popular mood
informed him that it would be safe. He resolved at the very
beginning to get rid of Bishop Fisher and Sir Thomas More,
the two most distinguished of his opponents, by implicating
them with the Maid of Kent. But the Lords showed signs of

revolt: too wise to risk a rebuff from a Parliament certain
to become more tractable as it grew more terrified, he filed
the pair away in the Tower to await developments. Shortly
thereafter, in June, 1534, he sent two wagonfuls of Francis-
can and Carthusian monks to the same destination. Whatever he intended, something warned him that to execute
reputable members of two orders whose rules forbade interference in politics would make martyrs of them. So he
starved them into submission instead, distributed them as
prisoners amongst rival orders, and impounded their lands
and chattels. Having thus gained a reputation for clemency
as well as some useful experience in monastic spoliation, by
April, 1535, he felt safe in hustling four especially distinguished Carthusians to a traitor's death at Tyburn via a
jury previously notified of the danger to themselves of an
acquittal. Before the country could sort out its various
emotions he had More and Fisher again before the Privy
Council, to decide whether they would swear to the Oath
of Succession or take the consequences.

Both preferred to take the consequences. Both towered
over the rest of Henry's subjects for moral and intellectual
grandeur. Otherwise they had little in common. John
Fisher, old, decrepit, violent, in the pulpit like some god
commanding the voices of music and thunder, was the arche-
type of fighting priest. He had fought Catherine's battle
in Wolsey's court and in Cranmer's. He had preached
resistance; he had even—though this was unknown to
Henry—intrigued for the assistance of foreign arms to bring
his own king back to his senses; he had so personified in
himself the remaining papal hopes of saving England that
Paul III, Clement's successor, either ignorant of the fact
that he was in the Tower or choosing to ignore it, created
him a Cardinal. on hearing which Henry grimly offered
to send his head to Rome for the red hat to be fitted on
to it.

Probably he was not altogether sorry for an excuse to kill Fisher. But only egoism swollen to the point of madness by jealousy of its own virtue and power seems able to account for his killing More. For More was his friend, perhaps his best friend, certainly the friend of his best self. Often had Henry strolled uninvited through the garden gate of More's little house by the river in Chelsea, to share his dinner and talk over things of state and of the spirit, or paced back and forth with him on the roof at night to discuss God, mathematics, and " the diversities, courses, motions and operations of the stars and planets " over their heads. He was a saint and a scholar, his *Utopia* far and away the most brilliant literary ornament to date of the English Renaissance. He had been Speaker of the House, with his wisdom and humour the King's indispensable moderator of its tumults during the earlier stages of the dispute with Rome; into his custody had passed on Wolsey's fall the Great Seal, carrying with it the title—quaint irony!—of " keeper of the King's conscience ". His own conscience being unable to approve the logic of Henry's, he had surrendered the Speakership and the Seal with the request to be allowed to retire to his studies. He disputed nothing that Henry did; he was quite willing to pray loyally for him and Anne " and their noble issue, so in such wise as may be to the pleasure of God, honour and surety to themselves, rest, peace, wealth and profit unto this noble realm ". Only he would not perjure himself by swearing to what he could not believe. Having been called upon officially in former times to persecute those whose consciences denied the papal supremacy, he was now prepared to suffer persecution because his own conscience denied the right of an unconsecrated layman to usurp such supremacy. On 6th July, 1535, a fortnight after Fisher and another batch of monks, his late friend and sovereign ordered him to the block with a parting curse upon his ingratitude.

First eminent and blameless priests, now the two most revered of living Englishmen, slaughtered for declining to affirm as true what all save a dubious minority of their compatriots knew before Heaven to be false. . . . To the whole civilized world it seemed a deliberate sneer in the face of decency—especially, of course, to the Catholic world, which wildly called upon its rulers to avenge the insult and deliver the faithful in England from their oppressor. The Pope at once transmitted the draft of a Bull of Excommunication and another of Deprivation to the two monarchs capable of carrying them out. Charles V, not unwilling to have a try, offered Francis I inducements to join him in a holy alliance before which even a united England would have been helpless. And England was far from united, as the Emperor discovered when he got into touch with the papal adherents there to see what chance there was of a rising with his help. Many of the old nobility offered to raise men, the monasteries to give money; the North in particular, steadfastly conservative and anti-monarchical as it had been in John's time, was reported to be awaiting only its feudal leaders' word to march. Outraged instinct joined hands with offended interests, and though their forces were diffused and unwieldy, it began to look, that autumn of 1535, as if they were really capable of cohering for Henry's destruction.

Nor was there very much he could do to prevent them. No army stood ready to nip rebellion at home, no allies to interpose a bulwark abroad. If he tried to anticipate events by attacking Charles, he would lose his only support at home, while the same tactics applied to Francis would merely drive him into the arms of Charles. Once again he made up to the German Lutherans, but they would have none of him unless he openly declared himself a Protestant: an impossible condition for a man who felt himself to be, and still trusted to avert the impending coalition against him by loudly proclaiming that he was, a more authentic Catholic than the Pope. Alone save for his growing navy and the incalculable fascination that his personality and his office still exercised upon his people, he faced the gathering of the crisis.

And save also for his luck. Even a far less self-assured individual than Henry would have been tempted to see in the events of the next few months conclusive evidence of divine approval. The kings of Spain and France came to a deadlock over Milan, which Francis demanded and Charles considered too high a price to pay for his aunt's and the Church's wrongs. At the same time Francis's Moslem allies broke out with such havoc in the Mediterranean as to render a Spanish naval expedition against the infidel of the north currently imprudent. Then on 8th January, 1536, Catherine died, wasted with suffering and disease. Whatever happened, she could no longer benefit, and her nephew, seeing no point amidst his other troubles in pressing a quarrel whose original cause had disappeared, persuaded the Pope to withhold his Bulls for some better occasion. Lacking sufficient impetus as yet to shift for itself, rebellion in England halted until autumn.

Before Henry had to meet it, however, he had the further luck to light upon the one victim (with the possible exception of Cromwell) whose removal could have won him the widest possible approbation of his people. He got rid of Anne.

It was both simpler and more complicated than getting rid of Catherine—simpler because he and his motives were both so much stronger, more complicated because of the awkwardness of repeating himself. He still had no son. Again he wanted to marry somebody else. But these motives, so impelling in the case of Catherine, were comparatively secondary in the case of Anne. Even if he had been certain of an heir by her, even if there had been no Jane Seymour, he would have snatched at any pretext for casting her off. For he had begun to hate her from the moment of possessing her. The ways that had once enchanted soon merely irritated: a shock particularly painful to a man so incurably naive as Henry about women and so sublimely assured that it was their supreme pleasure to make him happy. Barely six months after their marriage he had taken a mistress, and in answer to Anne's protest informed her that she would have to lump it as her betters had done. But mistresses could not soothe the hurt to his vanity rising out of the knowledge that she rather than he was the prime object of her own vanity. He suspected her of buying admiration by distributing the perquisites of royalty at his expense; he more than suspected her of laughing at him. What might for a normal man be no more than a salutary if uncomfortable experience was for an autocrat standing before the world as the heroic symbol of his people's will and ambitions an effect not only distressing but potentially dangerous. The conception of infallibility obviously precludes the sensation of being made to look or feel ridiculous.

That all this constituted unanswerable ground for divorce he did not doubt for an instant: to have made such a mistake in marriage he must, he argued, have been " seduced by witchcraft, and for this reason considered it null; and this was evident because God did not permit them to have any male issue ". But there were serious objections to acting on this assumption. Whatever steps he took to undo his marriage with Anne were certain to be construed by the simple-minded majority into a confession that he was still married to Catherine. Catherine's death partially removed the difficulty, but still failed to solve the problem of how to justify a second annulment without automatically discrediting the first. If Anne were to die, however . . . Cromwell, now extremely anxious to disavow his old connection with the Boleyns, contrived that she should as the best way out for his master. From reports on Anne's indiscretions gathered by his spies from her enemies, he compiled evidence of adultery amounting to high treason with seven lovers (later reduced to five), including her own brother Lord Rochford. The indictment being somewhat weak, he strengthened it with counts alleging that she had made fun to her paramours of her husband's appearance, clothes, and sexual shortcomings to such an extent as to cause him to fall ill to the danger of his life.

Oddly, Henry did not seem to mind having it advertised that he had been made a butt of. On the contrary, in the matter of his cuckoldry—a point on which a discreet sensitiveness might have been expected—he positively called attention to his horns by announcing that " more than a hundred had to do with her "; perhaps on the principle that when caught in an ignominious situation it may save the face to laugh first, or that the less to be said for her, the more to be said for him. On 17th May the lovers were hanged, drawn and quartered, all denying their guilt to the end save the musician, the lowest born of them, and he only confessing after a prolonged session on the rack and the dangle of a pardon. Two days later Anne herself, after a solemn mock trial by a jury of peers presided over by her uncle Norfolk, went to the block with no regret and a little peal of laughter at how easy the slimness of her neck would make the executioner's task.

Not many hours before her execution Henry had his marriage with her annulled by Cranmer on undisclosed grounds. The act relieved his conscience of the burden of his infidelities as well as his mind of any legal complications that might arise in the future, though it fails to explain how he could behead her for adultery if he was not married to her in the first place. The day before her death he gave a large party in honour of his betrothal earlier in the day to

Jane Seymour, and ten days later married her. She was the daughter of a Wiltshire squire with whom he had stayed the previous year, plain, not very clever, admiring, unostentatious in every way except, it might be, the least little bit in her disapproval of Anne and her devotion to the Princess Mary . . . traits all satisfactory to Henry, who in his own way was deeply attached to both his daughters.

This sentiment did not prevent him, however, from bastardizing Elizabeth as he had already bastardized Mary. The old Parliament having expired, he summoned a new one to deal with the consequences of Anne's downfall. The first item in its order of business was to thank him for putting the country before self by marrying again so soon after his previous marital deceptions. The next was to declare Elizabeth illegitimate, repeal the Act of Succession in her favour—thus restoring More, Fisher, and all those others to the status of law-abiding citizens—and give Henry absolute power to bequeath the Crown as he liked.[1] The old Parliament had, in diverting it to Anne's issue, asserted a control over the succession which had never yet pertained to king or parliament, either together or separately, but to natural priority of blood alone. The new Parliament now meekly divested itself of that high attribute of sovereignty and handed it over to Henry alone. Whether the deed was valid or not, however, remained for two hundred years of bitter debate and much bloodshed to determine.

[1] True, he could not will it away from any son he might happen to have by Jane, but since that was the last thing he ever contemplated wanting to do, the limitation was rather a sentimental tag accompanying, than an effective string attached to the gift.

CHAPTER VI

Rebellion

IN every great historical upset, as in every great tragic
drama, there is a point of rest, a moment when all the
forces in conflict seem to have attained a moment of equilibrium. The killing of Anne, in its impersonal or public
aspect, fell at such a moment. To the English people it
appeared as a sort of poetic atonement for the wrongs of
Catherine: one act of injustice cancelling out another with
an almost divine impartiality. By Henry, a connoisseur in
moral atmospheres, it was intended to serve as an object-
lesson of the highest urgency and timeliness, namely that
the revolutionary phase of his Reformation was over.

Against the unanimous sentiment of the country he had
divorced Catherine. In so doing he had divided it into a
majority which hated both the divorce and its consequences
and a minority which also opposed the divorce but welcomed
the consequences. Defiant of that hostile majority, he had
followed the consequences through to the separation of
England from the One Universal Church and its establishment as an independent unit of the Faith under his personal
direction. But though the process had elevated him, by
comparison with any of his predecessors, into something
more than a king, it had in another sense reduced him to the
status of a glorified party leader. As King of England he
commanded the traditional allegiance of his whole people,
but as a king who was also Head of the Church he was in
the position of factional chief to a radical minority. And

there was danger in the position; danger of estranging his faithful minority unless he carried the Reformation further, the certainty if he did so of active resistance from the majority. He had no desire to carry it further. For him the party programme had been achieved with the transfer of the spiritual power to the leader-king and needed only to be consolidated. But in order to rest at that point two things were essential: a final religious settlement sufficiently satisfactory to his opponents to reconcile them to the accomplished fact of the transfer, and the means of securing the adhesion of his followers to such settlement by solid advantages.

The second, and much easier problem, he had already taken in hand two months before Anne's death. During the previous autumn and winter various legal gentlemen in Cromwell's employ and armed with his instructions might have been seen touring through England to observe and report upon the condition of the monasteries. The reason given out for the visitation was the King's desire to discover for himself whether it was as bad as was generally reported and, if so, to see what could be done about improving it. The explanation may have been honest as far as it went; the complaints against the monasteries were quite long-standing and widespread enough to merit official attention. The worst that had ever been said of the parish clergy was genial compared with what was believed of the monks . . . for while the convent walls in no way excluded them from the more public vices such as extortion and the commoner forms of immorality, they obviously furnished them with a useful screen behind which drunkenness, sodomy, incest (since the nuns were vocationally " sisters ") and the blackest magic could be carried on unhampered.

But royal concern for the current state of monastic virtue did not entirely explain the descent of Cromwell's investigators. Henry felt it important to know a good deal more than he did about certain other features of institutions which historically and actually lay well outside the ordinary ecclesiastical discipline. The monasteries possessed their own organization and their own direct contact through their superiors abroad with the outside world. They were, therefore, natural centres of sedition. They also possessed their own incomes from lands left them in trust by pious founders and benefactors. Those lands, of enormous but unascertained value, would go far both to satisfy Henry's pressing needs and to create a vested interest in his completed revolution amongst a commercial aristocracy ravenous to become landed gentry.

On the other hand, to liquidate the monasteries outright would not only give serious offence to those of his subjects on whose affections they still retained a vital grasp, but would place government in the extremely embarrassing position of violating the sacred rights of property. Henry attempted to palliate the unpleasantness by infusing finance with morals. Cromwell's deputies set off with the prior intention of finding corruption and depravity sufficient to justify terminating the monasteries' existence, and found them. A raucous propaganda from pulpit and printing press dinned the findings into the public ear, together with the intimation that to dispossess such vileness of its hoarded wealth would automatically lower the taxes. Yet, despite these precautions, it was only after a prolonged debate, in the course of which he had alternately to accord modifications and threaten decapitations, that Henry obtained Parliament's consent in March, 1536, to his dissolving the smaller monasteries and taking over their belongings.

That a bill so comparatively modest in scope should have had so rough a passage through a legislature many of whose members expected large personal benefits out of it, indicated clearly enough the likelihood of opposition in the country taking a stronger form than words. But just at the time that the bailiffs were thrusting their way into the condemned Houses for purposes of inventory and expropriation, the popular attention was distracted by an event at once juicily scandalous and of scarcely less potential significance than the divorce from Catherine. To the jubilant reactionaries Anne's death and the bastardization of her daughter portended Henry's retreat from the evil ways into which his infatuation for " the concubine " had misled him: and with strained expectancy they waited to see how far the definitive religious settlement about to be formulated would consecrate her downfall.

Upon that settlement hung the decision as to whether Henry could revert from a revolutionary leader to a national king with all his gains intact; and that decision in turn would depend on whether, after having deposed the spiritual government of the Pope, he could establish another equally enduring in its stead. For until now he had done little more than install a new spiritual governor. Though everybody knew—or paid the penalty for not knowing—who was Head of the Church, nobody yet knew what the Church of England was, except that it had ceased to be part of the Church of Rome. Simply to go on reiterating that it was the same institution as before, apart from a change in the management, was obviously begging the question, since for one portion of Henry's subjects a Church under lay management was no Church at all, and for another it could never even become a Church until the last vestiges of the old institution had been scrapped and consigned to the devil whom they held originally responsible for it. A state in which belief was not uniform and compulsory was as inconceivable then as it seems to be rapidly becoming now. If the perplexed masses were not to be torn to a frenzy between the clamour of the extremes, it was essential to clarify for them the precise implications of a change which affected both their earthly peace and their immortal salvation.

And it had to be done without delay. Want of official guidance upon the grave topics in dispute was increasingly making itself felt in chronic outbursts of local disorder. Priests invoked the old disciplinary canons against their parishioners, and parishioners inflicted public insult or worse upon the priests. But what style of uniformity could cement peace between those to whom it was blasphemous to read prayers in English and those who considered it an impious mummery to read them in Latin—between those who would die rather than suffer the mass to be altered and those who would kill rather than suffer it at all? For Henry to offer to any of these conundrums a peremptory answer agreeable to the one side was to risk mortally inflaming the other, with fatal results to the existing equilibrium. Yet not to do so was to confess his inability to carry out a task which the papacy had performed with success for a thousand years. As often in turbulent times, the less the circumstances appeared to favour action, the more urgently they demanded it. Henry, natural man of action and gifted theologian, called his clergy together and instructed them to define the basic tenets of the Anglican doctrine. When they failed —being but noisy echoes of the general discord—he did the job himself, in Ten Articles " devised by the King's highness' majesty to establish Christian quiet and unity "

From Henry's point of view they did no more than give concrete application to the lesson implicit in Anne's death eight weeks earlier. Catherine had represented the Roman, Anne the Lutheran pretension: what had begun with the repudiation of the one must be deemed to have ended with the destruction of the other; and the net result, crystallized in the Ten Articles, to have determined that his Church was to be neither papist nor protestant, alien creeds both, but Catholic and English—his own exact image of himself. They preserved in substance the rites of the old faith with a few modifications designed to purify it of excrescent growths.

The saints were demoted, for instance, from objects of superstition to their original rank of models for veneration, and purgatory and the efficacy of paid indulgences to deliver the dead out of it were rejected; in short, what was essential to salvation was distinguished from ceremonial and " decent and politic order ". A list of supplementary injunctions from Cromwell stressed the teaching of the Bible in English to the laity, the devotional upbringing of children, the superior virtue of spending money on charity to wasting it on pilgrimages.

There was little in the Articles either to gratify the rabid reformers or to offend the fervently orthodox. But to the latter the point that really mattered was not what the Articles contained but who had written them. Whether inoffensive or not they finally codified the profane hypothesis that a secular person might rule sacred things. Acutely there confronted unnumbered thousands of souls the stark alternatives of burning in hell for ever or of fighting now.

Cromwell's agents again spread through the country, two separate swarms of them, the one to search out and punish infractions of the new code, the other to drive occupants of the monastic lands before them like vagabonds, in the process carting off the jewelled crosses and sacred vessels of gold and silver, even melting down the bells as if bent on silencing for ever the characteristic voice of the Middle Ages—as in fact they were: and those to whom the thought was bitter were at last constrained to recognize that the past was no more likely to return of itself than the pillaged goods. Only force could roll back force. In the North especially did this truth strike home. There, mediæval England still lived on, almost untouched by the breath of commerce, in love with its local liberties, passionately loyal to its native leaders, abominating the covetous, boastful, parvenu tyranny of the new England encroaching upon it. As Cromwell's scourge fell on the monasteries—no decadent survivals but living spiritual and bodily havens to the folk of those wide lonely moors—the call to resistance passed from mouth to mouth, then blazed in beacons from the hill-tops.

By tens of thousands the men of Lincolnshire, then of Yorkshire, snatched up their arms, pinned to their breasts the crusaders' badge depicting the five wounds of Christ, and assembled on the standard of the cross. The King's officials fled before them, his fortified towns surrendered with little resistance or voluntarily joined. The Lincolnshire rebels, confronted with a swift cavalry thrust under the Duke of Suffolk, fell back to parley, but the Yorkshiremen, gathering strength every hour of the way, swept on south.

There was nothing to stop them. The royal troops between them and London could be counted in scattered hundreds. Not until they reached Doncaster did Henry manage to concentrate in their path eight thousand militia under the Duke of Norfolk, forgiven the disgrace of being Anne Boleyn's uncle for the sake of flaunting his high lineage in the face of one of the rebels' chief grievances. But the Duke, whom a survey of the enemy's vastly superior numbers and morale quickly convinced that it would be hopeless to offer battle, sent back word advising his master to temporize.

Henry reluctantly agreed to receive the insurgents' demands. They turned out to be virtually unconditional surrender. The Church was to be reconciled to Rome, the orthodoxy of its doctrine and its personnel rigorously re-affirmed, all " villains' blood and evil counsellors " banished from the royal service, and certain special offenders, notably Cromwell, put to death; the monasteries were to be re-instated with compensation, various abuses, as of enclosures, remedied, the King's financial powers rigidly controlled, his right to fix the succession repealed and Princess Mary's name in it restored: all to be carried out by a freely elected Parliament which was to meet in some place well north of London, for which servants of the Crown would be ineligible. The fifteenth and seventeenth centuries, uniting their voices, required of Henry point-blank to resign the principle of the Reformation on the one hand and to submit to the principle of Constitutional Monarchy on the other.

That was the trouble with the terms. They were addressed not only to the wrong man but to the wrong age. They collided with another principle which the rebels themselves cherished as deeply as their faith and their traditional liberties—reverence for the person of the King. The very religion these " Pilgrims of Grace ", as they called themselves, were defending, taught implicit obedience to God's anointed, " His image on earth " in sixteenth-century phrase. In fact, " the preservation of the King's person from the villains " who were deluding him was one of the chief items on their programme. Never for a moment had they contemplated deposing Henry by violence; their demonstration of force was aimed as much at saving him from himself as themselves from him. But to be loyal to the King and yet disobedient to his will . . . the two impulses were utterly incompatible unless Henry were weak enough to adopt their will as his own.

Henry, no weakling, took full advantage of their dilemma. Between them and their purpose he interposed in his reply a vision of majesty so dazzling as to blind them to the fact that the material odds were all on their side. The Church? By what strange aberration did they, " the rude commons of one shire ", venture to tell him, the Defender of the Faith, what the true nature, teaching, and rights of the Church were? Who had ever heard of subjects dictating to their king the choice of his advisers? If any servant of his had unlawfully oppressed them, they had only to refer to their prince's notoriously impartial justice. As for a free Parliament, all his parliaments were free . . . though since it seemed better not to labour this point, he graciously authorized Norfolk to give way on it. He also granted the free pardon for which the pilgrims naturally stipulated when they had laid down their arms (and which until then he was scarcely in a position to refuse), " to show our pity if we find you penitent. . . . Now note the benignity of your Prince, and how easily bloodshed may thus be eschewed. Thus I, as your head, pray for you, my members, that God may enlighten you for your benefit." He sent for their leader, Robert Aske, a lawyer of distinguished reputation but far too gentle of heart and divided in soul to be directing counter-revolutions, turned the full current of the royal charm on him, personally confirmed the promises made through Norfolk, and sent him back in a perfect ebullition of loyalty. Ripping the emblem of the five wounds off their coats with a glad shout of " We will wear no badge nor sign save the badge of our sovereign Lord ", the pilgrims disbanded to their homes.

It was a tragic mistake. Either they should have been resigned to approaching Henry on their knees or made it their object to beat him to his. For between them and him —between their way of looking at things and his—no reconciliation was possible. To themselves they were freemen legitimately upholding, as against a misguided earthly sovereign, the charter of human rights inalienably instituted by their common Sovereign in heaven. To him they were wilful enemies of the commonwealth whose spiritual renovation he had been given a free hand by God to bring about. True, they held his pardon. But it was also true that they had conspired against established religion. Whoever did that was, by definition, guilty of schism and heresy; and, with regard to them, Henry was content to follow the papal rule that no faith need be kept with heretics. After the retreating pilgrims he sent a warrant for the arrest of

two aristocratic partisans of their cause—a direct violation
of the amnesty, and a deliberate incitement to fresh dis-
orders. This time, however, the outbreak was not serious,
the work of a few hotheads without support and easily
suppressed. Neither Aske nor his associates had taken part
in it, had in fact done their best to discourage it, but its
happening at all gave Henry all the pretext he needed for
revoking their pardons. In addition, letters captured in
their possession still harping on the free Parliament con-
clusively proved them, in Henry's opinion, " to persist in
a traitor's heart ". A batch of trials, a series of mass
executions——

" by the hanging of them on trees and by the quartering of
them and setting their quarters in every town great and small,
as they may be a fearful spectacle to all other hereafter who
would practise any like matter "——

and Henry's contention that England's distinctive character
as a nation was for him and him alone to determine stood
effectively vindicated.

The free Parliament went the way of the free pardon.
Instead of coming north to open it in person as he had
promised, Henry sent a crew of his trained bureaucrats to
take over the rebellious area almost like a conquered province,
with instructions to remove the local administration from
the hands of the native aristocracy who had monopolized
it from time immemorial, and to set up a sort of satrapy of
the Crown in York. A long while ago John had tried to do
much the same thing and had failed because England's
feudal liberties were too strong for him even with the support
of the Church Universal—herself mighty enough to have
previously subdued him unaided. Now, though joined with
the Church, they had succumbed to Henry. So far as any
power to qualify the Tudor despotism went, Magna Carta,
already superannuated in spirit before its last summoning

of energies in the Pilgrimage of Grace, was as dead a letter as a papal Bull . . . so dead that for a hundred years to come apparently no one as much as remembered its name.

Three months after the curtain fell on Henry's " fearful spectacle " Jane bore him a son. That she died as a result sincerely grieved him but in no way obscured his joy in the event's larger implications. God had set the seal of His approval upon him as upon Abraham.

CHAPTER VII

"Christian Quiet and Unity"

BY the ordeal of rebellion the dictatorship had been ratified. The King's religion was good enough for England—good enough, at least, to dissuade the miscellaneous majority of perplexed, irresolute, or indifferent Englishmen from making common cause against him with those for whom it was not good enough. More than that the collapse of the revolt could not be said to signify. If the country as a whole remained loyal, on this crucial point of religion it had been apathetically loyal; anxious for the King to master a threat to its order and security rather than aroused to any sense of precious convictions in peril. But that sort of loyalty, though sufficient to enable him to repel a sectional rising, gave no clue as to what would happen if he tempted the united Powers to similar violence—if Catholic Europe should decide in good earnest to take up the argument which the northerners unaided had so formidably poised. Would England's devotion still hold under such mighty physical and moral assault? Would her sense of unity as a nation under him prove stronger than her old sense of unity with Christendom? That question had not yet been squarely put to her. Until it was, Henry's decisive test lay before him.

It had in fact nearly come during the recent troubles, and had only been averted owing to Spain's resuming hostilities with France while still fighting the Turks in the Mediterranean. Arms and money destined for shipment to the Pilgrims by way of the Low Countries were diverted to other purposes; the Pope was left to act alone and he acted too late. In February, 1537, two months after the climax at Doncaster, he sent Reginald, Cardinal Pole, a self-exiled descendant of the House of York, to Flanders with instructions to cross over to England and as Cardinal-Legate assume the leadership of the insurrection. Earlier his presence might have given it the inspiration it lacked; as it was, far from sailing to England, he never even reached Flanders. Master again in his own house, Henry summarily informed Francis I and Charles V that he would consider the presence of his renegade subject on the territory of either an unfriendly act. Since neither was anxious while fighting the other to bring a fresh enemy down on him, Francis firmly escorted the Legate to the nearest point on the border of the Spanish Netherlands, which with equal firmness refused to receive him. After lurking a month in a neutral bishopric in danger of assassination and forcible extradition by Henry's emissaries, he stole by devious paths back to Rome.

It was a resounding diplomatic victory for Henry, but the papacy had suffered reverses of prestige before without being materially the worse for them in the end. That was its enormous advantage in the struggle to which Henry had challenged it. It was inured to vicissitudes which for him would have been fatal. The spiritual order which it governed, and had been governing when the Kings of England were vagrant tribal chiefs, was so ruggedly grounded in human habit as to be beyond the reach of organic injury, whereas the rival order which Henry was improvising out of his schismatic fragment could for a long while to come be at best no more than a ramshackle affair held together by external force and at the mercy of any grave mistake or accident. To defend his own weakness Henry, the original aggressor, had to attack and go on attacking. The papacy could afford to wait and he could not. All the victories he could win would barely suffice to stave off defeat, while his first defeat would mean its final victory.

So far luck had favoured his audacities . . . or else (what came perhaps to the same thing) by audacity he had made his own luck. Each emergency that he created he had overcome by creating another, with every risk dared Fortune to do her worst and hustled her into doing her best. But in November, 1537, three months after Pole's flight, she abandoned him to his own devices. Spain and France, dropping the quarrel that providentially had seen him through his worst crisis to date, came together to negotiate a peace—and, more ominous still, under the presidency of the Pope. What such an understanding portended for Henry a child could have told. In vain he tried to insert himself into the negotiations *vice* the Pope as mediator friendly to both sides. With equal unsuccess he next attempted to wreck the peace altogether with separate overtures to each.

Perhaps he went the wrong way about it. The sixteenth century was not squeamish, but Henry possessed the knack now and then of turning the most insensitive stomachs. His late queen was now already several weeks cold in her grave; his hand as indubitably free as his heart, he offered it simultaneously to Charles V's niece Christina of Sweden and Francis I's cousin Mary of Guise. But the latter was already engaged to his nephew James V of Scotland, whom she outspokenly preferred to her new suitor and whom, as the partner of an ancient and useful alliance, the French king did not in the circumstances care to offend. Unabashed, Henry then proposed that the beauties of the French court be dispatched in a body to some convenient spot like Calais for inspection with a view to marriage. The suggestion was for some reason resented, the refusal taking the form of an ironic counter-proposal from the French ambassador for an even more intimate pre-marital scrutiny of the candidates by proxy, at which Henry actually blushed before he recovered himself sufficiently to affirm that, " By God! I trust no one but myself. The thing touches me too near. I wish to see them and know them some time before deciding." Nevertheless he was apparently willing to take a chance on Christina on the sole strength of a portrait of her by Holbein. The enchanting sixteen-year-old widow, however, declined the honour with the oblique explanation (so it was reported) that if she had possessed two heads she would have been delighted to entrust one of them to Henry's keeping, and Charles V, who soon perceived that the wooer's political expectations from the match exceeded by too much his amorous inclination for it, did not press her. Meanwhile the Treaty of Nice between France and Spain reached the stage of signature in June, 1538, leaving Henry wondering far from idly to what extent the Pope had succeeded in imparting to it the character of prelude to a crusade.

However, to wait and see was neither in his disposition nor on his cards. Between the choice of sitting down under his rebuff or snapping his fingers at it he did not hesitate an instant, the more especially as an inspiration had come to him for a counter-attack upon the papacy in the inmost stronghold of its superiority, the past. Probably through no other means did Rome more firmly maintain her hold over the popular imagination than by the cult of the saints and of saintly relics. But they also laid her open to grave disparagement. Though in theory she discountenanced the polytheistic worship of the canonized dead, it was she, after all, who had canonized them and authorized prayers to be addressed to them for special conveyance to the Almighty. And however much she might deny miracle-working properties to the relics, she took the responsibility for them by the not inconsiderable profit she made out of them. Henry had already in the Ten Articles frowned upon these practices as popish apocrypha; he now proceeded to expose them as sordid frauds. A panel of experts looked into the phial containing the sacred blood kept at Hailes, at which shrine in Gloucestershire generations of pilgrims had laid their offerings for whatever blessing they most stood in need, and analysed the contents as simple gum. In Maidstone market-place the public executioner caused the holy Rood of Boxley —a crucified figure which when addressed opened and shut its eyes, bowed, nodded its head, and moved its lips—to do its tricks for the last time, only turned round backwards so that its adorers might see how the proprietary monks manipulated the wires. Before the new Elijah (who six years earlier had burned a batch of peasants for molesting a similar contraption) was finished, every traceable idol of the Roman Dagon, lovely or vile, had been torn from its place, held up to scorn, and dumped on the waiting bonfire in a tumult of expository sermons, ribald laughter, and gasps of fear.

The showmanship was masterly, the climax stunning. For the legends of marvels attached to it, for the number of pilgrims native and foreign who annually visited it, the shrine of Saint Thomas à Becket at Canterbury was the holiest spot in England, indeed one of the holiest in Christendom. But within it lay the mortal remains of the man responsible for the most impressive humiliation the Church Militant had ever inflicted on the English monarchy. The shrine itself, an exquisite unit of precious metals, jewels, and painted glass, Henry confiscated; the bones of the saint he summoned by proctor, as they had once summoned even in death another Henry, to appear before him and answer the charge of fleeing the realm in order to incite " the Bishop of Rome to procure the abrogation of wholesome laws ". When they failed to answer, he condemned them for contumacy and sentenced them to be burned. As a dramatic presentation of his fundamental dogma it would be hard to imagine a better. The traitor à Becket, who had betrayed his country's Church into bondage to an international gang of usurpers with headquarters at Rome, had at last received his just deserts from Henry the Liberator.

For an incredulous instant the world outside England refused to believe that such an act of desecration could actually have occurred; or if it had, that God had not blasted the offender at the moment of committing it. Then, with the assurance that the devil had again preserved his own, came the clamour, hysterical and exultant, for something to be done about it. For now surely, men felt, with Europe at peace, Henry's time had come . . . to brutal injury upon servants of the Faith he had now added wanton insult to the Faith itself . . . a taunt which even from a madman, a bellowing antichrist, the Church Militant for her own credit dared not ignore. The College of Cardinals resurrected and refurbished the Bull of Excommunication drawn up three years earlier, after the memorable session when they had burst into tears as one man at the tale of More's and Fisher's martyrdom. After sounding his two Eldest Sons, the rulers of France and Spain, the Pope in December, 1538, pronounced the decree severing Henry from the community of Christians.

Within a month the Bull had been rendered effective to the extent of a diplomatic quarantine. Charles V and Francis I refused to entertain any advances from him without the consent of the other. Behind the papacy also lined up Charles's satellites in Central and Southern Europe, behind Francis his ally Scotland, England's chronic enemy and the best base from which to invade her. Meanwhile Pole sped to the Emperor to concert more strenuous measures. The winter season being unsuited to military operations and the Spanish fleet being in any event engaged with the Turks, the plans had to be drawn with a view to their execution the following summer. They embraced, on the Emperor's part, an economic boycott to be followed by a descent of his fleet as soon as it could be disengaged; on the Legate's, a rising engineered through his kin, Poles, Courtenays, and Nevilles, scions of the old royal blood who might be expected to focus in themselves all the internal discontent with Tudor tyranny and impiety. Beleaguered from without, sapped from within, the Turk of the North (as the Vatican skilfully advertised him) could, it was reckoned, be speedily deposed in favour of a member of either the House of York or of France under joint French and Spanish protection.

The reckoning was out in one respect. Scarcely had Pole breathed the first word of his design to the Emperor than Henry demolished the important segment of it within his reach. Poles, Courtenays, and Nevilles he swept into the Tower, guilty and innocent alike. He bribed and tormented one into confessing on the others and, with the confession to vindicate his justice, had them executed as suited him, keeping the Cardinal's octogenarian mother to the last as a vain hostage for her son's reformation. Against the external menace, however, his advantages of speed and unified command were less availing. At the urgent advice of Cromwell he agreed, though it went much against the grain, to cement an alliance with the Emperor's Protestant subjects in Germany by marrying the sister of the Duke of Cleves—a lady of whom he knew little more than that her name was Anne, her age at least that of discretion, and her reputation both for comeliness and virtue excellent. But the Lutherans, even if they held firm against the seductions the Pope was holding out to them for a return to the Church, could scarcely be counted upon to neutralize the mighty papal coalition. Henry's supreme test was upon him. He must be prepared to fight for self-preservation. Would his people fight for him? If not, then he, and with him the whole Tudor experiment, would crash ignominiously.

It appeared that they would. They brushed the dust

from their long-disused weapons—pikes and longbows, bills
and axes even—and hurried to their village greens to march
and counter-march themselves into a citizen army. Willing
hands repaired the fortresses left to crumble through un-
martial decades and ran up fresh ones along the coast over-
night. The dockyards hummed, and in no time at all the
King's 150 ships were ready for sea. On many points Henry's
subjects might still be gravely divided, but on his fundamental
one—the First Commandment according to the Gospel of
Henry—he had taught them their lesson well. From whom
would they take their orders, himself or the Pope? Into
that terse query he had succeeded in dramatizing for them
as complicated a tumult of ideas as had ever set by the ears
not only England but all Christendom. And to it patriotism
found but one answer, thundered back at him in his own
slogan: as against " that pestilent idol, enemy of all truth
and usurpator of princes, the Bishop of Rome " and his
crew of foreigners seeking to mix into their English affairs,
they were ready to take on the whole earth for him if necessary.

And for that very reason they did not have to. The
Emperor contemplated the great battle fleet led by the
towering five-masted *Harry Grace-à-Dieu* and navigated by the
skilled pilots of Trinity House—Henry's creation all—and
decided to heed the warning his son Philip refused to receive
fifty years later from Henry's daughter. His armada he
left in the Mediterranean, his economic boycott he counter-
manded on a threat from Henry—now raised above the
need to manage the susceptibilities of his merchants—to
retaliate with an embargo on English trade with the Netherlands. Francis I sent an observer to verify the rumours of
England's military preparations and, on receiving his report,
instructed him to remain as ambassador for the renewal of
friendly relations. Even at Rome cold statecraft resumed
charge over crusading hysteria. The coalition had been

founded on the supposition that in England the will of the people was not the will of the King. And that supposition having proved unwarranted, its member princes dared not for their own sakes gainsay the dogma implicit in the new nationalism, that the voice of the people as expressed through their rulers was for practical purposes the voice of God.

Henry lived eight years longer, until 28th January, 1547, but they were chiefly years of repetition and revision rather than of fresh creation. In the spring of 1539, while the fear of invasion was still acute, Parliament at his request amplified the Ten Articles with a further Act of Six Articles which in effect erected his rigid personal orthodoxy—increasingly manifested in such forms as dragging his grotesque corpulence on its knees to the Cross on Good Friday and hanging a Londoner for eating meat on an ordinary Friday—into a test of any of his subjects' fitness to live. A diligent inquisition nourished by a legion of spies, professional and voluntary, saw to it that the test was not shirked, while a high but even-handed justice, which on one occasion united three heretics and three papists on the same gallows, relentlessly purged away those unable to pass it. There was no overt opposition and virtually no protest. By another Act granting him the rest of the monasteries, the larger and richer, Parliament made him independent of its financial control. Having thus abandoned its most potent function, it then decided that it might as well go the whole way, and after some grumbling practically divested itself, with a Statute giving his proclamations the full force of law, of any functions at all.

Cromwell had kept his promise. He had made his master, as he had boasted he would, an autocrat on the style of the Grand Turk and, if not the richest monarch in Christendom, as rich as the resources of England allowed. For that Henry rewarded him with the earldom of Essex.

Then, having no further use for him, he cast about for an excuse to be rid of him. The wife with whom the Secretary had saddled him during the late crisis provided it. She had proved a sorry disappointment at sight—nothing like "so young as was expected nor so beautiful as everyone affirmed"; in fact more like, according to her discontented fiancé, a "Flanders mare" than anything else. Desperately he tried to wriggle out of the marriage, but the offence to her relations would have been too serious. Groaning, he went through with it, to report the next morning that "I liked her before not well, but now I like her much worse". For a few months he brooded on his ill-luck, and then the responsible agent went to the Tower as a traitor and heretic, charged with having worked to undermine the King's religious policy. Henry kept him alive long enough to assist him in a divorce by swearing on oath that the marriage was invalid for "lack of hearty consent". Then he had his head struck off and retired Anne on a pension. The getting rid of a wife and a Prime Minister, once achieved only at the cost of a revolution, had become a mere matter of administrative routine.

He married twice more, once for passion and once for comfort. His fifth wife, Catherine Howard, deceived him, bruising his self-esteem and what little heart he had left to bruise, and her head, too, came off. His sixth and last wife, Katherine Parr, managed, however, despite open disagreement with his religious opinions, to survive him, a quickly comforted widow. Successful—too successful—in everything else, he could not somehow succeed in finding the domestic happiness he never ceased to yearn for—quite like ordinary men. Otherwise everything went pretty much according to his desire. Conspiracies to thwart his will melted automatically away in blood on Tower Hill. His army, sent to persuade the Scots into allowing the marriage of their infant princess Mary Stuart to young Edward,

Prince of Wales, and the annexation of her heritage to his, settled with brutal finality the ancient question of military superiority between the two neighbours, though the expedition led to the ultimate overthrow of his policy: a French effort to intervene in the quarrel was met with a shattering rebuke at the hands of his fleet, which swept on to the capture of Boulogne; and though the courtship came to nothing, since Mary ultimately escaped to France, Henry· never knew of this his sole failure, since he was already dead. His funeral was the most gorgeous ever given to an English sovereign.

He had been cruel, he had been greedy. But the age was cruel and greedy. The event showed that Henry represented his people far more than he repressed them. He had used the cruelty to extinguish old allegiances whose value had depreciated almost without awareness on their part; whereas his greed was no more than a flamboyant externalization of new energies and ambitions which had been subconsciously forming inside them. His original followers had long since, from observing the half-legendary potentates of Europe threaten and do nothing, become infected with a self-confidence bolder, if anything, than his. In various enterprising heads dreams had already begun to take shape of competing with the older empires for the domination of the New World—dreams realistically connected with the great oaken ships of the Royal Navy, which he had forged for the first time into a mighty instrument of national policy. Terror alone could never have fastened Henry's yoke upon a people so traditionally unruly as the English unless a dynamic nucleus of them had been willing to receive it for the exhilaration of being driven at so spirited a pace by so capable a hand in an instinctively desired direction.

And the terror, after all, affected only one department

of life. Only those who disagreed with the thesis that the
national king was the natural head of the Church had on
the whole suffered from his excesses. The ordinary man
was inclined to observe that the rites of his faith and the
priests who administered them remained in general the
same; and the priests themselves, once they took the pay
of the Establishment, were incomparable propagandists for
whatever differences it introduced. Ordinary justice had,
as Henry boasted, operated impartially between high and
low; familiar social habit had not been interfered with save
in so far as the general work of administration had been
steadily and remarkably improved. At the very height of
the Reformation, between 1534 and 1536, Wales had been
incorporated down to her last mountain fastness, Ireland
tranquillized, and peace maintained on the Scottish border,
with the result that during those tense and crowded years
England was rendered securer on her two islands than
perhaps ever before in her history. Obscurely aware of the
fact that some change in her religious orientation had in
any event to come, England preferred it to be carried
through by a despot who knew his business rather than leave
it to the hazards of a conflict between many ideologies and
interests.

That Henry felt himself called to the task by God there
can be no doubt. That he was entirely pleased with the
result is not so certain. In his last speech from the Throne
to Parliament—made when he was so aged and diseased
that his festering leg would no longer support his huge bulk
standing—he lectured his hearers with moving eloquence upon
the divine virtue of charity. He may even have meant it, for
he had begun to modify the rigours of his inquisition. At times
he regretted that circumstances had not permitted him to be
less Wolsey and Cromwell's king, more Erasmus and Holbein's, Skelton and Surrey's; that the wealth of the monasteries had gone so much to buttress power and so little to

endow learning, as the grandest episcopal ornament of his Reformation, Hugh Latimer, had urged; and hoped that what had not been vouchsafed to him, as to David that other man of violence, would be granted to the little Solomon his son to fulfil.

CHAPTER VIII

Elizabeth

THE fulfilment came, more splendid than the wildest flight of Henry's imagination—not through his son, however, nor through the eldest daughter whom as almost his last act he had restored to her inheritance in the event of her brother dying childless.

The monarchy, which had never stood so high as at his death, has seldom sunk so low as in the twelve years that followed. Having been made synonymous with dictatorship, it had forgotten how to function in any other way; and with the dictator gone it came near ceasing to function at all. That was the dangerous paradox in Henry's absolutism. The powers that he had concentrated in himself personally had of necessity become hereditary to the office and could no longer be separated from it, since their original owners—the Church, Parliament, the old system of local liberties—had been studiously rendered unfit to receive them back. But though Henry had thus been able to transmit his omnipotence *ex officio*, he was quite unable to transmit his aptitude for wielding it to the sickly nine-year-old boy and the ailing thirty-seven-year-old spinster who succeeded him. The opposing extremes, ultra-protestant and ultra-papist, which he had battered if not into uniformity at least into submission, seized upon it turn and turn about. From a supreme governing instrument it degenerated into the servile tool of party ferocity, to the loss of internal peace and almost national independence.

In the will executed a month before his death, and for precaution's sake formally ratified by Parliament, Henry appointed sixteen high officers of Church and State to act as a Council of Regents during Edward VI's minority.[1] But he himself had too deeply inculcated the habit of one-man rule for it to be supplanted at his posthumous wish by the rule of a committee. The sixteen Regents abdicated by arrangement in favour of a single protector, Edward, Duke of Somerset, Jane Seymour's brother and hence the King's nearest male relative. Of advanced religious views like most of Henry's " new " men, the Protector led England for the first time into open Protestantism. But even he proved not advanced enough for the stalwart minority of reformers who found the heart-caressing phrases of Cranmer's *Book of Common Prayer* an insufficient retort to the quasi-papistry of the Six Articles. Too moderate to please his followers, too lacking in Henry's brutal strength to suppress them, he was overthrown and in due course beheaded by a former colleague with neither of these failings, John Dudley, Earl of Warwick, an eminent soldier turned political adventurer.

For three years Dudley, promoted to be Duke of Northumberland, reigned by the liberal use of the axe and the fiction of a legal authority derived from the helpless King. But the fiction was valid only so long as Edward lived; and when it became clear in the spring of 1553 that he was in the last stages of consumption, Northumberland made a desperate effort to convert it into an unassailable fact. He

---

[1] The young King was, however, to have the power to call into question acts done in his name when he reached his majority. The will also decreed that Mary should succeed Edward if he died childless, and Elizabeth similarly Mary in the same event. If all his children died without issue, the Crown was to pass to the descendants of his younger sister Mary. It was this provision which formed the legal basis of opposition to the claim of the Stuarts—descendants of Henry's elder sister Margaret—during Elizabeth's reign. Margaret's son by her first marriage was James Stuart—James V of Scotland—her daughter by her second marriage married Matthew Stuart, Earl of Lennox; she was therefore the ancestress of both the Stuart branches, united when Lennox's son Darnley married James V's daughter, Mary Queen of Scots. Mary Tudor's daughter married Henry Grey, Duke of Suffolk, father of Lady Jane Grey.

induced the dying boy to sign a will leaving the Crown to his cousin Lady Jane Grey, whom he then married to one of his own sons and proclaimed Queen on Edward's death. Genius was on his side, as well as all the physical resources of government, army, ships, arsenals. Against him was merely a practically friendless woman fleeing for her life. Yet he failed, simply because the country worshipped the principle of legitimacy—of monarchy as personified in the Tudors—above all things on earth. It rallied to save Mary and refused, despite every temptation, to be a party to any of the attempts to deprive her of her throne during the five and a half disastrous years that she occupied it.

Henry, for all his autocratic temper, owned the precious gift of knowing what he could or could not do at any given time. Mary, with a similar temper, inherited none of the saving gift. Overwhelmed with the sense of a mission, nurtured in her devout, stubborn heart during the miserable years of isolation with her mother, to bring England back to obedience to Rome, she was able to do so outwardly with the aid of a Parliament ready to cringe to any wish of the Crown so long as the honourable members were not required to give up the former Church lands distributed by Henry. But practically such a reconciliation was impossible. Catholic by instinct most Englishmen still were, but not to the extent of welcoming back a Pope whom for a generation they had been taught to regard as their chief foreign enemy, while to the Protestants enfranchised under Edward he was of course anathema. Like her father, Mary tried to cure dissent by eliminating the dissenters, but where he selected his victims principally from amongst the prominent and condemned them for colourable offences against the State, she chose hers wholesale from amongst the humble, and recklessly irradiated them into martyrs for conscience' sake.

She made other blunders as well. She received Pole,

whom the country looked upon as a renegade and traitor, almost as a papal viceroy and installed him at her right hand as Archbishop of Canterbury. She engaged herself to the Emperor's son Philip and fell so passionately in love with him that she allowed him to commandeer her people for the prosecution of Spain's interminable quarrel with France. Prosperity, pride, and security alike paid the forfeit of her infatuation as England's credit collapsed. Calais—thriving souvenir of her former continental empire —surrendered to one French army, and another dug itself in on her Scottish border ready to invade almost at will. Meantime the fires of Smithfield consumed with appalling rapidity the Crown's diminishing reserves of popular affection. There was still enough left at Mary's death on 17th November, 1558, to ensure Elizabeth's peaceful accession, but whether it was enough to arrest the plunge of the once majestic Tudor inheritance towards moral and material bankruptcy many informed onlookers took leave to doubt. Unless there was a great deal more in this last living representative than met the eye, it very much looked as if the Tudors were destined to end as they had begun, in anarchy.

So far as the eye went, it could report nothing save what was in her favour. Her appearance had, to begin with, the great merit of recalling her father, by now transfigured into the presiding divinity of a sort of Golden Age, rather than her better-forgotten mother. The impression, derived at first glance from the reddish-gold hair that framed her high broad forehead, was fortified by penetrating grey-blue eyes, of the same shade as his but somewhat more prominent, over whose ready sparkle of amusement, glitter of anger, or mist of inscrutability, will appeared to exercise even greater control than mood, as with Henry. Almost as tall as he, though as slender as he was massive, with the

ELIZABETH

From the painting by Marcus Gheerarts

same superb carriage and, for a woman, remarkable bodily vigour, from both shone an equally formidable vitality. Of Anne Boleyn shè exhibited only the pale olive skin, which, however, by contrast with her so strikingly different general colouring, little suggested its origin. The oval line of face, the hawked nose, finely cut mouth, and long white hands, " of which she is so vain that she must always be displaying them ", were perhaps legacies from some distant Yorkist ancestress.

She possessed, too, her father's gift of popularity, as attested by the quality of her reception from the crowds that packed London's streets to observe and make up their minds about her in the early days of her reign. For her the gift was not only inestimable, it was indispensable, a *sine qua non* towards inducing a people sullen from the misfortunes of long misgovernment to defer judgment. But the elements of her popularity when analysed revealed nothing really very stable. Part only, and that perhaps the least, was due to a strong personal charm manifested not altogether artlessly in an appreciative eye, a direct tongue, and a free and easy manner wound round a core of natural dignity; all the rest she owed to the expectations aroused by her resemblance to Henry and to the fact that she was not Mary. To continue not being Mary was easy, a deduction from the nature of things that might be taken for granted. But that she would emulate Henry was equally taken for granted, and was an altogether more improbable feat.

For Henry had succeeded to a full treasury, trained advisers, a flourishing trade, and a long period of peace. Elizabeth took over debts, strife, hunger, and humiliation. Her revenues were mortgaged far in advance, and the public credit had sunk so low that the funds to meet current expenses had to be borrowed at 14 per cent. The debasement of the coinage, begun by Henry as an expedient and carried forward briskly by Mary, had all but demoralized

English commerce at a time when it was already having difficulty in adjusting itself to an era of rising prices and rapidly changing conditions of manufacture. War had completed the devastation, while the end of the war had thrown back upon the country hordes of discharged soldiers to swell the ranks of the able-bodied unemployed—dangerous recruits to the forces confronting one another in an apparently insoluble religious conflict. To the painful loss of Calais in a needless foreign embroilment was added the bitter knowledge that England had become of too little account either to compel the enemy to give it back or persuade her ally to co-operate in getting it back. Her border fortresses in decay, her fleet rotting in harbour, the once lordly arbiter of Europe found herself likened to " a bone between two dogs ", Spain and France, dependent for her bare security upon the good-will of the one and the forbearance of the other.

And whereas Henry had been carefully educated with an eye to his future responsibilities, Elizabeth, abruptly confronted at twenty-five with prospects as dismal as his had been brilliant, could scarcely be said to have received any preliminary preparation at all. There had seemed no reason why she should, when the chances of her using it had until very recently appeared so remote. Born her father's heiress, then officially bastardized, alternately made a fuss over and neglected to a point where her governess had to plead with his ministers for her simplest bodily necessities, she was awarded in his latest years the best available tutors for grounding in classical and Christian scholarship, languages, music, dancing, and riding. But it was after his death that she received what was to be the most valuable, though an unintentional, part of her education, a kind of education he himself had, perhaps unluckily, never known—in adversity, danger, patience, and self-control.

Arrested after Edward's accession for misconduct, at fifteen, with the Protector's brother and conniving at his

design to usurp the throne as her husband, she had managed
by a narrow margin to acquit herself, though he went to
the block. Again, in her sister's reign, a plot to depose Mary
in her favour had caused her to be thrown into the Tower,
but again she had managed to baffle her prosecutors. Set
free but still an object of suspicion to the sister who hated
her and hoped almost to the last to be succeeded by a child
of her own, she remained secluded from the world of affairs
till the moment of her accession, compelled periodically to
summon every resource of her wit to avoid being thrust into
marriage with some foreign princeling who would remove
her out of the realm for good.

But more serious than any of her other handicaps was
the one she had been born with—her sex. Though the law
did not as in other places prohibit female rulers, history,
instinct, and reason alike deplored them. Only twice before
had the experiment been attempted—once partially with
Matilda, occasion for a horrible civil war four hundred
years earlier, once with Mary of but too recent memory—and
neither could be regarded as anything but an impassioned
warning against the success of a third. The whole centralizing
tendency of Tudor government stressed the need of the
monarch to be strong, since " the king's will ", as a troubled
foreign diplomat observed, " is paramount here in all
things "; the existing situation, as unpromising as any
Henry had been called upon to meet in his full virile maturity,
intensified the need; and where was a woman, a creature
" painted forth by nature to be weak, frail, impatient,
feeble and foolish ", according to John Knox's current and
generally accepted definition, to find such strength?

Obviously only in a man. " Being a Maid she must
marry." That Mary had done so with unfortunate results
in no way affected the argument. Being superior to her
sister, Elizabeth must take care to marry better; in fact,
the success with which she chose her mate would constitute

an accurate measure of her superiority. " Everything depends on the husband this woman chooses," wrote the same troubled ambassador, the King of Spain's, and on that point alone if on no other her subjects were unanimously agreed. The right sort of husband would not only " relieve her of those labours which are fit only for men ", he would also, if her diplomacy were good, bring solid political advantages to the marriage contract. By thus placing her sex at her country's disposal she might yet convert it from a liability into a national asset of enormous potential value, and at the same time leave herself free to concentrate upon her primary duty of begetting the heir without whom her death would leave the reversion of her throne to be settled by another such long-drawn carnage as the Wars of the Roses.

It was therefore with a consternation easily imagined that her subjects heard from their new Queen's own lips her refusal to admit her handicap and the duty arising out of it. From the beginning, often and firmly, she announced that she had no intention of marrying. At least not yet; perhaps never. " It shall be a full satisfaction for my name and for my glory also," she declared, " if when I shall let my last breath, it shall be ingraven upon my marble tomb, Here lyeth Elizabeth, which lived a Virgin and died a Virgin." For she considered that she was already married and (making effective play with her coronation ring) that England was her husband. Her subjects' fears impressed her not at all. With her father's fervent love of power, she possessed his absolute self-confidence in her ability to use it for her realm's maximum good. She had waited a long time for it, surviving many obstacles that had seemed prohibitive, and now that it was hers she meant to enjoy it thoroughly. No man should interfere with that enjoyment if she could help herself. If by any chance passion or circumstances constrained her to reconsider her resolution, the only type of male she envisaged in the role of consort was one with no desire to dominate; in fact she said as much in her frequent stipulations that the husband she selected, if any, must be of her own unrestricted choosing.   Passion she felt sure enough of herself to keep in its proper subordinate place, and as for circumstances, however strongly they might seem to argue for marriage in general, they could always be made to argue with equal cogency against any particular marriage.

For whom, after all, was she to marry? A Catholic would estrange one half her subjects, perhaps to the point of revolt, a Protestant the other half. If he were a foreigner, he would naturally endeavour to exploit her in his country's interests, as Philip had exploited Mary; if a subject, his faction's, in the latter case without in any way adding to whatever resources she already possessed.   Unforeseen circumstances might arise to invalidate these objections, but until they did she saw no reason to anticipate them—an aversion to committing herself to anything in advance being the deepest-rooted principle of her nature. The child, too, could wait; she was still young.   Once she had him she would irretrievably have made over part at least of her authority to the father of the next king, while if she failed to have one her sacrifice would have been to no purpose.

For twenty-five years the quandary persisted, absorbing into itself virtually every other problem of her reign until age solved it by eliminating it altogether. Unless she married, her popularity, the indispensable buttress of her power, could not but remain precarious, subject to the reproach whenever things seemed to be going badly that her unnatural celibacy was the cause, and to the most scandalous explanations of its own cause. If she married the wrong man, she would lose her popularity altogether, and it was difficult to conceive of any man who would not be wrong. A husband chosen for her was likely to saddle her with a master, one of her own preference to prove a ghastly mistake. The whole of her reign—her relations with her people, her policy and her conduct, her achievements and her failures —was coloured, and often governed, by this decision she had to make yet would not make.

CHAPTER IX

The Sex Problem

SHE began well. By choosing her ministers from amongst the more pliant of Mary's and the less bigoted of their opponents in almost equal proportion, she allayed at the very start the pervading dread that her accession would inaugurate another violent oscillation. At their head, with the title of Secretary, she placed William Cecil, who had entered the royal service under the Protector, managed not to give offence and even make himself useful to Mary, and at thirty-eight combined an unrivalled grasp of public business with an incomparable instinct for the safe central point round which political cyclones could be left to rage until they blew over. With him to perform the liaison work between the Crown and Parliament that Cromwell had performed for Henry VIII, the Church of England was again established in independence of Rome, on a more Protestant basis than Henry had left it, though with Elizabeth as Governor instead of Supreme Head, in order to spare so far as possible the sensibilities of the Catholics . . . an all-round compromise both supple and solid enough to stand the wear of unexpected centuries.

Strict economy, skilful borrowing by the Queen's agent in Antwerp, Thomas Gresham, and a drastic restoration of the currency set the wheels of trade into confident acceleration once more. A hard sense of realities, which urged that England would in the end be better off without continental possessions to battle for, consented to the cession of Calais at an agreed price for the sake of a general European peace.

Only the urgently necessary was attempted, and that within the strict limits of the possible; a not exactly heroic policy (though it took courage to break afresh with Rome and affront national pride with the surrender of Calais), but so far successful that at the end of six months the prophecies of disaster overhanging the new Queen's head had lost some of their conviction. It was all that Elizabeth, a temperamental opportunist with great faith in time and very little in heroics, asked or expected.

Yet where caution would plainly not serve, she had no hesitation in resorting to audacity. The King of France, Henry II, died in June, 1559, at a tourney to celebrate the nuptials of his daughter to Philip II of Spain. The marriage had been expressly designed, on the part of France at least, to keep Spain benevolently neutral while England was invaded from Scotland. With French troops massed on the Scottish border, the enterprise was obviously feasible; and the new King of France, Francis II, indicated that he meant to go through with it by incorporating the arms of England with his own in the right of his wife, Mary Queen of Scots, nearest heir to the English throne by blood and with a better title to it in the eyes of Catholic Europe than the bastard heretic Elizabeth.

Elizabeth took advantage of the provocation to stir up a rebellion amongst the Scottish Protestants. When they proved unequal to the task of winning her battle alone, she thrust her army over the border in defiance of French might and Spanish remonstrances. Her pluck in the face of early defeat and the skilful eloquence of her State papers and speeches at putting the French in the wrong achieved the result of driving her enemy out of the British Isles and adding a highly valuable lustre to her reputation. The two guiding principles of her reign, timely aggression abroad and thrifty moderation at home, had been declared within eighteen months of its beginning.

England was delighted with her. Not only was she clever, she was a character. Her quips circulated through the realm to admiring guffaws and hearty thigh-slapping; a diplomatic adversary whom she out-fenced exclaimed in exasperation that she had ten thousand devils in her. If only she would marry and reproduce herself in a son, her people swore in chorus, there would remain scarcely a flaw on her perfection or their satisfaction. And even in that respect her actions belied her words so loudly that there was no reason for despair. She adored having men about her and visibly throve on proposals. From all quarters she brazenly enticed wooers, until she had before her the pick of the European marriage market in person or by proxy—a tribute to England's reviving importance which she insisted on enacting into so many separate homages to her own charms. Fast as they came she never found them too many, nor discouraged any because of the meagreness of what they had to offer.

There was her brother-in-law of Spain, the greatest king on earth because owner of a good part of it, whom she teased into torments before refusing him with a smile and a sigh on the ground that she feared she was too bad a heretic to be matched with so upright a Catholic. There were his two penurious Austrian cousins, the Archdukes Ferdinand and Charles, the latter to continue at or near the head of the list of possibilities for many years. There was Eric of Sweden, fantastically rich and even more utterly mad, and the irrepressible Adolphus of Denmark, who embroidered a heart on his sleeve and wanted to fight his rival, the petulant middle-aged Earl of Arundel, for her hand in her and the whole Court's presence. There was Sir William Pickering, a professional ladies' man and host of international celebrity on the slenderest resources, against whom the City bookmakers were prepared in the early spring of 1559 to give odds of no better than 4 to 1. And there were various others, foreign and domestic. Surely, reasoned her people eagerly, she would never have gathered this galaxy of suitors round her merely in the end to make fools of the lot—some of them members of reigning houses whom it would be in the highest degree imprudent to offend.

Yet as time went on, with Elizabeth still showing no sign of making a choice, an uneasy feeling began to spread that the grave business of courtship was to her no more than precisely. such a comedy. Else why did she not make up her mind, with every eligible bachelor and widower in Christendom at her feet? Not that her critics could make their own minds up, being themselves hopelessly divided on which of her suitors she ought to choose. But that did not affect the principle of the thing. The business of choosing was hers, all the more that she would not hear of anyone else choosing for her. Hesitation was a vice not permissible in a sovereign. As she continued to hesitate, the explanation took hold that it was a vice to which she was incurably addicted. She could not decide, because she never had and never would decide anything; when action could no longer be avoided, she still delayed until pushed into it rather than taking it herself; even to her triumph in Scotland she had only consented after endless recriminative discussion of the pros and cons, &c., &c.—a potent additional argument for submitting to a consort with an aptitude for the strong line before luck turned a contemptuous back on her shilly-shallying. But another school of thought was already holding to quite another explanation. She did not marry because she could not marry, knowing herself to be malformed and hence incapable of the marital relation. Her own physician (it was reported) had admitted that she was incapable of child-bearing; her flirtations were merely to gratify her vanity and throw dust in the world's eyes. Between the two theories the Tudors seemed doomed to sterility and England to anarchy. . . .

And then, at first whispered but soon shouted, came news that shattered both with a third more distressing than either. The Queen had fallen in love. She as good as confessed that she had found the man she would like to marry. Only he was utterly impossible.

He was Lord Robert Dudley, a grandson of Henry VII's chief extortioner whom Henry VIII had executed, and a son of the Duke of Northumberland who had tried to set Lady Jane Grey on the throne and forfeited his head to Mary as a result. Sentenced to death as his father's accomplice and his property confiscated, Robert had spent a year in the Tower, during a part of which Elizabeth, his schoolfellow in Edward's time, had been his fellow-prisoner and, according to the gossips, discovered in herself the beginnings of a tenderness toward him. Later, following his release in the autumn of 1554, he had withdrawn into obscurity until England's entry into the war on the Continent had given him the opportunity of attracting his superiors' notice to his soldierly merits and winning a royal pardon, though the Court, the sole gate to fortune for men of his type, remained stubbornly shut to him while Mary lived. Elizabeth's accession opened it: "mounted on a snow-white steed, being well-versed in managing a mounted horse"—still according to the gossips—he galloped through it.

"His beauty, stature and florid youth recommended him." A further recommendation, and perhaps more useful one at first, was his affiliation with Northumberland's old party, the extreme Protestants, whom Elizabeth was anxious to attach. Nevertheless there can be no doubt that she quickly fell in love with his looks, and very little that she was soon, and for many years, in love with him. Even on the admission of his enemies he was extraordinarily handsome: tall, dark, slender, mingling dash and grace in all his movements. His forehead was high and his hands long and fine, points she particularly admired because they were amongst her own best ones. They had others in common, not least a passion for sport, in which, whether at tilting, bringing down a bird in full flight with an arrow, or a deer with a lance at full gallop, he stood head and shoulders above his peers; Elizabeth, " like her father, King Harry, loved a *man* ". He was also, like her, witty, secretive, proud, arrogant, though unlike her he quite lacked the common touch—a defect of which she would instinctively approve, since it made it impossible for him ever to rival her in popularity. Openly gloating on " his many perfections ", she held him up as " the most virtuous and perfect man she knew ", and informed everyone within range of her remarkably audible voice that if she ever did feel like marrying, in him was embodied her ideal of a husband.

Her subjects could scarcely have taken a more utterly opposite view. Their dislike of Robert was as hearty as their desire to see her married was unanimous. The very traits that specially recommended him to her rendered him odious to them. Politically the name of Dudley stank for them of greed and cruelty, corruption and usurpation, with which for two generations it had been associated. Personally they looked upon him as an arrogant upstart, an unscrupulous schemer whose good looks and soft-spoken tongue had enabled him to exploit the Queen's natural feminine weakness. They suspected him of poisoning her private ear with evil advice, of wheedling out of her to the detriment of better men the honours, offices, and wealth she showered upon him in her infatuation. If looks could have killed, he would have died every time he rode out in public behind her carriage in his glittering panoply of Master of the Horse. In fact foreigners, baffled as often by English political usages, marvelled outspokenly that no man had yet been found with enough spirit to run a poignard into him.

The only consolation, and that of a very double-edged sort, was that Elizabeth could not for the present carry her infatuation to the length of marrying him since he already had a wife. Some ten years earlier, at the age of seventeen, he had married Amy Robsart, daughter of a Norfolk squire since deceased. It had been an ordinary marriage of convenience arranged between the two fathers, though on her side at least theré appeared to exist a certain affection strongly mingled with awe. They had no children, and of late years had mostly lived apart, Amy, on the meagre evidence, a somewhat simple, extravagant soul, moving about as paying guest from one country house to another.

But if Amy's existence prevented him from marrying Elizabeth, his prevented Elizabeth from marrying anybody else. And in the meantime the scandal of the relationship could scarcely help cheapening her matrimonial value. What the exact nature of the relationship was nobody knew, but the spies who reported on the matter on behalf of interested foreign Powers tended to believe the worst; while amongst those who believed her incapable of normal misconduct some surmised even worse than that. Elizabeth furiously denied or uproariously ridiculed these slanders, according to her mood. God forbid, she exclaimed, that she should ever have the will or find pleasure in such dishonour. To a protest of one of her confidential ladies at her so compromising her reputation, she retorted by pointing at the regiment of retainers who surrounded her day and night. Nevertheless, it seemed there were ways of evading their vigilance; at least, it sounded a flimsy pretext giving Robert apartments on her own floor of Whitehall Palace because his on the ground floor were too damp. One could well imagine the reaction of the more fastidious of her royal wooers if ever she were caught out with a subject whose quality even in his own country was not considered of the best.

And what if, imitating her father, she decided to eliminate the impediment between her and her desire? If, like Henry in so many respects—" Like her father, she means to have her will in all things "—she emulated him also in this? He had divorced one wife in order to marry a second, beheaded the second to clear the way for a third. Irresistibly the memory of his example hardened into a fixed dread lest his daughter yield to some analogous expedient with regard to Amy Dudley. Plainly, Amy could not be tried on any capital charge. Divorce, which was at one time mooted, was soon seen to be out of the question, since it was obvious that the Church, reflecting public opinion, would never agree to clear the path for its head to disgrace herself by so unseemly an alliance. A discreet murder remained the only alternative. Artful rumour was credited with preparing for it with a tale that the unwanted wife was suffering from a mortal cancer of the breast. Her husband, " who is assuming every day a more masterful part in affairs ", was quoted as having in an unguarded moment told somebody, " who has not kept silent, that he will be in a very different position a year from now, if he live . . ." A slow poison had been, or was to be, the method employed, and meanwhile " the Queen . . . in the matter of her marriage is only keeping the country engaged with words until this wicked deed is consummated ". The law in the sixteenth century accorded considerable leeway to resourceful rulers, but something always more important in England even than respect for law, that unwritten code which protected Robert from his enemies' daggers, strictly forbade private assassination. Only if Amy died could Elizabeth marry the man who possessed her heart, the one man she admitted any inclination to marry. Yet if she contrived at Amy's death and were found out, she ran an excellent chance of losing her throne and perhaps her head.

So matters stood when the Spanish ambassador, Alvarez

de Quadra, Bishop of Aquila, rode from London to Windsor, where the Court had lately taken up residence, on Friday, 6th September, 1560, the eve of her—and according to the astrologers Robert's—twenty-seventh birthday. On that same day or the next he talked to her earnestly about the Archduke Charles, the official Spanish suitor, whom she had half-promised to marry in order to keep Spain quiet during her Scottish adventure. He found her ill at ease, wrought up, looking unwell, and controlling her nerves only with an effort, though still able to dodge his efforts to pin her down with her usual tactics of mingled innocence and mockery. Baffled and disquieted, he sought an interview with her chief minister, Cecil, which, if his account of it is at all trustworthy, took as extraordinary a turn as any ever recorded in history:

"After many protestations that I would keep it secret, he told me that the Queen was conducting herself in such a way that for his part he thought it best to retire. . . . He begged me for the love of God to warn her as to her irregular conduct and to persuade her not to abandon her business as she did. . . . Then he repeated twice over to me that Lord Robert were better in Paradise. . . .

"And finally he said that they were thinking of putting Robert's wife to death, and that now she was publicly reported to be ill, but she was not so, on the contrary was quite well and taking good care not to be poisoned."

Next day de Quadra learned from Elizabeth herself that Amy, recently installed as a guest in the house of her husband's steward, Anthony Forster, at Cumnor in Oxfordshire, had been found dead of a broken neck at the foot of a staircase.

How she died, or whether anyone was guilty of her death, was never discovered. The coroner's jury which sat on the case brought in a verdict of accident; the meagre evidence that exists seems to point to suicide. But in the circumstances it was not the truth that mattered but what Elizabeth's subjects took to be the truth.

Robert they held to be guilty of his wife's death because they hated him and because ostensibly he had most to gain by it; Elizabeth they acquitted because their affection and their self-interest alike shrank from the consequences of implicating her. But had she gone on to marry him, the presumption in her favour would have instantly collapsed. It would then have been taken for granted that this was the end she had in view all along, and outraged morality might well have verified de Quadra's prediction that " she is in a fair way to lie down one evening the Queen and wake up in prison next morning plain Madame Elizabeth ". Though ready enough to champion Robert's innocence, she was not prepared to run such a risk for any man. She loved her throne and her power, not to mention the peace of England, too much. There was nothing for it but to wait for her people to see him as she did and meantime to go her way alone, trusting in her woman's wit to accomplish what they considered beyond a woman's strength, and to acquire for herself such absolute sway as to be able to frustrate all efforts to impose a man upon her.

CHAPTER X

Parliament

ELEVEN months after Amy's death there entered into Elizabeth's immediate orbit the woman who was to affect her reign and her fame more profoundly than all her lovers and suitors put together.

She was Mary Stuart, daughter of James V of Scotland by the Mary of Guise for whom Henry had unsuccessfully proposed in the interval between Jane Seymour and Anne of Cleves. Nine years younger than Elizabeth, she had been Queen of Scots since the age of one month as the result of her father's death after his defeat by his uncle at Solway Moss in November, 1542. At five she had been spirited away to France to avoid capture by the Protector's advancing armies come to betroth her by force to Edward VI. At sixteen she had been married to the French Dauphin, a sickly lad of her own age who succeeded his father in June, 1559, as Francis II. Seventeen months later he died and his widow, seeing no future for herself in France owing to the hostility of her mother-in-law, Catherine de Medici, returned to Scotland in August, 1561, after an absence of thirteen years. Endowed with a natural gift of fascination and polished up to the highest French Renaissance standards, she already enjoyed the reputation of being the most attractive woman in Europe.

Natural female jealousy alone would have inspired in the two cousins thus thrown together as neighbouring Queens feelings not of the most cordial. Mary's greater youth and physical charm touched Elizabeth's vanity, Elizabeth's superior prestige and strength Mary's eager ambition. But there existed even profounder reasons for mutual distrust. Henry VIII's will, ratified by Parliament, had deprived the descendants of his elder sister Margaret of their normal place in the succession on the ground that they were not English. Except for that provision Mary, as Margaret's eldest living descendant, would now have owned an undisputed title to be considered Elizabeth's heir so long as she remained childless. She felt herself wronged, and in that the majority of people agreed with her, including a great many of the English who felt that Henry's act offended against the legitimate order of nature. But Mary went even further: she believed and openly proclaimed Elizabeth a bastard and hence usurper of her own rightful place. As Queen of France she had flaunted her pretensions by taking the royal arms of England, an act which furnished Elizabeth with her best excuse for her recent stirring-up of trouble amongst Mary's Scottish subjects, and though in the subsequent Treaty of Edinburgh Elizabeth's objections had been allowed by the French plenipotentiaries, Mary had steadfastly refused to recognize the agreement. In that refusal lay the fundamental cause of all the future discord between the two.

For though Elizabeth could not, and never did, deny the merits of Mary's claim in theory, she dared not admit it in practice. Definitely to name any heir was, according to all precedent, to proclaim a sort of lawful rallying point for every kind of discontent and lawless ambition, but specifically to name Mary would, in her own terse phrase, have amounted to preparing her winding-sheet forthwith. Her other possible successors were at least likely to wait round more or less patiently for her to vacate the throne in God's good time; Mary made no secret of the fact that she regarded her as an interloper under an invalid will

who might properly be removed from a throne to which
she had no right at all. Her power to enforce this belief
was at present restricted by lack of means, but once
acknowledged as next heir the means might easily become
available. With every facility for building up a party to
exploit each grievance as it arose, she would be at hand
should a Catholic reaction set in or some policy of Elizabeth's unfavourably affect England's mind or interests.
And if a sufficient number of Elizabeth's subjects called her,
it could be taken for granted that Scotland, France, possibly
Spain as well, would assist her to respond.

Her return to Edinburgh made it imperative for Elizabeth to choose between the two possible ways of dealing
with her—to treat her as a friend or an enemy: to allow
that she had the best title to the succession if she acknowledged
Elizabeth's superior title to the throne, or to render her
powerless by estranging her potential allies on the Continent
and stirring up trouble amongst her Protestant subjects at
home. Against the advice of her principal ministers, Elizabeth chose to try the method of friendliness. Though declining to have Mary officially proclaimed heir by Act of
Parliament, she championed her claim negatively by forbidding any other even to be mentioned. She wrote
affectionate letters to the younger Queen and received
equally affectionate ones in return; they exchanged valuable
and ingenious gifts; in the summer of 1562 they planned
with joint enthusiasm a meeting near the border, an idyllic
week during which, face to face for the first time in their
lives, they would speak their minds to one another fully and
frankly. Even the outbreak of civil war in France, which
aligned Mary's kin the Guises against Elizabeth's sub-
sidized friends the Huguenots, though it postponed their
meeting, failed to mar their cordiality.

For two years they cultivated goodwill with determination, watchfulness, and apparent sincerity. But antagonism

and distrust were too deeply rooted in their interests and temperaments. Elizabeth still dallied, refusing to give a straightforward answer to Mary's repeated requests for a public acknowledgment of her rights. Mary, irked by the other's prolonged evasiveness, discontented with Scotland for its poverty and backwardness and with the Scots for their growing disrespect towards her both as a sovereign and a Catholic, resolved to improve her prospects by a brilliant marriage. Three consorts in particular commended themselves to her. One was the King of France, Charles IX, her thirteen-year-old brother-in-law; the second was Elizabeth's perennial suitor the Archduke Charles of Austria; the third, and on the whole most desirable, was Don Carlos of Spain, Philip II's demented son and heir.

To all three Elizabeth entertained strong objections. She wanted no closer tie than already existed between Scotland and France. Even less could she tolerate Scotland becoming linked to Spain and thus to the Netherlands, then as always the vital key to England's security. In the effort to dissuade Mary from these marriages, she threatened her with war in the event of any of them, at the same time herself inviting proposals from the parents of all three of the prospective bridegrooms. Being the more desirable match, she was successful in procuring for Mary a snub all round. Mary, stung but undiscouraged, retorted by shifting the struggle on to Elizabeth's own soil.

Her cousin, Henry Stuart, Lord Darnley, was also the grandchild of Henry VIII's elder sister Margaret, by a second marriage. He was now (1564) nineteen years old; he had been born in England and brought up at the English Court; and to many of Elizabeth's subjects who preferred the Stuart claim, yet agreed that Henry had been right in disqualifying Mary as a foreigner, he seemed the most eligible and proper heir. It occurred to Mary that if she married him their combined claim would be difficult if not impossible for Elizabeth to resist. Those who yearned for a Catholic restoration would certainly support her; those who dreaded her succession would be unable to unite on any other candidate with anything like her strength, and if they did not support her at least they would be afraid openly to oppose her. There was, however, Elizabeth to reckon with, to whom the idea was scarcely likely to appeal. Without her permission Darnley could not even be brought to Scotland. Mary sent her ablest minister, William Maitland of Lethington, to reinstate the policy of friendship. As younger cousin to elder, she placed herself and her happiness unreservedly in Elizabeth's hands, vowing prettily that she asked nothing better than to be guided by her and please her in all things, even—indeed especially—her marriage. Meanwhile she got secretly into touch with Darnley's father and mother. A suit over the family property in Scotland, previously confiscated for rebellion, was decided in their favour. The award necessitated Darnley's presence in Edinburgh. He applied to Elizabeth for permission to go.

The stratagem was too transparent. Elizabeth's ministers expected her to reject the application straight out as an insult to her intelligence. But she was fearful that by thwarting Mary's ambitions in England with such crude finality she would goad her into further and perhaps successful search for an alliance on the Continent; she also believed in her own superior insight into Mary's character. The response she gave to Mary's advances was so effusive as to be positively embarrassing. To Darnley as a possible husband for Mary she expressed no objection whatever, quite the contrary, and would give his request her best consideration. But, as an elder cousin anxious to be worthy of the confidence reposed in her by a younger, she would do better for Mary even than that. She would give her

" the most honourable and virtuous man she knew ", the only one she herself could ever conceive of marrying if her inclination had happened to run that way: Dudley, in short, whom she created Earl of Leicester to qualify him for the honour of wedding with royalty.

Mary at first declined to believe that she was serious. To offer *her*—the Queen of Scotland, Dowager. of France, heir (to say the least) of England—a discarded lover, a low-born adventurer, as one might toss a poor relative a cast-off garment! Tears of burning rage rose to her eyes and scathing epithets to her pen. But presently she thought better of it, as Elizabeth had perhaps anticipated. If with Leicester came a firm offer of the succession, she intimated that it might be worth considering. She had the question put to Elizabeth with a demand for an unambiguous yes or no. Elizabeth answered yes, certainly . . . that is, in a sense; loving Mary and Robert both so dearly, it was unimaginable that she would not wish her crown to go to them and their children; a definite promise sealed by Act of Parliament she could not at present undertake to give, though in time undoubtedly. . . . Meantime, as an earnest of her dis-interestedness and her complete faith in her cousin, she granted Darnley's application over her advisers' horrified protests. Mary still hesitated, naturally, to stake her future on anything less than a hard-and-fast contract; nevertheless she allowed her eagerness plainly to be seen. The English ambassador in Edinburgh and her intimate councillors formed the impression that she was quite prepared to have Robert if her terms were met. And then it transpired that she could not have him. Some said he would not have her, others that Elizabeth had never meant to let him, nor did either condescend to explain. To Mary the appalling fact stood out that she had been tricked into demeaning herself for no other purpose than to receive an outrageous snub. Beside herself with humiliation and fury, she accepted

Darnley, who had already caught her fancy, and married him in almost the same breath.

On receipt of the news, Elizabeth sent a special envoy to Scotland to forbid the marriage on pain of her enmity, and to recall Darnley home. It was too late. The envoy, a diplomat of long experience named Nicholas Throckmorton, believed that he had been deliberately sent too late, because Elizabeth had all along intended things to turn out exactly as they did. She knew her Darnley well: in the opinion of Throckmorton and various others who turned out to be wise before the event, she had coolly gambled on him proving more of a liability to Mary than a blessing. But the more general opinion was that she had been outmanœuvred, that Mary's rage was all put on, and that she had from the beginning merely pretended an interest in Dudley so as to cozen Elizabeth into giving up Darnley. At any rate she was now the undisputed successor for the unnumbered multitude who still yearned for a return to the ancient faith; and it therefore became a matter of the utmost urgency for the men whose property, privileges, and even lives were staked on the existing religious settlement that Elizabeth, whose health had been none too good, should place a first lien upon the future with an heir of her own body. Instead it was Mary who did so, in the shape of a son born in June of the following year, 1566. The cry for Elizabeth's marriage became so shrill that even Leicester was swept into echoing it. The stage was set for a decisive conflict of will between the Queen and the dominant faction in the State. It came when Parliament met in September of that year.

She would have postponed it if she could, but she had no choice. Unlike her father, with his huge inheritance at the beginning of his reign and the proceeds of the monastic confiscations in the latter part, she possessed no resources beyond her ordinary revenues. Out of an annual income of some £200,000 derived chiefly from the Crown lands supplemented by a grant on the customs duties known as tonnage and poundage, she was expected to defray the expenses óf her Court, the civil service, and the military and naval establishment in peace-time. For extraordinary expenditure she had in each case to call upon Parliament. In 1563 it had voted her a subsidy (a kind of occasional income-tax) to equip an expeditionary force in support of the Huguenots in the French Civil War, but the cost of that unlucky intervention had been far greater than the anticipated yield, while a rebellion in Ireland had so piled up the deficit as to leave her in urgent financial need. Whether she liked it or not, Parliament had to be faced.

The Commons at once showed their temper by electing as Speaker one Onslow, " a furious heretic ". The choice was a criticism and a challenge. It expressed the House's disapproval of her religious policy and its determination to have it changed. In the opinion of the majority, which believed, like Henry VIII, in unity by repression, Elizabeth was fostering papistry by neglecting to enforce the anti-Catholic tests. Whereas she, believing in unity by pacification, held that " the law touches no man's conscience so as public order be not violated by external act or teaching ", and openly boasted that " she made no windows into men's souls ". The rift between the sovereign and the legislature could scarcely have been cleaner. They were resolved not to pay out money which would enable her to do as she liked regardless of their wishes. She was resolved that they should.

The ministers of the Crown laid their finance bill before the Lower House. The House countered with a petition praying the Queen either to name a successor (other than Mary, of course) or to marry forthwith. Elizabeth sent it back with a demand that they cease minding her business and get on with their own, which was to vote the necessary supplies. The House adjourned in a huff. At the end of a fortnight it met again to hear the Comptroller of the Household open the debate on the finance bill. His opponents drowned him out with cries for an accounting for the previous subsidy, and with charges of peculation against all and sundry. The effort of the ministers to appease the tumult with facts and figures merely caused the diversion they sought to avoid: the House, shelving finance altogether, rose to its feet shouting that it was " far more necessary for this kingdom to speak concerning an heir or successor to their crown and of the Queen's marriage than of a subsidy ". The frantic ministerial promises that these matters should be considered once the needs of the treasury had been taken care of fell on deaf ears. The members refused to be snared in that trap again. Various of them swore that their constituents would have their heads if they returned home having voted the tax without having obtained the desired assurance.

The ministers in despair notified the Queen that the House had got out of their control. Either she must give way or the subsidy was lost. Elizabeth refused to give an inch. " The Commons," she snapped, " are very rebellious. . . . It was not for them to impede her affairs and it did not become a subject to compel the Sovereign. What they asked was nothing less than wishing her to dig her grave before she was dead." The opposing points of view were as sincere as they were irreconcilable. The Queen saw in the legislators' demands a threat to England's peace both internal and external, which so far she had procured by leaving the world balanced between hope and uncertainty as to how she would dispose of her hand and throne; the legislators saw in the Queen's pretensions a threat to their constitutional rights as well as to their future security. " I know not what these devils want !" she exclaimed in honest exasperation to de Silva, the friendly Spanish ambassador who had succeeded de Quadra, and he with singular acuteness responded that " what they wanted was simple liberty, and if kings did not look out for themselves and combine together to check them, it was easy to see how the licence these people had taken would end ". In the altered circumstances of seventy-five years later under a monarch less adroit than Elizabeth it ended in a Civil War.

The Lords intervened to arrange a compromise. Elizabeth would not hear of it. To take the Commons, that " knot of hare-brains " even partly into her confidence on a matter of such great importance was to sacrifice the whole principle of the Crown's exclusive jurisdiction over high policy. On this answer the Lords retired discomfited though by no means unanimously persuaded. The Duke of Norfolk, their most conspicuous ornament by rank and wealth alike, permitted himself the caustic observation that the Queen took " no other advice than her own ". Suspecting (justly, as events proved) a malevolent intention behind the words, Elizabeth angrily threatened him with arrest. The Duke had a strong following: to prevent the situation from becoming even more embroiled, four of his fellow-peers with a call upon her good graces, the Marquis of Northampton, the Earls of Pembroke and Leicester, and the Lord Chamberlain, waited upon her in a well-meant effort to condone the offence. They merely succeeded in annoying her further. That the hereditary lawmakers should not appreciate the issue that had arisen between her and the elected ones opened up abysmal possibilities of a renewal of the secular, now happily dormant, strife between king and barons. She called Pembroke a swaggering soldier and advised Northampton to save his breath to explain how he happened to be married to a second wife with the first still living. Her adored Leicester she tried to let off lightly with the reproach that she had always supposed she could count on him even if all the world else abandoned her. To prove that the supposition was still correct he offered to die at her feet, but she irritably rejected the offer as irrelevant. The four slunk out bearing her promise to arrest the lot of them if they dared approach her on such an errand again.

A delegation of Bishops she disposed of in similar fashion. Then followed, as a last resort, a mixed commission of both Houses. A little weary by now, she shifted her ground slightly. There was no need their pressing her to marry, since she had determined to marry simply to spite them, but God help them when they saw the husband she had chosen. Who he was and when they would see him she did not say, except to imply that he was a foreigner who would take care that they should règret it " if I, your lawful Queen, am to be so treated ". The hint was enough for the class that hoped to profit by standing in well with the King-Consort whoever he might be. The Lords, spiritual and temporal, withdrew from the struggle.

Not so the Commons. However much the other two Orders might now and then bicker with the Crown, the question of supremacy between them was settled: their very existence had, when all was said and done, been made dependent on it. Whereas the Third Estate had never submitted because it had never yet properly fought. Dimly its representatives felt that they had to fight now lest the theory of Divine Right supplant the old English principle that the Crown itself was a mysterious coincidence between the will of God and the will of the people—something that even Henry VIII had not dared to deny in so many words and Elizabeth at her accession had expressly affirmed. Undismayed by finding itself alone, the House reiterated with greater vehemence than before that the Queen's marriage and the succession were its public rather than her private concern: not a penny till one or the other was assured. To Elizabeth's reminder that she had forbidden the topic to be discussed, a member retorted that unless the ban were removed " she would see something she would not like ". Another member, a Mr. Dalton, defied the injunction in a furious onslaught upon an anonymous book recently published hailing Mary's son James as heir-presumptive: " Prince of England, and Queen Elizabeth having as yet no child! Prince of England, and the Scottish Queen's child! Prince of Scotland and England, and Scotland before England! Whoever heard or read that before this time? . . . If our mouths shall be stopped . . . it shall make the heart of a true Englishman break within his breast."

Elizabeth's answer to this flagrant disregard of her command was to throw Dalton into the Fleet prison. In so doing she raised an issue far above the realm of mere policy, however great. The right of members to exemption from arrest during a session was the very cornerstone of parliamentary privilege. If they could be punished for speaking their minds, then Parliament itself became a myth. Her supporters and opponents alike, frantic with indignation, refused to discuss any business whatever until Dalton was released.

Elizabeth saw that she would have to retreat. Perhaps she even foresaw it when ordering Dalton's arrest. In any event, having shifted the battle on to the field of principle, she gracefully broke it off for the sake of gaining the object of the original dispute, precisely as her father would have done in like case. Dalton was released with a pretty apology to the effect that nothing had been further from her thought than to trespass on her loyal Commons' freedom of speech. The Commons, relieved and delighted, at once voted her the subsidy she asked for with no strings attached either to her marriage or to the succession or—after a short further struggle—to her right to deal liberally with religion. For their complaisance she voluntarily reduced the appropriation by a third; for their conduct she told them off in one of her resounding matriarchal addresses from the

Throne. Both the gesture and the speech were characteristic and help to explain the near-idolatry she was capable of provoking in her subjects when she set herself to it. The speech ran in part:

"I have in this assembly found so much dissimulation, where I always professed plainness, that I marvel thereat, yea two faces under one hood, and the body rotten, being covered with two vizors, Succession and Liberty. . . . But do you think that either I am unmindful of your surety by succession, wherein is all my care, considering I know myself to be mortal? No, I warrant you. Or that I went about to break your liberties? No, it was never in my meaning, but to stay you before you fell into the ditch. . . ."

The point of view of Authority, vigorous and self-confident, as against a distrusted and self-mistrustful Liberty could scarcely have been more succinctly put.

The relative scope of the two had been determined for the duration of Elizabeth's reign. Roughly she could do as she liked provided Parliament could say what it liked. Its right of criticism might become uncomfortable or dangerous, but she could prevent it from exercising the right by refraining from calling on it for financial support. On her ability to make her money stretch depended her continued enjoyment of playing the dictator while yet remaining a virgin.

CHAPTER XI

The Feudal Revolt

MEANWHILE Mary's marriage had turned out even worse than Elizabeth had been suspected of wishing it to. A month had been sufficient to initiate her into the knowledge that her husband was a liar, a drunkard, and (by common report) a pervert—a vicious and conceited oaf whose one idea was to feed his ego at her and her kingdom's expense. Loathing him and for a time herself for having become involved with him, she presently gave her whole confidence to her Italian secretary, a former choir-singer named Rizzio. Darnley, tormented by a jealousy more apprehensive than amorous, joined with others of the Italian's enemies to kill him and take over control of the government.

Mary's superb courage and address after the first purpose had been achieved in her very presence frustrated the second: she seduced Darnley away from his fellow-assassins and sent them flying for refuge to England, where they received it from Elizabeth's ministers with suspicious warmth. Their hostility made it the better part of wisdom to remain on outward good terms with her husband, which she did until after the birth of her son. Then she fell in love with one of her own nobles, James Hepburn, Earl of Bothwell, an audacious adventurer recently returned from France. She gave him her whole heart and he gave her the strong, single-minded support she so conspicuously needed. Between them they arranged for Darnley's destruction, which Bothwell accomplished by blowing him up with gunpowder at Kirk o' Field in Edinburgh on 10th February, 1567.[1] Shortly afterward Bothwell kidnapped her with her own consent in order to beguile the public, and went through the motions of forcing her to marry him. The public refused to be deceived. The Lowlands rose. In a single battle the pair were overthrown, Bothwell driven into exile, Mary made captive. She abdicated in favour of her son, escaped, withdrew her abdication. Then after another battle she fled in disguise for safety on English soil.

There had been no other place for her to go. France and Spain, disgusted with Darnley's murder (of which nearly everybody still believed her guilty) and her marriage with the murderer—a Protestant at that—had washed their hands of her. Only Elizabeth amongst the sovereigns of Europe had shown her the least sympathy in her recent troubles, and to Elizabeth she had blindly turned for protection from her own subjects panting after her. Penniless and almost friendless, she was now in Elizabeth's power.

Yet in another sense Elizabeth was, paradoxically, in hers. For what was she to do with her? To restore her forcibly to her throne, as she proposed, involved crushing England's own best friends amongst the Scots, a war which even if successful would have turned them into mortal enemies. To send her to France—her next request—would inevitably have tempted the French sooner or later to the same enterprise, thus bringing them back to the Scottish border and undoing all the good work of seven years before. To allow her to circulate freely in England was a standing incitement to those who considered her the rightful heir to consolidate round her—some were doing it already and becoming alarmingly upset by her beauty, charm, and distress. To imprison her or put her quietly out of the way, as the

---

[1] This is, I believe, the more generally accepted modern conclusion derived from the Casket Letters and other evidence in this much-debated affair.

stronger-stomached of her English critics suggested, or hand
her back to the vengeance of the Scots—which in their
present mood came to the same thing—would have had
the effect of obliterating the evil she had done in the enormity
of what Elizabeth had done to her.

Moreover, Elizabeth had a strong aversion on other
grounds to dealing with her severely. What excuse could
she give? That Mary was a criminal justly deposed by her
own people and therefore liable, like any other criminal,
to trial and punishment? To admit that was to admit that
sovereigns might be called to account for their acts by their
subjects—an admission which would betray the whole
divinely instituted order of monarchy and create a precedent
which no Tudor could tolerate in England. For Elizabeth's
sake as well as her unwelcome guest's, it was necessary to
treat Mary as a Queen in misfortune and accord her the
right to negotiate for terms like an equal. But what terms?

The quandary was aggravated by the time of her arrival.
Since the reign of Henry VII, England had, save for a few
intervals under Henry VIII, been a friend of Spain, often
an ally, for a while under Mary virtually a vassal. Interest
and sentiment alike contributed to maintain the friendship:
not only did the Spanish Crown govern the Netherlands,
England's most valuable market by far, but it had absorbed
through marriage the House of Burgundy, England's ancient
helper against the still common enemy France. Various
factors had, however, tended of late to modify these considerations. There was religion, irresistibly casting England
for the role of enemy to Christian civilization in the eyes of
the ordinary Spaniard, and Spain for that of champion of a
decadent superstition in those of his English opposite, though
their respective rulers had on the whole remained aloof
from these emotions. There were the fabulous resources of
the New World, held by Spain in jealous monopoly, to
arouse increasing envy in enterprising English breasts. And

now, on top of these slowly crystallizing animosities, had
come the Revolt in the Netherlands which, after simmering
for several years, broke out shortly before Mary's flight,
and abruptly confronted Englishmen with the problem of
whether and how far to take the side of their co-religionists
and best customers, the Dutch, or of their Spanish masters.

On the answer to this, the crucial foreign problem of
Elizabeth's reign, depended in the last analysis the treatment to be accorded Mary. So much so that when the
answer was finally given after twenty years of intense indecision, and not till then, was Mary's fate determined.
For if England plumped for Spain it would be idle to argue
that Mary, the nearest heir by blood, was ineligible to
succeed by reason of her religion. Whereas if England ranged
herself on the side of the Dutch, thus assuming the leadership of a united Protestant front, there was not the remotest
possibility of her accepting a Romish sovereign. In one
event English policy would have been committed to Mary's
friends, in the other to her enemies.

Elizabeth wished to commit it irretrievably to neither.
Without the slightest trace of the crusading spirit herself,
she damned those who would have dragged England into
support of the Dutch on grounds of faith as heartily as
those who on similar grounds were intriguing to align
England in a sort of Holy Alliance on behalf of international
order with Spain. Ideologies she detested, and if religion
could not be entirely separated from politics she preferred
that it should be subservient to them rather than the other
way round. So far as in her lay, she took the line that the
rebellion was a clash not of irreconcilable beliefs but of hard
worldly differences between rulers and ruled, a struggle in
which her own sympathies lay on the side of traditional
authority but England's best interests in a somewhat elastic
neutrality.

It was not an easy course to follow. English sentiment,

appalled alike by the cruelty of Spanish vengeance upon
the Dutch rebels and the peril to English livelihood from
the Spanish effort to strangle Dutch trade, made itself
powerfully heard at the Queen's Council Table, deploring
her supine indifference. It was no easier to remain neutral
with regard to Mary. But about her, at least, something
definite might possibly be done, some compromise worked
out which, considering that she was physically in Elizabeth's
power, she might be prevailed upon to accept. If, for
instance, she were restored to her throne with English help
under proper guarantees for her subsequent gratitude, then
Elizabeth's position would in every respect, domestic and
foreign, be enormously simplified. To do this, however,
involved getting round Mary's enemies, who would object
strongly to the restoration, and her friends (including Mary
herself), who would kick violently at the restriction on her
freedom implied by the guarantees. Plainly nothing less
than a masterpiece of duplicity would persuade both even
to discuss such a project.

Such a masterpiece Elizabeth proceeded to concoct. To
Mary was now conceded the right she had more than once
demanded—of publicly stating her case against her rebellious
subjects. At the same time the Scots, headed by their
Regent, her bastard brother the Earl of Murray, were
invited to come to England and submit their answer. The
proceedings envisaged were in no sense a trial. Elizabeth
did not pretend to any jurisdiction over either of the parties,
nor to regard them as on an equal footing; she merely
offered them a convenient forum in which they might, under
her neutral presidency, appeal to the world at large for a
verdict upon their conduct to one another. But what she
did not tell Murray was that she had induced Mary to take
part in the proceedings with the intimation that once she
had cleared herself—an easy matter, since her adversaries
would in no event be permitted to introduce harmful counter-

charges into their defence—English help would be forth-
coming to reinstate her on her throne. Nor did she inform
Mary that she had induced Murray, naturally frightened
of just such a result, to appear on the secret undertaking
that he would be allowed to make any accusations he could
substantiate, and if they established Mary's unfitness to
rule she would be kept indefinitely under restraint. Decep-
tion could have gone no further than enticing two suspicious
antagonists to come together by promising each a favourable
result in advance. But it is difficult to see how good politics
(an art consisting, as someone has remarked, of the choice
between unpleasant alternatives) could in the circumstances
have avoided bad ethics.

The meeting took place at York in October, 1568. Mary's
representatives delivered her accusations against her subjects
to Elizabeth's commissioners, headed by Cecil. Murray
submitted his answer. It consisted in the main of a silver
casket abandoned by Bothwell in his flight. A lesser effect
would have been produced by a bombshell. Inside the
casket were various letters and sonnets addressed to him by
Mary proclaiming her love and her pressing eagerness for
Darnley to be put out of the way. Mary's representatives
objected to their introduction as contrary to the promise
that she should be the accuser, not the accused. They also
declared the documents to be forged. Murray and his
colleagues naturally contended that to prove Mary a mur-
deress by instigation constituted a proper defence of their
conduct towards her and undertook to prove the documents'
genuineness. The English commissioners, having been given
no power to arbitrate, referred the matter back to their
Queen. She, after another and larger but equally futile
conference at Hampton Court in December, took it under
advisement—where it indefinitely remained. She had not
broken her agreement with Mary, since she had not allowed
the casket's contents to be published nor warranted their

authenticity. On the other hand, the world, knowing that they existed, could now draw its own conclusion . . . and of course drew the worst conclusion from Mary's own objection to having them examined. It thus fell out that her reputation was sufficiently blemished to excuse Elizabeth from treating her as an injured fellow-sovereign entitled to help, but not too utterly ruined to make it impossible for her to threaten to do so should Murray's government fail to toe the mark. She held the Casket as a hostage for Mary's good conduct, Mary for that of the Scots.

To Mary's enemies in England this "verdict that was no verdict" was on the whole satisfactory. Not so to her friends. She was as much a prisoner as before, her title further, if anything, from being allowed. Their discontent and alarm were further intensified by another event that occurred in that same month. In order to pay his forces in the Netherlands, Philip II had borrowed a large sum of money from some Genoese bankers, who contracted to deliver it to the Spanish viceroy in Brussels, the Duke of Alba. Coming through the Channel the vessels bearing the precious freight sighted pirates and took refuge in the nearest English ports. The pro-Dutch party in the Council, detecting in the incident the visible hand of Providence, hastened to point it out to Elizabeth. If the money were in her coffers, they urged, it would considerably lighten her financial embarrassments, while its absence from Alba's would correspondingly hamper his putting the finishing touches to the almost moribund Dutch cause. Elizabeth demurred: to steal Philip's money might be construed by him into an act so deliberately unfriendly as to call for serious chastisement. Cecil, ranging himself for almost the last time on the side of temerity, reminded her that the money was not yet technically Philip's; to appropriate it, substituting her own promissory note for his, would be borrowing, not stealing; and in any event he was far too preoccupied with other troubles to do more than complain. Impressed by this reasoning, Elizabeth, in the midst of vowing that her mind was still far from made up, ordered the money to be removed to the Tower for better safe-keeping. From there it could either be reshipped to its original destination or transferred to the nearby mint for recoinage, depending on how things fell out.

Spain squared herself to retaliate. Alba impounded all English goods within his jurisdiction until the money should be released. The measure failed of its full effect because Elizabeth retorted by sequestering the far more extensive Spanish property in England. But meanwhile Philip II's ambassador, Don Guerau da Spe, threatened war and instigated rebellion. He found many thousands of Englishmen ready to listen to him: men sick with yearning for the old faith, with sympathy for Mary, with loathing of a government seemingly frivolous enough to risk a breach with Spain by a meanly dishonest trick. In the North particularly, conservative and ardently Catholic as in Henry VIII's time and currently suffering as well from the hindrances to the overseas trade in wool, its incomparably most important product, unrest wanted only leadership to solidify into revolt. Such leadership now appeared in the person of Elizabeth's first subject, the Duke of Norfolk.

As a member of the English delegation at York he had been smitten with the idea of marrying Mary Stuart and through her becoming king not only of Scotland but ultimately of England. The prospect was so dazzling that at first he was frightened of it, with the poltroonery of the man whose ambition is three-fourths conceit; knowing with what displeasure Elizabeth would view an alliance between the chief of her nobility and her principal enemy, he had not dared even to broach it to her. But his friends egged him on, Don Guerau promised the support, if necessary military, of Spain; and the total of his debts, enough to paralyse even the largest private income in England, contributed a further incentive to desperate enterprise. Before he was quite aware of what had happened, he found himself enmeshed in a vast conspiracy with Alba through Don Guerau, with Mary Stuart (who stimulated his courage in a series of letters simulating love and admiration with practised genius), and with the feudal chieftains of the North—Percies, Nevilles, and Dacres.

The conspiracy was as diffused as it was vast. The Northerners desired primarily to restore the Catholic faith and their old local liberties, Norfolk to marry the Queen of Scots and obtain the controlling voice in the government; Mary was interested in none of these motives except as they bore on her personal fortunes, the Spaniards in any or all of them in so far as they assured England's deference to Spain. The only denominator common to all of the parties was an active dissatisfaction with things as they were. One factor, however, distinguished Elizabeth's subjects sharply from the rest. Unlike Mary and Don Guerau, they did not even contemplate a change of sovereigns; they merely aimed at compelling the sovereign to change her ways. Cecil and all that he stood for must go, Elizabeth, reduced to dependence on ministers not of her choosing, might remain. Consciously or not they had been drawn together in resistance to a principle rather than to a person—the Tudor principle of centralized despotism. Disbelieving in it, either they had to obey where they did not believe or to fight; fight in the literal sense, with arms, since by its nature the principle allowed no other form of expressing disagreement. It was the contingency foreseen in Magna Carta—the lawful right to rebel consecrated by their ancestors after successfully disputing the same principle with John.

But Magna Carta was long out of date and, since the last unsuccessful attempt to vindicate the right in the Pilgrimage of Grace, to all intents and purposes forgotten. Between it and this new age towered almost to heaven the divinity that hedged about a king. Norfolk hesitated, hoping against hope to gain his ends by what then passed for constitutional means—Cecil's forcible removal from the Council Table to the Tower, perhaps, followed by a unanimous petition to Elizabeth from the rest of her overawed ministers to grant what the Duke and his followers wished. Momentarily Cecil confused him by bribing away one of his most influential supporters in the North. But all Cecil's acumen on top of his enemy's moral timidity could not overbalance the sheer physical weight of the forces accumulating on Norfolk's side as the spring of 1569 advanced. Even the Queen's most trusted servants, amongst them advanced Protestants like the Earls of Leicester and Pembroke and Nicholas Throckmorton, thought it prudent to enter into secret overtures with him and Mary as men converted to the project of their marriage. Mary herself felt so confident that she haughtily rejected a fresh proposal from Elizabeth to help her back to her throne on terms. The French Government, eager to claim a stake in the conspirators' victory, handed Elizabeth a tentative declaration of war; the Pope, Pius V, made ready to unite the whole moral force of Catholic Christendom in their support. So probable did the success of the anticipated *coup* seem by midsummer that Cecil took steps to transfer his family and whatever property he could abroad to spare them from his own imminent fate.

But his antagonists still had the Queen to reckon with. Though she occasionally doubted the wisdom of his policy, it never for a moment occurred to her to sacrifice him at their behest. To have yielded to opposition except at her own pleasure would have amounted to a betrayal of her sacred prerogative; for opposition to attempt to coerce her was in her Tudor eyes rebellion, and rebellion *per se* treason. Patiently she waited to collect the fullest possible measure of information about her critics' designs; then she struck first and struck hard. She ordered Norfolk to Court to account for himself. Frightened, he ran away to his family stronghold in the county whose name he bore. She commanded him to return with the threat to send and fetch him if he dallied. Wildly he turned to his friends for help, but they were not yet ready; nor was he, when it came to defying outright God's anointed. He started for Windsor, was arrested on the way, and escorted to the Tower. The moody silence of the crowd which from the banks of the Thames watched him being carried by barge to his destination showed how little the populace had yet made up its mind between the old easy-going feudalism and the masterful new monarchy.

Then the storm broke. Elizabeth issued the same summons to the Earls of Northumberland and Westmoreland, heads respectively of the clans of Percy and Neville. Less awed by her, and with Norfolk's example before them, they refused and turned for help towards Spain, as he had turned towards them. But Spain was no readier than before: Don Guerau, who had all along outrun his instructions, was forced to advise them to temporize. It was too late. Their peril had already set their followers on the march. As in 1536, the beacons blazed from the hill-tops, humble men in the Pilgrims' home-made uniform of red and blue ran by thousands to assemble on the standard of the cross, pinning the badge with the five wounds of Christ on their breasts as they ran. They took Durham, where they ceremoniously destroyed the Anglican symbols—the Bible in English, the Book of Common Prayer, and the Communion Table—and heard the mass in all its traditional splendour. One detachment sped westward to rescue Mary from Tutbury, whither she had been removed in the nick of time for better safekeeping to the care of Elizabeth's cousin the Earl of Huntingdon. The rest flowed on south in a gathering torrent.

No more than her father in a similar situation did Elizabeth flinch. Like him, she enjoyed the advantage of one mind with one purpose over many minds distracted by many purposes. A prompt command closed the ports to any communication with the rebels from abroad. Another whisked Mary to Coventry far out of her deliverers' way. Another cousin, Lord Hunsdon, operating in concert with the Earl of Murray on the Scottish border, advanced with a small regular force to harry the enemy from the rear, while to meet them in front the territorial musters were called out in greater strength than ever before attempted in civil strife. Caught between the two fires, the rebels halted, bickered, retreated, and dispersed.

The trouble was not yet over. It had arisen from causes too deep and too widespread for it to be stamped out so swiftly. Leonard Dacre, the northern leader whom Cecil had temporarily bought off, turned round and partly succeeded in rallying the insurgent forces. His sympathizers in Scotland assassinated Murray. At the same time—February, 1570—the Pope launched a Bull declaring Elizabeth not only excommunicated but deposed—a measure his predecessor had never dared take against her father—and summoned the Powers to execute it. But again Elizabeth struck first. Redoubling her vigilance over Mary, who alone gave coherence to the whole wide-flung scheme, she assured the loyalty of the Scots by procuring the nomination of Darnley's father, Mary's most implacable enemy, to be Regent in Murray's place. Hunsdon swooped down on Dacre before he could concentrate more than his own personal followers and annihilated him in a single charge. By the time the Bull came to the notice of those to whom it was addressed, the enterprise it had been intended to consummate was so plainly bankrupt that the interest it evoked on the Continent was scarcely feebler than the effect it was able to produce in England.

Thirty-three years—a full three-fourths—remained of Elizabeth's reign, but organised rebellion was at an end. Supreme within, whatever serious challenge she had henceforth to face came strictly from without. Shortly after the collapse of the revolt the Pope and Philip of Spain backed a plot between a Florentine banker, resident in London, named Ridolfi and his debtor, the Duke of Norfolk, to have her put out of the way; and though it failed, the same potentates continued for twenty years to hope that a successful assassination would spare them the expense and uncertainty of an invasion. It was tantamount to admitting that there remained no way of estranging her will from her people's short of destroying her—or them. The ascendancy of one human being over several million could scarcely have gone further.

Viewed externally, her power certainly looked less imposing than her father's. But that was only because she paraded it less ostentatiously. Save where it was attacked by force, she never yet armoured it in force. Though in a spasm of anger and nerves she dealt out shocking punishments to the rebels of the North, there normally existed no systematic machinery of repression, no secret police and corrupt or brow-beaten juries, to ferret out and rid her of suspected opponents. In all the first dozen years of her reign the only public figure to be put to death for a political offence was Norfolk, for his share in the Ridolfi plot; and even him she nearly pardoned, while Mary she insisted on letting off despite the vigorous disapproval of Parliament and the City. Unlike Henry, she tended to identify herself with the law rather than the other way round; to interpret it with the minimum of severity necessary to keep it in respect rather than to treat it as an instrument of personal infallibility. She neither created crimes by edict, nor sought by inquisition to erect irregular opinions into criminal acts. So far as any despotism could rest upon consent, hers did.

CHAPTER XII

The Uses of Time

THE second decade of Elizabeth's reign settled down to a peace unknown since the early days of Henry VIII. No violent internal controversy or foreign complication threatened seriously to upset it, though the differences were still many and acute as to the shape into which the spiritual and material amalgam of English life, so long fluid, should be made to harden, and though, just across the narrow waters, in the Low Countries and France, Catholics and Protestants were slaughtering one another for motives very close to English hearts. In almost miraculous immunity from the disintegration that beset her neighbours like some mysterious plague, England was able to obey the sudden stirrings within her towards expansion.

During the previous three-quarters of a century Spain, Portugal, and France between them, with the first well in the lead, had discovered, in part explored, and begun to colonize the Americas, opened a sea-passage to China and India both by the east and the west, girdled the globe with their ships. In that time England's maritime enterprise had been limited to a tentative trade with Russia through the Baltic, and the efforts of John Hawkins to cut in on the slave trade between Africa and Spanish America. Moreover the last Russian venture, Anthony Jenkinson's, had broken down and Hawkins had run into disaster at the hands of the Spaniards in Mexico in 1568—an event that had in large part influenced Elizabeth to seize the Genoese loan to Philip II by way of reprisal. Now Thomas Banister, going far beyond Jenkinson, succeeded in carrying his bales of English cloths to the bazaars of Samarkand and bringing home their selling price in carpets and silks. Two years later, in 1571, Jenkinson himself established a regular exchange of English woollens against Muscovy furs. Hawkins triumphantly landed his " black ivory " in defiance of the Spanish monopoly and returned with gold and spices to prove it. Shortly afterward young Martin Frobisher, in an attempt to find a short-cut to the Indies outside Spain's jealously guarded routes, led three expeditions in three successive years to look for a north-west passage through the polar ice. Between the second and the third Francis Drake started, in December, 1577, with no such scruples, on the raid into the Pacific that took him, loaded to foundering-point with gleaming loot, round the world.

And all this was only a beginning. Soon the first English ambassador ever to be received in Constantinople testified to his country's growing importance to the Power commanding the old overland route to the East; in the towns of the Barbary Coast resident consuls chaffered with the local pirate Deys and Beys over her new rights and interests in the Mediterranean; while on the other side of the world, on a strip of marshland called Virginia in the Queen's honour, a company of emigrants struggled to justify the beliefs of certain capitalists at home in the possibilities of an English colonial empire. Nor did this sudden and unparalleled energy exhaust itself upon mere geographical space. More slowly but no less exuberantly it spread its activities into hitherto unexplored regions of the mind. It caught the wakening imagination of Spenser, Sidney, and Raleigh, none of them over fifteen at the beginning of Elizabeth's second decade, of Bacon, Drayton, and Shakespeare, respectively eight, six, and five. On the assorted pabulum brought home by the adventurers, the strange

objects of richness and beauty and the even stranger tales
of men and places, they and the rest of their astonishing
generation—Kyd and Webster, Hakluyt and Marlowe (to
mention but a few)—cut their wisdom teeth.

But not only the imaginations of the poets were nurtured
by the achievements of the adventurers. The ambitions of
statesmen and merchants were also; and at such a rate
that before long they became incompatible with the peace
that had cradled them. For beyond a certain point England's
material expansion could only continue at the expense of
other nations, notably Spain, whose prior claims more or
less embraced the earth. Those reluctant to allow her
claims on selfish grounds began to ask themselves how far
they could be justified on moral grounds. The answer was
satisfactory. The Spanish title to the Indies, East and West,
and to the routes leading to them derived originally from
the award of a Pope [1]—that " enemy of all truth and usurpator of princes " whose fraudulent pretensions to mundane
authority it was every true Englishman's duty to denounce
along with the " detestable superstition " on which they
rested. The collision of interest thus evolved by natural
transition into a conflict of right: to the attraction of profit
was added the virtue of smiting the enemies of truth. And
since it was obvious that if Spain succeeded in crushing the
revolt in the Netherlands she would be free to give her
undivided attention to contesting this theory, those who
held it most strongly laboured to erect their desire that she
should not succeed into a cardinal principle of national
policy.

This forward group was still, during the 1570's, a small
minority, but it made up in vigour and leadership what it
lacked in numbers. Its early nucleus, though consisting of
the extreme Protestant sect popularly derided as " hot

[1] The Bull of Demarcation issued by Alexander VI in 1493 divided the whole
of the unexplored world, very unequally, between Spain and Portugal—whom
Spain in 1580 overran and absorbed.

Puritans ", recruited a disproportionate strength from amongst the powerful financial circles in the City. Its most prominent member at Court was the Queen's own adored favourite the Earl of Leicester. Its directing brain was Francis Walsingham's, a swarthy, secretive young man who, after an eventful term as ambassador to France, in 1573 succeeded Cecil, recently appointed Lord Treasurer, to the post of Principal Secretary. Most important of all, as time went on, it gathered to itself the ablest and most ardent of the younger generation, including the poets. Also, as time went on, it altered its character. From a faction of courtiers and merchants it developed into something like an organized political party, the first in English history. Its original objective, an intervention in Holland for the dual purpose of aiding the Protestant Dutch and keeping Spain well occupied, swelled into a vast design for an all-Protestant offensive under English leadership upon the Roman-Spanish power in every quarter of the globe.

Against this enterprising policy stood nearly all England outside London and the seaports of the south and west: not only the countless secret Catholics whose last hopes it would necessarily destroy, but the miscellaneous multitude of squires, yeomen, and artisans who, once reconciled to the Elizabethan revolution in Church and State, asked nothing more of it than to follow their individual ways in comfort and quiet. At their head and typical of them was Cecil, now Lord Burghley, who had devoted six months to carrying through the revolution, a dozen years to consolidating it, and was now determined that it should stop. Though circumstances had given him the opportunity to overthrow an existing order of things repugnant to his interests and convictions, he was by temperament no revolutionary. Having substituted a new order as satisfactory to himself, his family, his class, and his country as he could reasonably expect in an imperfect universe, his every instinct opposed jeopardizing it by further experiment. To put it to the hazard of a holy war with Spain, the world's first military Power, seemed to him irresponsible fanaticism egged on by wanton greed. The exploits of the adventurers appealed to him no more than the enthusiasms of the sects. Though he had used the pretext of the injury inflicted upon Hawkins in Mexico to justify the seizure of the Genoese treasure, he had in that affair acted rather from the belief that the occasion, in view of Spain's other troubles, was too good to be wasted than from any notion that English rights had been abused which must at all costs be vindicated. On the contrary, having the sort of mind that computes rights in terms of tangible value proportioned to risk, he profoundly doubted whether Spain's remote preserves would ever yield enough profit to be worth the cost of a quarrel with her over them. Better fifty years of Europe, in his and his followers' estimation, with steady trade and profits safe, than a cycle of Cathay.

Meantime in the Netherlands Spain's incomparable infantry, aided by Italian engineering genius, recovered town after town, province after province. The Dutch, breaking their dykes and taking to their ships, transferred their main line of resistance to the sea. The Huguenots in France, also beaten in every battle by the royal troops under the leadership of Spain's paid protégés the Guises, Mary Stuart's close kin, did the same from their impregnable privateering base at La Rochelle on the Atlantic. Ever more swiftly and thoroughly Europe dissolved into two hostile camps—Catholic versus Protestant, land-power versus sea-power, authority versus change; and ever stronger grew the pull of the factions in England towards one or the other. Each victory for Spain evoked from the interventionists a passionate clamour to oppose her before it was too late, from the isolationists a more stubborn resolution to avoid giving her offence; every triumph of her enemies was jubilantly exploited by the former as England's providential opportunity to strike, by the latter as her absolution from any possible reason for doing so.

With an obstinacy equal to their own the Queen disagreed with both parties. No more than she would permit her people to be dragged into what seemed to her an irrelevant war would she consent to what she considered their legitimate energies being thwarted. " *Point de guerre!* " she shrieked at Walsingham when in a moment of crisis he recapitulated the case for intervention, and flung her slipper at his head to emphasize the inalterability of her decision. But to forestall Cecil's making difficulties about Drake's voyage into the Pacific she kept him in ignorance of what was afoot until the expedition was equipped and well out to sea. Between the limits indicated by those two incidents she steered her course, firmly if crookedly, during the years of mounting tension till the last possible moment of them. Her adventurers could count on her blessing, a substantial investment from her purse where a good return seemed likely, and her uncanny skill at lying to frustrate hostile inquiry into their doings. They had to be prepared, on the other hand, to be disavowed as irresponsible rascals if they were caught in an act likely to land her in international complications. Though she turned a blind eye 'on the volunteers who for conscience' sake followed Humphrey Gilbert and others to fight for the Dutch, she demanded as strict an accounting from William of Orange's government for depredations on English commerce as from Philip II's. Avoiding either excessive truculence or apologetic passivity, she sought from an aggressive neutrality to extract the benefits of both with the risks of neither.

It was a day-to-day, a hand-to-mouth policy, if indeed it could be called a policy at all. It got nowhere because it was intended to get nowhere, aiming rather to cope with the present than to modify the future. It boasted no moral purpose because its directress declined to recognize that any

moral issues were involved. To her it appeared, or so she
insisted, a case of Spaniard and Hollander proclaiming rival
dogmas of religion and actually meaning the rival claims of
business: and in fact the Dutch, by shifting the ancient
trade of Ghent and Bruges to Amsterdam and Rotterdam,
were making a very good business out of their rebellion.
Yet her policy had a morality of its own which could be
summed up in the single word peace. Peace primarily for
England, of course, whose welfare was her personal trust,
but also for the distracted belligerents if they would have it.
Repeatedly she did her best to end the conflict on the basis
of the Dutch acknowledging the sovereignty of Spain if
Spain would respect the local Dutch liberties whose infringement had precipitated the revolt. Why not, she demanded of Philip II with regard to their religious grievances,
let them " go to the devil in their own way "? Her efforts
were unsuccessful because her latitudinarian detachment
under-estimated, as Oliver Cromwell was one day to over-
estimate, the moral passion burning in the breasts of both
antagonists underneath their more obvious material considerations. Nevertheless she did try, with her eyes fully
open to the fact that the dangers of peace might well equal
—in the opinion of many already exceeded—the dangers of
war; that if the strife in the Low Countries were composed,
Spain would be free to turn its attention to herself and a
formidable commercial rival have risen (as the next century
was to prove) in Holland.

For six critical and invaluable years, from 1572, when
Spanish might on land drove the Dutch to the sea, until
1578, this policy kept England, despite the terrific and
growing strains within and without, from the tempting
excesses of fear and folly. They were years of rest, regenera-
tion, and self-discovery; a precious span of quiet allotted at
a moment of historical unfolding, a breathing spell between
the internal convulsions of the two previous generations and

the approaching exertion of a mortal struggle for place
in the unending tourney of the nations. Circumstances,
however menacing or shifting, lent themselves to the art of
balance, and balance happened to be the art in which
the mistress of England was at her best and happiest in
dealing with circumstances.

In 1578 a new Spanish viceroy of vigour and genius,
Alexander Farnese, Prince of Parma, took over the task of
subjugating the rebellion. Almost immediately he broke
the southern provinces off from a tentative federation with
the northern (very roughly modern Belgium and Holland)
achieved two years earlier with Elizabeth's encouragement
after much labour and in the face of seemingly insurmount-
able differences. Alone and exposed, the' Dutch could
plainly not continue their resistance indefinitely. The
impulse in England towards intervention acquired a fresh,
in some quarters a hysterical, momentum. Drake's spec-
tacular career in the Pacific powerfully fortified the interventionists' argument while rendering it more difficult for
Elizabeth, unless she was willing to forgo the 4700 per
cent profit Drake was accumulating on her investment in
his voyage, to maintain towards Philip II the appearance
of friendly impartiality. Glib words would no longer do.
Either she had to contrive somehow to restore the balance
with help to the Dutch or resign herself to seeing Spain,
the injured colossus astride every road of English expansion,
securely re-established within a few hours' sailing of London.

But that was not the whole or even the worst of it. From
the very beginning of the rebellion the most dangerous
complication for England was the active intrusion into it
of France, the largest and, had she been united, potentially
the strongest single state in Europe. That danger had been
averted by the series of civil wars which had prevented her,
ever since the third year of Elizabeth's reign, from playing
any considerable part in general European affairs. It would

be almost impossible to exaggerate how much of her immunity Elizabeth owed to those wars, nor did she fail to
acknowledge her debt in the form of assistance, usually
secret and financial, but once, in 1563, open and military, to
the small Protestant minority to enable them to keep going.
For if the ultra-Catholics, led by the great ducal family of
Guise, won outright, it was their unconcealed purpose to
bind France in a rigid coalition with Spain and the papacy
for the extermination of Protestantism everywhere, including Holland, England, and Scotland, the easiest approach
to an invasion of England.   In other words, the prime
article of their domestic policy was to unite France by the
appeal of that Catholic crusade which constituted, as it had
in Henry VIII's time, the deadliest threat to England's
independent existence.

Yet, on the other hand, no more could Elizabeth afford
to have her Huguenot protégés win outright.   For being a
minority—perhaps a thirtieth of the population including a
third of the nobility headed by the Bourbons, first princes
of the blood—they could not expect decisive victory by
arms alone.   Their only hope of saving themselves and their
cause was to merge it in some great national enterprise
which would command the imagination of their more
moderate Catholic fellow-countrymen.   And that enterprise
could only be the glorious deliverance of the Netherlands
from Spanish tyranny and their equally glorious annexation
to France.   But how could England, anxious enough when
the Netherlands belonged to Spain, from whom they were
separated by an immense tract of sea, allow them to belong
to a Power to whom they were joined by a long land frontier
which made it far easier to hold them in subjection?   The
history of a few months of 1572 had vividly exposed the
underlying dilemma.   In the course of that spring, while
Elizabeth was still fearful of retaliation from Philip II for
the seizure of his pay-ships, and while the young king of

France, Charles IX, was temporarily under the influence of the Huguenot chieftain Coligny, she had concluded an important defensive and commercial treaty with him. But when Coligny, having led his sovereign to the verge of sending an expedition to Flanders, besought Elizabeth's co-operation, she had, in spite of pleasant words, withheld it. The result had been a melodramatic reversal of French policy: the marriage of Henry of Bourbon, King of Navarre, to the King's sister—high point of Huguenot ascendancy—followed within a week by a general Huguenot massacre on the fearful day of St. Bartholomew's.

Now, in 1578, the dilemma asserted itself again, more acutely than before. The unstable, neurotic Charles IX was dead. He had been succeeded in 1574 by his fascinating but languorous brother, Henry III. Their mother, the amiable and unscrupulous Catherine de Medici, still exercised such powers as the strife of the factions had left to the Crown, using them primarily to assure its preservation for her children. The Guises, recovering their nerve and their almost idolatrous popularity with the extreme Catholics after a temporary eclipse in the reaction against St. Bartholomew's, had begun to assemble a vast quasi-secret society known as the Holy League to be used as an instrument for imposing their will on the Crown and ultimately transferring it to Duke Henry, the head of their House. The King, or rather his regent the Queen-Mother, had the choice of fighting—a very dangerous choice, seeing that France was preponderantly Catholic—or trying to compound with them. She would have preferred, following her life-long instinct, to compound. But resolutely barring the way to such a composition stood the disconcerting figure of her youngest and last surviving son, Francis Duke of Alençon, next heir to the throne so long as Henry III remained childless, which in view of his history seemed all too likely.

Frantically ambitious, suffering constant agony from the sense that his mother and brother failed to appreciate him, the young man yearned to escape from their authority and, by exploiting his nuisance-value to the full, force them to revive the policy of Coligny for the purpose of carving out a throne for him in the Netherlands. Already he had endeavoured to forward this purpose by running away to join his brother-in-law the King of Navarre, now titular head of the Huguenots and next heir to the throne after him, in the perennial civil war against the Guises, taking many moderate Catholics with him. He was in close touch with elements hostile to Spain in Flanders and of keen interest to an important party in Holland which, disgusted with Elizabeth and despairing of English help, were urging an appeal to France. It began seriously to look as if the French royal family, in order to prevent itself and the realm it ruled from being torn in two, would be compelled to keep Alençon quiet by adopting his scheme as the national policy.

What was Elizabeth to do? If she opposed Alençon, or even as the chief Protestant monarch simply denied him her countenance in his venture, she would discredit him in his own country and almost certainly drive it into the hands of the enemies vowed to her destruction, as she had done before in 1572. In the measure that she assisted the heir to the throne of France to take to himself the throne of the Netherlands she would be helping to plant the most dangerous of neighbours within pistol-shot (to adapt Napoleon's phrase) of the heart of England. While to hold aloof altogether and accept the consequences however they fell out was positively to assure an evil outcome either way.

But if one were to assist while at the same time opposing— launch Alençon in pursuit of his ambition on her money but his own responsibility, without engaging either England's or France's? The only parties whom he would then be in a

position to harm were Spain and himself. He was un-
married; so was she. He must, therefore, go forth as her
knight errant, not his brother's heir-presumptive. Once
more she called on her sex for its last and greatest service
to her statecraft.

He had been offered to her by his mother seven years
earlier, when English horror at the St. Bartholomew's massacre had brought negotiations to an abrupt stop. A hint
from Elizabeth was sufficient to reinstate them as if by
mutual consent. Catherine de Medici longed to get her
troublesome younger son married and if possible settled;
the Queen of England was still the greatest catch to which
the parent of a royal bachelor could aspire; while if the
marriage failed to settle him, it was on all counts better
that Elizabeth rather than her adored elder son Henry
should be saddled with his vagaries—a consideration of
which Elizabeth was fully aware and prepared to make the
utmost. She proposed to her ministers to send for the
young man and look him over. The moderates, led by
Cecil, cautiously approved because of their paramount
desire to see the Queen married while it was still conceivable that she might have a child. The forward party,
concentrating on the fact that Alençon was a professing
Catholic, were aghast. There were scenes, reproaches, even
threats. In the country the Puritan preachers hurled
furious tirades from the pulpit against the suitor's being
allowed into the country: one of them circulated his objections in a pamphlet so inflammatory that he lost his right
hand for sedition, and Leicester's own nephew, Sir Philip
Sidney, was banished from Court for sponsoring him.
Leicester himself unintentionally brought on the crisis in
a manner that all but deprived him for good of the favour
which had been his life's chief stock-in-trade. Alençon's
personal envoy revealed to the Queen the well-kept secret of
his recent marriage to one of her cousins. At a stormy

session of the Council, where in the ordinary way she rarely appeared in person, Elizabeth reminded her listeners, with tears of rage streaming down her cheeks, of how long and how often they and the whole country had implored her to marry: yet now that she had found a husband who combined every qualification she could desire both as a woman and a Queen, a little group amongst them, led by the trusted friend who had betrayed and deserted her, were attempting out of sheer partisan selfishness to deny her the happiness which he had not scrupled to take. Seizing Alençon's passport from the table before her, she scrawled the decisive signature authorizing his coming.

If it was not sincere, it was superb histrionics. Probably the truth, obscure even to herself, was that partial sincerity heightened a natural gift of histrionics to bring off a perfect performance. The main thing was that it should be convincing, and it was so because it was entirely in character. Her interest in young men had not waned with the years —to that her versatile flirtations with her courtiers and the caresses she was even then lavishing on Alençon's tell-tale envoy, Simier by name and simian in appearance (she called him her " little monkey "), were notorious and conclusive testimony; there was nothing inherently improbable, altogether the contrary, in her being thrown into a state of genuine excitement by the prospect of a most eligible suitor come to tell her how beautiful, clever, and altogether desirable she was—nor was there in Alençon being taken in if she gave a good enough outward demonstration to take in others who knew her better. True, even he could not have flattered himself that he was an Adonis, being short, ungainly, sallow, and deeply pock-marked, with an enormous bulbous nose that his detractors described as two noses carelessly thrown together. But then he was twenty-four and she forty-five, to the critical eye somewhat scrawny, raddled, and grotesquely bewigged, so that he had no reason to feel at a comparative disadvantage. And, though shrewd, he was intoxicatedly vain, his vanity being, indeed, the short explanation of his readiness to gamble the welfare of his country and his family's dynastic existence on his own glorification. Add to that the bleeding stump of Stubb's right hand, Sidney's banishment, and Leicester's humiliation, and the total yielded an irresistible presumption that the middle-aged virgin who set such store on his visit would not be too difficult a conquest.

She laid down the condition that he should travel, at least this first time, as a private personage, *incognito*. Her actual motive for the stipulation was to avoid committing herself or further exacerbating her people, but she gave it the flavour of a love-tryst that concerned nobody except themselves. When he arrived, in the late summer of 1579, she all but swooned like one transported by expectation unimaginably surpassed. She took him apart into corners and even into her private chamber, kissed and fondled him in public, showered him with jewels: brazenly scorning, as she did not neglect to point out, maidenly modesty, royal dignity, or care for reputation in the first rapture of love realized and plighted. With such abandon did she fling herself into her part that she herself certainly lost track of where calculation ended and sensation began, while for the spectators, including the cold-hearted little wooer, it was a case of succumbing perforce to a flawless dramatic illusion. Less conceited men than he have undergone similar experience in the conduct of a love affair off-stage with a consummate actress who lived not only for but in her art.

While they bandied tenderness they talked business. Assuming their marriage to be agreed, it was Alençon's idea that it should cement an Anglo-French alliance to eject Spain from the Netherlands and award him its crown. Elizabeth, without rejecting the idea in principle, insisted on first fixing the details in their proper order. How much would France contribute to the venture? Henry III and Catherine de Medici, when referred to, proved desirous of contributing as little as possible, preferably nothing. Elizabeth expostulated at length on the unfairness of a wife bearing the entire burden of financing her husband when his family would obviously expect a large share in the returns. With convincing assurances of her eternal devotion Alençon returned to the Louvre to explain her attitude to his mother and brother. Much time was consumed. More elapsed in lengthy discussions as to whether Alençon should be entitled, in the face of native feeling, to practise the Catholic faith in England and under what conditions—the old stumbling-block which had proved so serviceable in slowing up the pace of most of Elizabeth's previous serious courtships.

Growing impatient, the suitor flung off to Brussels on his own in answer to a somewhat ambiguous local invitation and was presently flung out again, though not without inflicting damage on the Spaniards and placing a strain on Franco-Spanish relations. Elizabeth now had all the necessary data about him as a man, a soldier, and a statesman—the same sort of useful insight into his character and availability for her purposes as she had once had into Darnley's. Worthless for the purpose of leading a united France into a war of conquest, and therefore innocuous to her, he could still be of considerable use in aggravating Spanish difficulties. When he came again in 1581, she shovelled a woman's balm on to his injured self-esteem and kept him up to the mark with elaborations upon the successful idyll of two years before. So thoroughly did she do it that she found herself under the embarrassing necessity of redeeming her repeated and public promises to marry him or else buying them back. She preferred to pay, and so, with a goodly sum of her money and Leicester to do the honours of escorting him across the North Sea, she sent him off to a second expedition in Flanders which was as

useful to her and as barren for himself as the first. Two
years after that, in the spring of 1584, he died of the common
phthisical affliction of his family.

"I have let time pass, which I generally find helps
more than reasoning," Elizabeth wrote to Henry III on a
later occasion. In those casual thirteen words—or, more
exactly, the first five of them, since the rest are but a subordinate explanatory clause—she confided her political
testament. They furnish virtually all the necessary clue to
her technique as a ruler and the dominant instinct of her
being of which it was the expression. They explain not
only the success but the character of her reign, of which
so striking a feature during so large a part of it was the
absence of drama. To the best of her ability she avoided
drama because she abhorred its elements of emotional
violence, large risks, and surprise. The practice of it she
left to her adventurers and her poets, herself merely afford-
ing them the necessary scope within the limits of the public
safety. Only when events had finally defeated her genius
for procrastination was it able (and even then not without
her step-by-step resistance) to intrude into the activities of
the State. Unlike her father, who, since his business was
change, had to keep on inventing novel circumstances in
order to circumvent existing ones, she, whose task it was to
preserve, waited to let adverse circumstances cancel one
another out. She did it intuitively because she was by nature
cautious and thrifty. She did it deliberately because her
common sense told her that what her intrinsically poor,
under-populated country trying to expand in a fiercely
competitive, passion-racked world most required of fate
was the most generous allowance of simple duration. It
was a method which, just because of its lack of heroics, she
felt to be best adapted to minimizing the disadvantages
and exploiting the accident of her sex.

The Alençon courtship was its most finished example, her masterpiece. By the not very pretty spectacle she made of herself she helped to gain six more precious years. In the course of them English sea-power grew out of all proportion, as did that of Holland, while in Huguenot France there rose to maturity a very great leader to redress the balance against the Guises, Henry of Navarre, now heir to the throne. And as the delay reinforced England's strength, so it served to clarify the issues in the minds of her people. Thanks to it, the gratuitous crusade preached in the 1570's by a small and unpopular minority became in the 1580's the solemn answer of a virtually united people to a challenge it neither dared nor cared to evade.

Suddenly, with the crack of a pistol-shot, Elizabeth's patient and fruitful alliance with time snapped. The shot, fired just three months after Alençon's death by a bigot in the employ of Spain, struck down William of Orange, the illustrious protagonist of the Dutch cause from the very beginning. The loss was irreplaceable: for Elizabeth it created a new situation impervious to any of her tried stratagems. Dutch capacity to continue the struggle in the face of Parma's reinvigorated forward drive relaxed as Dutch unity disintegrated. One party in the unhappy Provinces was ready to sue for peace. Another turned desperately to France, but the French King could no longer have given help even if he had been disposed to: Guises and Huguenots had already hustled him into the three-cornered civil war which was to destroy him and the Guises in turn before Henry of Navarre ended it by saying a Mass ten years later. A third, and momentarily the dominant party, crossed the North Sea to pray Elizabeth to accept their country's Crown in return for taking it under her protection.

The Crown she did not want, as she had made clear when it was offered her once before. Unlike her predecessors, she had no mind to saddle England with permanent responsibilities on the Continent. But help of some sort she knew she would now have to give, much as it went against the grain, lest the Spanish military power, borne on the tide of the Catholic Reaction, should sweep across all Europe, Britain along with the rest. The Dutch mission landed in June, 1585. For two months she haggled with it and scolded those of her advisers who, in the impatience of their triumph, were trying to hurry her on—Walsingham for religion's sake, Leicester for glory's. She was not greatly interested in either. She wanted only to determine what would be the smallest outlay necessary for success and the most she could obtain from the Dutch in the way of fortified towns and harbours as security for her money. While she bargained, Antwerp—England's chief port of entry into the continental markets, whose delivery from a Spanish siege was the immediate point of the negotiations—fell to Parma. She might have been dismayed; some were. Instead she rose to the occasion, cut short the bargaining with a substantially increased offer, and signed an alliance with the Dutch binding her to see the thing through. Having exhausted every resource of delay, having made herself universally distrusted and often ridiculous and even contemptible, she finally by her own will and yet against it accepted her hour of destiny . . . " taken the diadem from her head ", in the words of the friendly King of Sweden, " and set it upon the doubtful chance of war ". As in most supreme political decisions, the question had become no longer one of whether the act itself was right but whether the moment chosen for it was right.

Shortly afterwards an expeditionary force, the first to leave English shores for a long generation, set sail under the command of Leicester, still the first man in her heart though white-bearded, red-faced, a little paunchy, and chronically rheumatic. But before the kingdom's full strength could be deployed for the struggle by land and sea, there remained an urgent precaution to be seen to. For several years Spain and the papacy had been trying to forestall the decision which Elizabeth had now taken by undermining her from within. Jesuit seminaries on Flemish or Guise-controlled French soil, or more latterly at Rome, had trained young English exiles for the Catholic priesthood with the express intention of smuggling them into England again to reconvert it piecemeal to the old faith. Some had consecrated themselves narrowly to that task and by the beauty of their lives, the courage of their devotion, and the eloquence of their preaching performed it even to the apprehensive admiration of their enemies. They were perhaps the more ultimately dangerous, but less immediately so than various of their colleagues bent on swifter results: men who plotted to overthrow the government and to earn, or instigate others to earn, the martyr's crown promised by the Holy See for the heretic Queen's assassination. One of them operated even from the privileged precincts of the House of Commons. Supervising them from Rome was Father, later Cardinal, Allen, an exile who aspired to emulate the function of Pole in Henry VIII's time.

The individual priests Walsingham's secret agents—skulking everywhere, in every nest of English malcontents whether at home or in Brussels, Rheims, Paris, Madrid, Rome itself—could track down and frequently bring to a horrible end on the scaffold, high-minded and red-handed alike. But they were more than individuals: they were the virtually inexhaustible human counters in a resolute and infinitely resourceful purpose; and that purpose, so far as it regarded England, centred round the captive Queen of Scots. To the great majority of Catholics everywhere she was the sole and natural alternative to Elizabeth. It was in her interest that any conspiracy to overthrow Elizabeth by death or otherwise was conceived; it was she whom Elizabeth's enemies counted upon to provide the rallying point should the throne be vacated by an act of violence and thrown open to competition.   Therefore from the English war-party's point of view it was imperative now to fulfil their long-cherished determination to get rid of her.

She unwittingly co-operated.   She became involved in a plot headed by a priest and a young English Catholic of fortune to abet Spain in the gathering conflict by loosing an insurrection in England, with the Queen's assassination as its signal.   Walsingham and his spies, aware at every instant of what she was up to, encouraged her to incriminate herself beyond any possibility of escape.   They facilitated, read, deciphered, and passed on each item of correspondence between her and her accomplices.   When they had what they wanted, they swooped.   Their evidence sent the accomplices to the gallows and put Mary on trial for her life. Granted the genuineness of the evidence and the existence of any jurisdiction to try her at all, both of which she ably contested, there could be no doubt of the verdict.   The Court of High Commission, which included a number of her partisans, unanimously found her guilty.   Caught in the predicament she had been dodging for eighteen years, Elizabeth tried frantically to find some way out short of execution.   She could not: England, indeed the world, had grown too small to contain both herself and her cousin safely.   Tormented and tearful, unable to sleep and wildly furious with the servants whose vigilance had forced the decision upon her—and who were urging her on with sinister tales of further conspiracy—she signed Mary's death-warrant (executed on 10th February, 1587) and at once visited her wrath upon them, ungenerously but not altogether indefensibly, for having caused her to do so.

What she hoped was to disengage herself, in order to shield the Crown and Majesty of England from the odious consequences of her servants' useful act, by throwing the responsibility on them, as she had so often done before;

as she had, by another confusion of responsibilities, involved herself without involving England in the Alençon affair. But it was too late for such ruses; her failure was as inevitable as the effort was ugly. She had become too great a person to be able any longer to escape by such petty loopholes. In those two tremendous decisions, intervention in the Netherlands and Mary's execution, she could no longer avoid speaking for Elizabeth because in them she spoke for her people. There could be no mistake about that. Her voice was theirs, their will hers. If the Pope was to reclaim England and Philip II his Netherlands, they had to treat the English people as jointly accountable and forcibly master them along with their sovereign. True, in the Netherlands her campaign was not going very well. Perhaps she had chosen the wrong man to lead it. Certainly she gave him too little leeway and not much more trust, fearing his ambition to make himself king there against her interests. Out of jealousy that the Dutch were doing too little, she was overcareful not to do too much. Her army, like so many English armies after a long period of peaceful neglect, had much to learn before they became a match for the enemy's veterans. But she could send reinforcements as she liked so long as the supply held out, whereas he could not while her fleet held the seas through which they must pass. The only way to drive it off the seas and keep it off was to overrun the many-harboured island on which it was based. Hence the pooling of Spain and the papacy's money for the construction of an armada powerful enough to force its way through the Channel to the mouth of the Scheldt and thence cover the transport of Parma's infantry for the invasion of England.

In English legend the defeat of the Invincible Armada is (as in legend it ought to be) ascribed to a spontaneous, improvised putting forth of the nation's strength under the kindly protection of a Protestant weather-god. It was not

altogether so. The keenest of neutral observers agreed that
the Spanish flotilla (delayed in harbour a year as the result
of a smashing raid by Sir Francis Drake) was most unlikely
to reach its appointed destination. The victory had been
prepared long before, in the quiet cementing of English
unity and the inexorable development of English sea-power.
To swell the sturdy little royal navy, made ready against
the day of need with tireless forethought and patience by
Sir John Hawkins, came hurrying in their swift little ships
the hardened smugglers and pirates of the southern and
western coasts. Commanding the main fleet off Plymouth
was Lord Howard of Effingham, commanding the secondary
line of defence in the Straits of Dover was a Seymour—the
one a member of the great ducal Catholic House of Norfolk,
the other of its once deadly rival, the arch-Protestant
Protector Somerset's. Under Howard served Drake from
Devon and Frobisher from unruly Yorkshire, as great a
pair of fighting seamen as the age had to show. And over
them all, inspiring them and the nation standing to arms
behind them with the magic of her words and the greater,
more mysterious magic of personality, towered the Queen
herself, in so many ways the very incarnation of the eternal
England they were fighting for—its vitality, its humour and
common sense, its respect for realities and horror of ideologies, its essential good-nature and delight in eccentricity
. . . and yes, its love of liberty, if liberty be regarded not
as an empty abstraction or a fixed relation to the ever-
changing framework of the State, but as that condition which
favours individuals best serving the general weal by being
most fully themselves.

The fourteen years that followed, till Elizabeth's death
in 1603, are often treated as a sort of epilogue. In the
general shape of the reign they were. Its important problems
—the relation of Crown and Parliament, the Catholics, the

orientation of England's foreign policy—had for the time being been more or less resolved; the new problems that arose in the course of them—the growth of the Puritans, the increasing hostility of business to the Crown's self-profitable interference in England's commercial expansion by the award of monopolies to favoured companies, the underlying social transition—as well as the old problems that were to crop up again, were more the affair of the reigns that followed. In the long and agitated history of dictatorship in England those closing years of Elizabeth's reign may in retrospect be fairly taken, despite war and the monitory rumblings of vast changes to come, as the high, tranquil point of culmination and rest.

CHAPTER XIII

The Despotism by Habit

THE precept by which Elizabeth had ruled so many emergencies in her life quietly regulated the most dreaded emergency of all—her death. For forty-four years, with what had often seemed a frivolous disregard of logic's inexorable warning that if she died without a recognized heir the reversion to her throne would have to be settled by civil war, she had preferred to wait and see rather than to borrow trouble in the present by saddling herself with a rival for the sake of the unknowable future. . . . " I have let time pass, which I generally find helps more than reasoning." So it turned out. The rival was averted, the successor in good time materialized. By degrees so slow as to be almost imperceptible the evolution of events had oriented the pointer of common sense towards the candidate already designated by the sacred principle of legitimacy, James VI of Scotland, Henry VII's senior descendant through his mother Mary Stuart. Shortly before Elizabeth's death an influential group of her ministers and courtiers, headed by William Cecil's hunchbacked son and successor Robert, entered secretly into negotiations with him to exploit the current of opinion in his favour in return for his promise to maintain intact the Elizabethan settlement, including their own solid interest in it, and in due course were able to carry out the bargain with scarcely a show of opposition.

Relief at being let off a second War of the Roses disposed the English people to enthusiastic expectations of their new sovereign which in most cases failed to survive closer inspection. To look at he was a sad come-down from the Tudors—hideously ugly, bandy-legged, scrawny, and uncouth. To listen to he was even less prepossessing. His voice, the sound of which he dearly loved, grated on less partial ears as harshly as his manner on the sensibilities. Opinionated, pedantic, tactless almost to genius, he conceived talk, despite the impediment of a tongue too large for his mouth, to be the most proper form of exercise, and argument the one congenial form of talk; delighting in his own cleverness—upon which the foremost wranglers of his native country had for thirty-six years lavished equally their energies and their applause—he revelled in the royal privilege of airing it in monologue. Nor did what he said tend to mitigate his way of saying it.

Like the Tudors, he assumed monarchy to be for all intents and purposes synonymous with divinity. Only, unlike them, he made the mistake of trying to prove it. Where they, with clairvoyant understanding of the English character, had been content to accept power as a fact, James, exaggeratedly Scottish, insisted on exploring its theory: the system which they had imposed as a pragmatic necessity justified by results he endeavoured, through incessant instruction of the least metaphysically minded race on earth in the philosophy of Divine Right, to erect into an Article of Faith grounded upon dialectic. To talk of the King being subject to the law, ran his argument, was paradoxical nonsense. For there to be a law there must obviously be somebody to make the law. Who that somebody was reason and the authority of Holy Writ, notably the two Books of Samuel, alike made plain. To assert that any creature of the law—Parliament for instance—might assert a will contrary to the King's, its earthly source, was a contradiction in terms, an impeachment of the order of nature, not to mention the good order of the State.

There was no flaw in the reasoning provided one granted the premises. But they had already been granted by implication under the Tudors; all that James achieved from his efforts to render them explicit was to incite his hearers into examining them afresh. One of James's Scottish subjects had bluntly reminded him that he was " God's silly Vassal " like anybody else. And now the critics whom Elizabeth had squashed by judicious inattention rebounded to the challenge. One of them punctuated a harangue in Parliament with the warning, none the less—perhaps all the more—pointed for its innocent begging of the question, that " England is the last monarchy which yet retains her liberties. Let them not perish now." His first Commons put it even more succinctly. On the ground that " as to dispute what God may do is blasphemy, so is it sedition in subjects to dispute what a king may do ", he forbade it even to discuss the limits of his prerogative or any other topic save at his pleasure; by unanimous resolution the House retorted that its privileges were a matter of right and not of grace, it being " an ancient, universal and undoubted right of Parliament to debate freely all matters which properly concern the subject. . . ."

On that ground, from which Elizabeth had gracefully retreated without loss in 1566, followed clash after clash for the rest of the reign. So far as specific legislation went, James, with Tudor tradition and contemporary tendency still strongly on his side, in every instance had his way. Yet the net result for the Crown was a pyrrhic victory. A new and incalculable element had been drawn into the controversy—the nation of cultivators, artisans, and adventurers whose attention had long been diverted from such issues by the satisfactions of profits and glory. For the first time since the Protestant Revolution the question as to whether the sovereign power was really the King's by divine appointment or their own property held in trust by him on mutual agreement, had been posed before them in terms demanding their consideration, not as passive auditors merely, but alert assessors capable not only of reaching but enforcing judgment in the light of their best interests. From a fact ingrained in habit, Divine Right had been reduced to the status of an arguable claim, the always latent impulses to conflict between ruler and ruled lifted from the level of the material on to the plane most dangerous to any form of despotism, that of ideas.

James's acts, moreover, recommended his thesis as little as did his presentation of it. The efficiency of government declined, the cost rose. Partly the rise was due to a general European fall in the value of money resulting from the influx of precious metals from Spanish America, but alongside this somewhat subtle cause was the more easily visible one of royal waste and extravagance. The increase had actually begun under Elizabeth, but at least with her there had been something to show for the money—a great and victorious war in the conduct of which she had been more severely censured for stinginess than for overspending. James, without this excuse, for the struggle with Spain lapsed shortly after his accession, managed regularly to equal or exceed her costliest budgets. Moreover Elizabeth, shrewdly mindful of the prejudice crystallized in the historian Fuller's description of the English yeoman " not caring how much his purse is let blood, so it be by the advice of the physicians of the State ", throughout contrived to share responsibility for taxation with Parliament. That James on principle disdained to do. Where the Tudors had, under the appearance of free co-operation, directed the working of Parliament through leading members of it like Thomas Cromwell and Cecil, thus utilizing it as a controlled safety-valve for public discontents, James haughtily demanded its dumb consent to his wishes or contemptuously did without. Parliamentary sessions, virtually annual under the Lancasters and on the average frequent if irregular under the Tudors, became an increasing rarity. More and more when in want of funds he came to depend on ingenious exactions suggested by his favourites, a rackety group of familiars whose crimes and perversions devasted his reputation as thoroughly as their corruption his treasury.

Meanwhile Parliament, left to its own devices and unsupplied with " those good matters to set at work " which Francis Bacon urged upon the King " that an empty stomach does not feed on humours ", learned to shift for itself. Within the contracting limits of its activity it took the initiative in devising legislation, chose its own leaders, and evolved a system of committees to provide it with the specialized knowledge for which it had hitherto been dependent upon the ministers of the Crown. An efficient instrument of opposition began to take shape. As the tone of the country progressively deteriorated with the government's shabby peace-at-any-price policy—of which the execution of Sir Walter Raleigh, last of the Elizabethan paladins, to placate Spain, was the crowning humiliation— this nucleus of opposition attracted to itself the nostalgic elements of aggressive nationalism. The notion of domestic liberty became identified with that of external respect, with the monarchy the obstacle to both. No autocracy ever existed that could have fostered that combination with impunity.

Nevertheless, so vast was the monarchy's accumulated credit that the prodigal drafts made upon it by James for twenty-two years scarcely affected it in the eyes of the majority. A vigorous instinct of loyalty repaired the outward ravages of thought, and in the liturgical cadences of Shakespeare, Drayton, and the Dedication to the Authorized Version recited a doxology of kingship beside which the raucous polemics of the King and his critics alike sounded remote and irrelevant. The great administrative machinery of the Tudors ran on under its own momentum, a priceless asset to the Crown and a discouraging answer to the radicals in Parliament, enabling James at one and the same time to advertise his care for security, justice, and efficiency in the common man's everyday affairs, and to restrict the expression of unwelcome opinion under the guise of guarding him from the discomfort inseparable from the spread of unpopular heresies. Moreover, though many of the leading men in England disapproved of his supine attitude in foreign affairs, the large section of the public which had undergone the inevitable reaction from the heroics of the Elizabethan Age was grateful to him for stopping a war of which it had grown weary and fretful. When, owing to a complication of circumstances, hostilities broke out again in 1624, his earnest efforts to avert them further strengthened him with these admirers, while his failure to do so automatically suspended the opposition's monopoly of patriotism. His learned encyclicals on the evils of tobacco brought to many the comforting assurance that the throne stood for the old-fashioned virtues against the intrusion of smart newfangled vice; many more were solaced by the insight and ruthlessness with which he attacked the problem of witchcraft, the flourishing peril Elizabeth and her father had derisively tolerated as puerile superstition. And—conclusive rejoinder on behalf of the *status quo*—business on the whole remained good.

It was still an age of men rather than of institutions. In the long process of emerging from the feudal wreckage the State had received such character as it possessed largely from its current governors instead of, as in more stable times, impressing its character on them, with the consequence that to its subjects its virtues seemed to reside rather in those rugged individuals than in itself, their plastic creation. The same was true of its shortcomings, and at James's death in 1625 few even of the most implacable of his late adversaries imagined any more serious amendment in it than a superior compound of qualities in his successor.

By that criterion the auguries promised well. In almost every observable respect the young man who ascended the throne at the age of twenty-four afforded a most pleasing antithesis to his predecessor. His fine dark features were as thoughtfully distinguished, his bearing and manners as graceful and charming as his father's had been uncouth; in place of James's aggressive pedantries he nourished a passion combined with taste for pictures, buildings, music, and books rare even amongst the princely amateurs of the Renaissance. So striking was the contrast that in the light of what followed it seems like an ironic trick of nature to heighten only the more dramatically to explode the delusion which lulled James's enemies into equating the prospects of the State with the person of its ruler.

Though it is possible that if they had had the chance to take a hand in his education the explosion would have been less violent. Close intimacy between the heir and the opposition was an almost natural phenomenon of monarchy, a species of mutual attraction between two unsatisfied ambitions out of which both parties not infrequently gained some permanent influence over and at the least some useful knowledge of one another. But Charles had not been born the heir; it was to his elder brother Henry that the politicians had addressed their hopes and the scribes their flatteries until his death in 1612, leaving a vacancy that his radiant promise rendered too large and too late to fill. And Charles, consigned to the exclusive supervision of the born pedagogue his father, victim as well of a stammer that had bred in him a miserable sense of inadequacy for popular contacts, grew up not only singularly uncontaminated by any contrary influence but practically unknown to the men prepared to nurture it.

CHARLES I

From the painting by Van Dyck

But though better acquaintance might have softened their subsequent shock of disappointment, it would probably not have resulted in any deep and lasting impression on Charles. He was not a rebel by nature. The strength of his affections corresponded too deeply to the nearness of their objects for him to be attracted by the distant and the novel. With an inordinate, an almost sensually protective tenderness towards family and friends and old familiar things and ways, anything which threatened their well-being aroused in him instinctive repugnance and distrust. Like a dutiful son, he received his father's precepts as unquestioningly as he accepted, though already King and free to choose for himself, the wife his father had designated for him, and like a devoted husband thereafter raised her to be his most cherished counsellor. She was Henrietta Maria, daughter of Henry IV of France and consequently of that House of Bourbon whose capacity for learning nothing and forgetting nothing was to shape its destiny along lines so curiously parallel to the Stuarts'.

Yet no more than nature had fitted him to be a rebel against the tradition in which he had been reared had she fitted him to be its champion. The very fact that the autocratic principle rested on no mystic religious sanction or dispirited submission to force—nor even, thanks to James, any longer on passive acceptance—demanded something more of him than mental and moral refinements: something of the exuberant vitality, the boisterous self-assurance, the downright commonness which had made Henry VIII, Elizabeth, and his own father-in-law, though otherwise so different, each a " character " to captivate the vulgar. They could command the multitude because they were at the same time of and above it, a magnified expression of itself. Charles, aristocratically apart from it, was debarred from expressing what he was temperamentally unable to understand. No man could have had a higher sense of duty towards the people placed in his care, none could have had a much feebler sense of them as *people*, a living, breathing conglomeration of four million tangled cravings, energies, fears, sensibilities, and visions of salvation. Unable to forget himself in them, he had been denied the magical faculty of making them at supreme moments of stress forget themselves in him.

There, in its essentials, lay the root of his tragedy. For tragedy it was, in the true poetic sense of the word, more nearly than any other reign in English history can show—the spectacle of a thoroughly well-meaning wilful man propelled by fatal misunderstanding towards inevitable disaster. In all sincerity Charles believed that he could do as he liked provided he did it with the selfless approval of his own conscience—an illusion unconsciously shared by the very antagonists whose effort to correct it brought on the disaster. The one element originally missing, a lack of the full tragic stature in the hero's character, was before the end to be supplied by the reflected immensity of the circumstances with which he contended.

It took fifteen years to complete the prologue—years in which Charles floundered in the vicious circle of trying to restore James's dilapidations by emulating James's methods. Committed to a fresh struggle with Spain, of which he had been partly the instigator, he sent forth the fleet to assail Cadiz in the grand Elizabethan manner. But long disuse and misplaced economy had reduced the royal navy to little more than a collection of leaking hulls and rotting spars. The expedition collapsed with horrible loss, for which an outraged public held accountable primarily the King's appointment of his father's former favourite and his own bosom friend, the handsome young Duke of Buckingham, to the post of Lord Admiral. Various other undertakings to which Charles, unbeknown to anyone except his confidential circle, expensively pledged himself to his German and Danish allies met with similar disasters.

To carry on required money, great quantities of it. Confident that his policy was the best and most honourable for England, he turned to Parliament for co-operation. But Parliament was more interested in knowing the whys and wherefores of the sums already squandered on a series of national humiliations. Also the business community, which had never liked the war and whose trade was suffering from it, could make its influence felt in that quarter and did. Instead of voting the supplies demanded, the Commons launched an attack on the royal enterprises and the way in which the royal ministers, Buckingham in particular, carried them out. The King's haughty reminder that policy and the conduct of his ministers alike transcended their competence failed to silence them, and to his lofty plea of the country's urgent necessities they conceded nothing more than the renewal for one year only of the customs revenues known as tonnage and poundage—a perquisite which the Crown had taken for granted from time immemorial.

It was derisively insufficient. In his straits the King levied a forced loan·on the City, the very stronghold of dissatisfaction, and went on collecting the tonnage and poundage by his own fiat after his parliamentary warrant had expired. Vainly Parliament protested that these impositions were an evasion of its lawful powers, the victims that they infringed the basic rights of the subject. Frustrated in the effort to control the King by restricting his income, Parliament moved for a critical examination into his expenditures. This manœuvre Charles, indignant, and not altogether unfrightened at what such an examination might disclose, blocked with a flat denial of the right of anyone to question his servants on the performance of their duties; whereupon the Commons, as another way to the same end,

drew up for presentation to the Lords articles of impeachment against Buckingham accusing him of corruption,
incompetence, and neglect of the King's interests. This
was even worse. If the King's advisers—the most trusted
and dearest of them at that—could be hauled before Parliament to answer for their doings and dismissed or punished
at its will, it followed that he would in the end be compelled to take such advisers as it approved, and the royal
authority, as he understood it, be reduced to a mockery.
To head off the proceedings he called upon every resource
of a harassed tyrant, including the arrest of too-outspoken
members of both Houses—a violation of privilege neither
condoned nor forgotten after his subsequent release of
them under joint pressure from their colleagues and the
courts. Unable finally to prevent the impeachment, he
manipulated his favourite's acquittal by a blend of trickery
and terrorism.

The same tactics were used to overawe popular objection
to the forced loan. Hoping to obtain judicial sanction for
it, Charles had it submitted to a bench of judges for their
favourable opinion, which he failed to extort even by the
removal of the Lord Chief Justice and threatening the rest.
Nevertheless he proceeded with the collection and, when
large numbers of the City merchants, basing themselves
on the adverse decision, refused to subscribe, had the more
respectable of them flung into prison and the humbler sort
drafted into the army. Five of the former, all knights and
men of substance (by no means the same thing necessarily
since Elizabeth's death), thereupon sued for their release on
bail by writ of *habeas corpus*, requiring the Crown to show
cause for their imprisonment. Counsel for the Crown declined: to the defendants' citations upon the point from the
majestic precedents of the Common Law, they opposed the
more recent and still unclarified doctrine of the Reason of
State—the thesis that in the last analysis orderly rule was

impossible unless the esoteric necessities of government (of which it was itself the sole valid judge) were the supreme and inscrutable law. Muttering confusedly in their beards to the effect that their decision in this case must not be constructed into a general licence to the Crown to imprison its subjects indefinitely on any pretext or none, the Court, with one eye timidly on the Crown and the other ashamedly on their professional oath, dismissed the writ and returned the defendants to their cells.

A growing unrest spread through the country. It was only the beginning.

Yet of themselves Charles's foreign misadventures and his high-handed treatment of his subjects' persons and property would in all likelihood not have accomplished the gigantic triple operation of magnifying, fusing, and directing resentment into open revolt. Elizabeth had suffered military defeats and on occasion abused strict justice: an Elizabethan precedent had been tellingly cited against the five knights. To the public the words liberty and tyranny still partook rather of the nature of arresting slogans coined by a small group of extremists than of symbols for real and mortally irreconcilable forces; the underlying issue, confused by the very multitude and vividness of the details that were creating it, seemed as yet to consist of no more than the old intermittent struggle for power between Sovereign and Parliament, a conflict which Charles might, had no additional complication entered in, have maintained in his own lifetime at least as successfully as had his father. But another cause of unrest was at work, which he had also inherited and was further to aggravate, powerful enough presently to overshadow and eventually to unify all the rest—religion.

Like most other great changes in human affairs, the Reformation in England had evolved by a series of violent and contrary oscillations, varying its form with its current direction. One dominant clique had, after much chopping and changing, given it in Henry VIII's time a form most nearly described as Anglo-Catholic—an autonomous sprig not only betraying but boasting its resemblance to the mother-stock. Another had essayed to graft it on to radical Protestantism in Edward's; a third had succeeded in abolishing it altogether for a while under Mary: and all the warring impulses responsible for those fluctuations were still furiously alive in it. ˙Elizabeth had tried to reconcile them in her broad, insular, on the whole easy-going compromise, but the fighting retreat of the papists from open to secret resistance during the first two-thirds of her reign, and the rising aggressiveness of the Puritans at the end of it, plainly indicated that the compromise owed less to its intrinsic coherence than to the strength of the secular authority for holding together as long as it did. ˙James, in whom a Calvinist upbringing partially offset an exaggerated respect for the orthodox Anglicanism which uniquely embodied the principle of royal supremacy, was able to maintain it by intermittently repressing his Catholic and Puritan malcontents at home while lavishing cordialities impartially on their friends abroad. But all the while the animosities between the various creeds grew, embittered by˙ the impact on English emotions of the fearful Thirty Years' struggle then raging to determine the religious complexion of Europe for good and all.

In Charles's mind was no reflection or understanding of nor sympathy for these divisions in his people's. Like Henry VIII, only more warmly and imaginatively, he was a tradionalist on every question which divided the lawful Church roughly in two; between those who dreaded lest the Reformation go too far and those for whom it had not gone nearly far enough, he was unhesitatingly on the side of the former. The old ceremonies which the Puritans and their kind despised as impious mummery he cherished not only for their rich appeal to the senses, but as tokens of

continuity and deep accumulated wisdom otherwise in-
expressible; the stately hierarchy of bishops and priests
whom they detested as impostors, deceitful muddlers for
gain of the limpid waters of scriptural truth, he venerated as
the divinely ordained interpreters of that truth and the
indispensable framework of social decency construed from
it. Naturally the priesthood returned the compliment,
adulating the monarch and the monarchy to the point of
nausea, and equally naturally their enemies held both him
and it in deepening suspicion. Already they muttered that
in his heart he was a papist, intriguing like his grandmother
Mary Stuart to bring back the Pope.

The accusation was untrue: it would no more have
accorded with Charles's religion than with his political
beliefs to put the Pope once more over the King in England.
But there was enough in the charge to give it colour. His
Queen was a devout Catholic, he himself and the theologians
with whom he was filling the commanding offices of the
Church openly adhered to the teachings of the Dutchman,
Arminius, which in the bosom of Protestantism repudiated
the Calvinist doctrine of predestination in favour of the
Catholic doctrine of free will. So the uncompromising
zealots of the new religion drew together and became one
with the rising critics of the absolute monarchy; while the
upholders of the Elizabethan compromise, the heirs to the
monastic lands distributed by Henry VIII and all the solid
moderate men who, seeing and loathing the excesses, the
bumptiousness and pretentiousness of the sectarians, should
have been the monarchy's instinctive supporters, seeing also
the disposition towards reciprocal indulgence between the
King and the remnants of the papistry they and their fathers
had fought to exorcise, became distraught and uncertain.

" Remember," Charles had told his second Parliament
when dismissing it, " that Parliaments are altogether in my

power for their calling, sitting and dissolution: therefore as I find the fruits of them good or evil, they are to continue or not to be." He would much have preferred them not to be, but, with his expenditures hopelessly outrunning every possible source of income, he once more for the third time summoned one in a last hope of obtaining better fruits than from its predecessors. The hope was vain as it was blind. The elections returned an overwhelming majority against him in the Commons. The new House took up where the old had left off and laid down a demand for the redress of grievances before even listening to the question of supplies. Arbitrary taxation and imprisonment of the subject must cease; the King must abandon the practice of quartering troops on householders in time of peace—a new and particularly odious grievance, for if the practice of raising a standing army and maintaining it at private expense were persisted in, not only would insufferable damage be done to households which harboured such ruffians as composed the armies of the Thirty Years' War period, but the Crown would be well on its way to fashioning a military despotism contrary to all English precedent; and lastly the Arminian clergy (of whom far too many in any event enjoyed appointments which the parliamentary majority would have liked to see filled by austere divines) must discontinue propagating from their pulpits the dogma that the King was infallibly right. Charles, anxious only to get his money and be rid of this impertinent meddling, offered, after a stiff reminder that the security of his subjects was his own exclusive and sacred trust, to give his word of honour for the preservation of its traditional safeguards. But the royal word of honour was no longer enough: the legislators felt, not without reason, that a king who thought himself answerable only to God was not likely to take too strict a view of a promise given to men he disliked in order to relieve a temporary necessity. After considering various devices, the Commons induced the Lords to join with them in a solemn petition embodying their grievances which the King should be invited formally to ratify. This, the famous Petition of Right, Charles was constrained to give his assent to on 7th June, 1628.

Having signed, he justified only too quickly his adversaries' suspicion that he would not feel bound to keep faith with them. A law is but a form of words, its effect lies in the acts that stem from its interpretation, and Charles could argue that the Petition was not even properly a law. His will and the ingenuity of his advisers found immediate means of going through and round it. He continued to appoint priests of his own way of thinking to serve as sole licensed commentators on his way of doing, and to dismiss and punish the others; to raise revenues which had not been voted him; to silence opposition by imprisonment on the one hand and the immense patronage of his office on the other.

In vain Parliament tried to recall him to his promise. The fatal stabbing of Buckingham by a young army officer whose wits popular hatred of the favourite had unsettled, further alienated him from the men to whose unprincipled provocation his grief and anger attributed the blow. When over his prohibition they locked the doors of the Commons to draw up a public remonstrance against his violated pledges, he anticipated the strategy which was to bring on the catastrophe twelve years later by dispatching an armed guard to break down the doors and forcibly disband the sitting. On this occasion, however, the House rapidly brought its business to a close (two members holding the Speaker in his chair till it had) and adjourned on its own motion. That ended the first phase of the struggle. Convinced that there was no possibility of an understanding with a body which, though ready enough to clamour for vast and expensive projects of government, was unprepared to make any other contribution to them than incessant carping, Charles abruptly ordered a dissolution. Nine of the members he imprisoned for what they had said while the House was in session—a flagrant breach of privilege which cut at the very root of the parliamentary function—of whom six secured their release after humble submission, two remained in prison until another Parliament was able long afterwards to command the keys, and one, the most illustrious, Sir John Eliot, died there. From 1629 until 1640, the longest uninterrupted period in its history, no Parliament sat in England.

As the years rolled on it began to seem not improbable that none would ever sit again, except perhaps as a listening-gallery stocked with the King's puppets to nod a mechanical approval of his will on behalf of what might pass for public opinion. Beyond any of his predecessors Charles was absolute. All the attributes of power to which Henry VIII and Elizabeth and James had attained or pretended were his without even concession to forms. As final effective authority in Church and State, no voice could be raised in either to gainsay his ordering of his people's beliefs and conduct whether in the spiritual or the temporal sphere. He was pope, king, parliament, prime minister, and supreme court of justice combined in one person.

To help him carry this enormous burden, he presently found two energetic and highly capable assistants in thorough sympathy with his way of thought. William Laud, a pugnacious little prelate of vast learning and no fear, whom he had previously translated in rapid turn by way of two lesser bishoprics to the diocese of London, was in 1633 promoted to the Throne of Canterbury, whence he proceeded by rigorous purgings of the clergy and the liberal use of the secular arm on the laity to make the Church a haven for all that was reactionary and a hell for those who

were not. As his opposite number in the secular administration Charles a little later appointed Thomas Wentworth,
a distinguished convert from the parliamentary opposition
who, after a highly successful term as President of the Council
of the North and an almost uniquely successful one (from
the conquerors' point of view) as Viceroy in Ireland, was as
Earl of Strafford to bring his master within sight of the
promised land where a large standing army and an ample
flow of revenue mutually sustaining one another should
jointly make and keep him (in Strafford's words) " as
absolute as any Prince in the world can be ". Collaborating
unofficially with them in Charles's innermost Councils and
exerting a continually greater because subtler influence than
either on a mind whose narrow obstinacy increased the
further it withdrew from the realities of popular feeling, was
Henrietta Maria, more royalist than the King and more
Catholic by a good deal than the Pope.

All three were intensely disliked; the regime which
they upheld fitted most awkwardly the spirited, notoriously
independent race on whom it was compressed. But the
English were no more than most races wedded to any abstract
theory of government or disposed to jeopardize the solid
comforts of what was after all a tolerable present for the
perilous and painful quest after ideal perfection in the
intangible future. The abuses which outraged the affected
or enlightened left the average man unperturbed unless he
too became enlightened by becoming affected. Money
incomes were small, the country still being preponderantly
agricultural and locally self-sustaining, and those with
sufficient substance to be worth the attention of tax-collectors
constituted a very limited class whom he could see mulcted
with equanimity. Not only were they rich, but their wealth
was in many cases fairly new and not untainted with corruption, those squires and merchants whom the King's
ingenious lawyers compelled under an antiquated statute to

buy themselves off the feudal burden of knighthood and whose lands by a loophole in another ancient statute they brought within the charges and penalties of the Crown's forest domains. Even the famous ship-money case probably excited acute interest in only a comparatively small part of the community.[1] As for the Puritans, though the average man disapproved of Laud's treatment of them, the disapproval was mitigated by a strong dislike of their notions, appearance, and conspicuous disinclination to suffer in silence. The wrongs of others may inspire uneasiness but they seldom incite to spontaneous revolt. Unless and until an unforeseen circumstance made it imperative for Charles to turn for assistance to the class whose interests and self-respect he had injured and recall the Parliament which had become almost its private preserve, there seemed no reason to suppose that his system of personal government would not remain the vogue in England as it was practically everywhere else.

But in 1640 such circumstances arose. Money, as usual, was at the root of them. Despite all his efforts, Charles had not yet had time to hack out through old and rugged precedents and prejudices enough new channels for the steady and sufficient flow of revenues, while like so many other autocrats he lived on a scale of chronic emergency, his utmost income failing to cover his normal expenditures. His tastes, displayed in the sumptuous splendours of his

---

[1] Extending the old right of the Crown to the provision of ships by the maritime cities for the defence of the realm in time of emergency, Charles demanded of the inland cities that they compound in money for the ships they did not provide, and renewed the demand in successive years until it began to seem clear that the tax was intended to become a permanent addition to the King's resources instead of a special contribution to the navy in war-time. John Hampden, a rich Buckingham landowner, refused to pay on the dual ground that no tax was valid unless voted by Parliament and that in any event no such emergency existed as would justify the levy of ship-money. The exchequer court before which he was tried held by a vote of 7 to 5 that the King might do anything he deemed necessary to protect the realm in time of danger, of which he was the sole competent judge—a decision resented as apparently enabling him to act as if the realm were in a chronic state of war and to use his powers accordingly.

Court and an outburst of building which alike dazzled the age, were extravagant, the necessary costs of his centralized administration and its self-preservation top-heavy. Nothing remained over for the unexpected, such as the outbreak of armed conflict; the country's glaring military weakness had reduced it to a negligibility in European affairs unknown since the Wars of the Roses. So that when the Scots, goaded to fury by the efforts of a king of their own blood to impose a quasi-Roman episcopacy on their jealous Presbyterianism, dispatched an invading force over the border, Charles had nothing wherewith to meet them.

He tried to negotiate; their terms were too stiff. He turned to Ireland, where the enthusiastic Catholics of the native Parliament voted him money and men to stem the Calvinist menace, but they were not nearly enough, apart from the danger of importing papists to fight on English soil. Pressed on all sides, he dubiously followed the advice of Strafford to summon Parliament and appeal to it on the highest and narrowest grounds of patriotism. His doubts proved only too well founded: it went for him with all the pent-up venom of eleven years, and within three weeks had been peremptorily disbanded, thus going down in history as the Short Parliament. Again Charles turned to the Scots. They demanded a round indemnity, amongst other things, as the price of their retreat. He had no option but to pay it or suffer their advance into a country already alarmed into riot and confusion. To pay it, or else to resist, however, required the immediate generosity of the English Parliament. For the second time that year writs went out for an election, as a result of which virtually the same members who had been dismissed in the spring returned in the autumn determined this time to stay until they had got what they came for.

CHAPTER XIV

Parliament Takes Over

IN the modern sense the Lords and Commons who met at Westminster that 3rd of November, 1640—and remained there intermittently, a shrinking fragment of themselves, until dissolved with their own weary approbation nearly twenty years later—could scarcely be described as a Parliament at all. They came not to participate in but to reassert their assembly's historic right to supervise the conduct of government. They possessed no party programmes to one of which the majority of the electorate had given positive assent, nor any developed party discipline to carry through such programmes; they were merely five hundred individuals, elected (apart from the handful of hereditary and ecclesiastical peers) on an antiquated and absurdly ill-apportioned franchise, who had previously deliberated amongst themselves, in manor house and counting-room, riding to circuit and to hounds, upon their common grievances and ways to remedy them.

That they were able to arrive at the substantial agreement which was to give them such astonishing force as an opposition was due to the existence of one firm and certain bond between them: property. It was the basis of the franchise which had elected them, its protection the chief animating purpose of their grievances. It rendered them proudly independent of the power they were about to assail, while exercising a restraining influence upon them as men possessed of a stake in the good order of the realm. Though they were out to curb the monarchy, none but a few cranks amongst them dreamed of seriously undermining, let alone overthrowing it, or would have refused his subscription to the out-and-out royalist's future party-cry of " Fear God and Honour the King ". Far from harbouring thoughts of revolution, they looked upon themselves as conservatives lawfully delegated to repeal the reckless innovations of a legally uninstructed King.

Significant of the changing times as well as of their underlying unity was the notable proportion of lawyers, spokesmen for the new property in money, sitting side by side with the spokesmen for the old, exclusive property in land. The two men already singled out for leadership accurately reflected both this balance and relation between town and country. To the exertions of John Hampden, hero of the ship-money case and lord of one of the greatest estates in England, largely belonged the credit for the over-whelming majority at the polls; upon John Pym, ex-Treasury Clerk and company promoter, devolved the task of leading it on the floor and in the lobbies. Hampden, lofty of soul but awkward of speech, " a supreme governor over all his passions and affections ", " *Pater Patriae* " to the legions of his idolaters, in appearance a patrician of patricians, re-presented all that was appealing in the parliamentary cause; Pym—massively square, shrewd-eyed, thick-nosed, full-lipped, a great orator and even greater organizer and wire-puller, known as " the Ox " for his forays amongst the ladies—its ruthless driving force. Conspicuous amongst their colleagues were Oliver St. John, Hampden's counsel in the ship-money case; Sir Arthur Haslerigg and Sir Henry Vane, upon whom Pym's mantle would in turn fall; Edward Hyde, the little lawyer who was to outstay them all and as Earl of Clarendon liquidate and chronicle the Great Rebellion he would have spared them; Sir William Waller, their general-to-be, and Edmund Waller, their poet laureate (until their greater general employed an even greater poet in John Milton), and various others: nearly all related to one or other of their chiefs and to one another, as kinsmen, neighbours, business and professional associates, most of them veterans of the fruitless parliamentary struggles of the early years of the reign.

Less conspicuous, but unmistakably entitled by connection, training, and previous reputation to a place in this ruling group, was the newly returned member for the borough of Cambridge, Oliver Cromwell. " By birth a gentleman," according to his own description, " living neither in any considerable height nor yet in obscurity," he could trace his ancestry through a series of opulent East Anglian squires on both sides and count in the present Parliament no less than seventeen, later to be augmented to twenty-one, relatives by birth and marriage, including Hampden, St. John, and the Wallers.[1]

The opulence had somewhat diminished in his immediate family through his father's being only a younger son, but enough had remained to provide him with the typical education of his class—the local grammar school, Sidney Sussex College, Cambridge, a term at Lincoln's Inn to absorb as much law as would be helpful to a landed proprietor in the management of his estates and his probable duties on the magistrates' bench and in the House of Commons. First elected to the Parliament of 1628 for his birthplace, Huntingdon, he had proved a sturdy, if somewhat silent, asset to the radical opposition. Since then, in 1631, he had sold his inherited estate and bought another at St.

---

[1] The name of Cromwell came into Oliver's paternal family when Morgan Williams, rich Welsh brewer of Putney, married the sister of Thomas Cromwell, Henry VIII's famous minister, who adopted their son Richard and made him his heir. Richard's grandson was Sir Henry Cromwell, known in Elizabethan times as the " Golden Knight " for his lavish hospitality, one of whose younger sons became the father of Oliver Cromwell. The family preserved the original name in legal documents until fairly late, Oliver signing himself in his marriage contract " Williams alias Cromwell ".

Ives in Huntingdonshire, where, while pursuing with modest fortune his calling of cattle-grazer, he had won himself the suffrage of his adopted constituency by vigorous interventions on the side of his poorer neighbours against the encroachments of grasping magnates and Crown officials. He himself had been fined for refusing Knighthood and arrested by the Privy Council for resisting an enclosure of common lands. The estimate of his capabilities entertained by his colleagues in the new House could be somewhat gauged by the fact that when it was fully organized he was called to serve on eighteen of its general committees.

More than that, they marked him closely, though he was no Cicero, when he rose to speak. They saw a man about five feet ten inches in height, " well-compact and strong ", looking rather older than his forty-one years; sober, when aroused even grim, of expression, with steel-blue eyes under shaggy brows, a long, thick, slightly aquiline nose so over-sized as to be a topic of jest, a wide, firm mouth, with a large mole prominently beneath it, all framed in thick light-brown hair worn long but severely cut after the common Puritan fashion; as to his clothes—" very ordinarily apparelled, for it was a plain cloth suit which seemed to have been made by an ill country tailor; his linen was plain, and not very clean, and I [the recorder is Sir Philip Warwick, a royalist member] remember a speck or two of blood upon his little band, which was not much larger than his collar; his hat was without a hat-band, his sword stuck close to his side; his countenance swollen and reddish; his voice sharp and untunable [he suffered from a chronic weak throat, which he often kept wrapped in red flannel], and his eloquence full of fervour ". Altogether a characteristic specimen, to the outward view, of the country gentleman already widely designated by reason of his style of hair-dressing by the name of Roundhead. The topic of his discourse on this occasion was equally characteristic—a

plea for the release of a servant of the notorious Puritan
Prynne, who with his master had been scourged and imprisoned for having " dispersed libels against the Queen
for her dancing and such innocent and courtlike sports ".

But if outwardly the member for Cambridge was more
or less cut to the pattern of the Roundhead squirearchy,
there was already within him matter that, if known, would
have tempered his fellows' respect with consternation and
fear. They tended to divide into practical men and idealists,
politicians and bigots: in him an instinct for action schooled
by a habit of deep meditation had achieved a fusion of the
practical and the idealistic so nearly final and effective as
to have left him too rigid for the politicians and too supple
for the bigots, with an impatient fundamental scorn for
both. His enthusiasm for their " great, warm ruffling
Parliament " depended strictly on the kind and amount of
business it got done, not on any mystical properties or
abstract natural rights currently claimed for it; it was an
instrument like another, if perfected obviously the handiest
for paving the way towards the new heaven and earth he
at times visualized as concretely as his native fens, but even
when perfected no more sacred than any other instrument.
On talking assemblies in general his intrinsic opinion was
not far off Strafford's, who quitted a brilliant career as
virtual leader of the Commons largely because its muddle
and twaddle disgusted his sense of efficiency. The moment
his colleagues completed their immediate task and either
decided to rest there or broke into wordy theories as to
what to do next, it was fated that he should part company
with the lot of them.

For wordy theories, like accepted fervours, were impossible to him because personal experience was his only
valid test for anything. " True knowledge," he informed
his son, " is not literal or speculative but inward, trans-
forming the mind to it." To that inward digestion of ex-

OLIVER CROMWELL

From a crayon portrait by Samuel Cooper

perience he owed his religious and political convictions, as in the end his astonishing self-fulfilment. As a student he had neglected the conventional academic fodder of classic literature, language, and philosophy to concentrate on history (his favourite book was Sir Walter Raleigh's *History of the World*), mathematics, and geography, since " these ", as he wrote to the same son, Richard, his successor-to-be, " fit for the public services for which a man is born ".

As a young man pulled in one direction by a love of crude physical effort, boisterous horse-play, and the ordinary temptations of the flesh, and in the other by a brooding melancholy " splenetic and full of fancies ", he had sought and found grace, not by an orthodox retreat into or an intellectual effort after faith, but by a lone and purposeful striving for direct revelation, until at the age of twenty-eight it was granted him. " I lived in and loved darkness and hated light! I was chief, the chief of sinners. This is true, I hated godliness and God had mercy on me," was the exultant conclusion of his report of this experience to his cousin, Mrs. St. John.

That his conversion took the form it did—" My soul is with the Congregation of the First-born, my body rests in hope "—probably requires no more recondite explanation than the fact that Puritanism had been as emphatic a feature of external reality as the headmaster's rarely idle birch at the Huntingdon Free School or the bright new stones of Sidney Sussex College, denounced by Laud as a particularly virulent nursery of the creed. And meanwhile the yet unreleased part of him, the man of action craving an adequate outlet, found food for his imagination in perusing translations of Swedish books on the art of war—most pragmatic of all the arts—as displayed in the campaigns of his hero Gustavus Adolphus; studies marvellously adapted to serve him for vicarious experiences when the need came until he had gained his own. It is not impossible that a Commons still concerned to keep religion prudently subordinated to politics and detesting the very notion of armies would, had they surmised that they were harbouring in their midst one seriously cogitating the fusion of all Britain into a militant Congregation of the First-born, have moved to expel him as they did not many years later.

In less than six months Parliament had stripped the Crown of more powers than it had accumulated in thrice sixty years. The same necessity that had compelled Charles to summon it deprived him of all hope of controlling it. The presence of Scottish troops on English soil not only revealed the ineffectuality of the government in the elementary duty of national defence, but offered to the domestic enemies of Laud's Church too enticing an opportunity of starting in conjunction with them a civil war of religion. Only money could buy them off or furnish an army to drive them out, and only Parliament could raise the money without exciting a dangerous resistance on the part of those who would have to pay it. The immediate conditions it laid down for doing so—an end to arbitrary taxes and arrests, the trial and punishment of those who had perpetrated them, an existence for itself independent in the future of the King's will—were such as to enlist the widest support from public opinion. Charles was not in a position even to put up a good fight against them.

What followed was for him a time of indescribable pain and humiliation. Wanting Strafford, then commanding in the north, at his side before the opening of the session, he summoned him to London with a promise to be personally responsible for his safety; Strafford, though well aware that he was " with more danger beset than ever any man went with out of Yorkshire ", obeyed, relying on the King's word and his own inner resolution to rend his enemies if possible before they could rend him; but the promise and

the resolution alike came to nothing before the swift action
of Pym, who procured his arrest in the House of Lords and
his imprisonment in the Tower without his friend and
master being able to raise a finger to protect him. Three
weeks later Laud was sent to join him by the same irregular
procedure. Two other of the King's most valued counsellors,
Sir Thomas Windebank, the Principal Secretary of State,
and Sir John Finch, the Lord Keeper, who as Chief Justice
had given the decision against Hampden, took the hint and
fled to the Continent. The various taxes by which Charles
had maintained himself since the last Parliament were proclaimed not only illegal but criminal, and heavy punishments
enacted to be visited retrospectively on his servants who had
done no more than carry out his orders. To show that it
had no faith in him to carry out in letter or spirit the acts
it constrained him to sign, Parliament further forced upon
him a bill providing for its own renewal at least once every
three years and a consecutive sitting of not less than fifty
days to be secured by an elaborate machinery over which
he had no control. A vigilant check was placed on his
expenditure of such revenues as were allowed him, and with
it upon his immemorial, almost mystical, attribute of
sovereign captaincy over the armed forces. No offence
was spared either to his principles or his feelings. Powerless
to befriend those who had trusted in and served him, his
authority in the State reduced to a blasphemous caricature
of itself, his religion was next assailed in a huge public
petition demanding the " root and branch " destruction
of the, to him, divinely instituted Episcopal Church of which
he was the appointed Defender, a proposal to which Parliament showed every sign of giving serious consideration the
moment pressure of other business allowed.

Most pressing of that other business, and most horrible
for the King, was the fate of Strafford. The unbelievable
had happened when the royal word had failed to protect

him from imprisonment; it was still unthinkable that the royal power should not be able at least to safeguard his life. Nevertheless his life the Commons had determined to have, though the difficulties in the way were formidable. The only capital charge which could conceivably be brought against him was treason, which consisted of making war on the King or attempting to subvert his government; obviously a ludicrous accusation since everything he had done had been on the King's behalf and by his authority. Undeterred, the House dug up hearsay evidence of one of its own members to the effect that Strafford had urged the King in Council to bring the Irish army into England, and used this evidence as the basis of an impeachment in which for the first time the now familiar distinction was made between the King as a person and as a symbol for the State. Even so, the indictment would not hold water: the words alleged were ambiguous, there were not the necessary two witnesses. The Lords, judges of the impeachment, hesitated. The Commons did not. Outdoing even their prisoner and his master in contempt for the due process of law, they fell back on Henry VIII's useful precedent, the Act of Attainder —a sheer arbitrary device of power whereby a simple majority in the legislature voted an antagonist unfit to live. The Lords and the leaders of the Commons, Pym himself (though he later, like many a leader, fell in with his followers), protested. But behind the majority in the Commons stood the mob in the City, as 150 years later the mob of Paris rallied at each crucial moment to the extremists of the Convention. It marched on Westminster, an ominously organized horde, crying for the blood of the members opposed to the attainder. The bill, despite Charles's frantic effort to avert its passage by dismissing Strafford, was voted and sent up for his signature, without which it was of no effect. He could refuse and invite insurrection; he could agree and sacrifice a friend whom he had sworn on his royal word to defend. Distracted, he sought advice, but the opinion of those he turned to merely reflected, naturally, the divisions in his own soul. In the end it was Strafford's word, as so often before, that carried the decisive weight: with quiet nobility he wrote Charles to yield for the sake of peace. The advice he could not decently follow Charles accepted because he could not safely decline it and, with the heart-broken regret that he could not change places with him, signed away the life of the man who had lived to raise him beyond all human compulsion.

Years later, when it came Charles's own turn to stand at the block, he remarked that if he deserved to die, it was not for anything his enemies had against him, but for having sacrificed a loyal and dutiful friend to selfish necessity. It was a truth that only a man of exquisite sensibility would have perceived, even at that solemn moment: the great truth to which the high tragical happenings of history and the inventions of the tragic poets alike bear recurring testimony, that evil done that good may come of it still remains evil, demanding to be expiated without extenuation by the good that it had sought. Charles was surely right in so far as giving way over Strafford spared everything he held dear, " my wife, children, and all my kingdom ", from being swept away in an orgy of bloodshed. Parliament was also right, knowing that, so long as Strafford lived, its reforms and its individual heads would be in constant and imminent danger. So was Strafford right, who stood for order and reverence in the State and combined with a loyalty to his King a consideration for the " meaner sort " of subject to whose welfare his class-proud foes were largely indifferent.

But in their pursuit of right all three were guilty of hideous wrong—violence, treachery, infidelity to their own professed ideal of law on the part of Parliament, to that code of honour whose keeping was his distinctive compact

with God on the part of the King; and all three were paid
in precisely the same evil coin they had distributed. In
their brazen subordination of means to ends, they ignored,
the fact that means are the very process of life itself, the
manner of its unfolding to experience, while ends are but
the innumerable tentative patterns capable of being ab-
stracted from it; and that to seek even the fairest ends by
a brutal disregard of means is, from any point of view except
the seeker's own possibly squint-eyed one, rather like spitting
in the unchanging moral face of the universe to improve its
appearance for a local occasion.

No one in his senses could have expected the King to
put up with his indignities indefinitely. He had no intention
of doing so: Parliament never deluded itself that he would:
and so it went on to devise ever more potent, and therefore
more resented, shackles for him, and the keener grew the
distrust and bitterness between them. Barely had Strafford's
headless body been removed from the scaffold than the
Commons proceeded to take up again the "root and
branch" bill for the suppression of the bishops and the
transfer of the ecclesiastical power out of the King's hands.
Apart from its religious implications, the idea behind the
bill was to ensure that the Crown should not, through its
satellites in the high diocesan offices, enjoy the enormous
influence wielded by the Church through its courts—whose
rulings the State was bound to enforce—its revenues and
above all its incomparable opportunity for direct appeal
through the pulpit to the popular mind. Only by uprooting
that influence did the movers of the bill feel that they could
regard themselves and any part of their previous gains as at
last safe from the reaction in the King's favour which they
mortally dreaded.

But the bill could not be separated from its religious
implications, and through their very dread they provoked

the reaction. In its secular reforms Parliament had commanded the almost unanimous approval of the country and unity within itself; when it came to religion it forfeited both. Most people would have agreed, as in pre-Reformation days, that many of the Prelates were corrupt, worldly, and prone to get above themselves, but only a small minority desired, also as in pre-Reformation days, to purify them by straightforward extermination. The bleak Establishment which that small minority of Presbyterian Puritans proposed to substitute attracted the rest of their countrymen little more than the Romanism of which they stridently proclaimed the bishops to be the secret and sinister agents. Even the accredited leaders of the Commons were not with them, though perforce inclining somewhat their way lest the withdrawal of their support disrupt the House's solidity. But the Lords, less susceptible to their influence, for the first time refused to collaborate. A preliminary bill from the Commons to deprive the bishops of their seats in the Upper House they threw out; the " root and branch " bill they never even entertained. The rift in the Commons between moderates and extremists began perceptibly to open. With the country now as uneasy over legislative tampering with sacred matters as it had formerly been with executive trespasses on civil rights, men once more instinctively turned to the King as their natural bulwark against obnoxious novelties.

Had Charles been a better psychologist, he might yet have spared himself and England the worst. But because a people already tiring of change were willing to follow him for the sake of a system of worship which they still cherished despite all its faults, he assumed that they must be eager to return to his system of government *with* all its faults. Instead of using such advantages as he had to strike a durable bargain with the more reasonable of his adversaries, he went off to Scotland to make terms with the Scottish leaders in the fond belief that he had but to return with a Scottish army at his back for England to rise joyfully and join in the discomfiture of his enemies. But from the hyper-Protestant Scots he received only a rebuff, while his going incurably deepened Parliament's suspicions. Meanwhile the Queen carried on secret negotiations with Rome for help in exchange for an abrogation of Catholic disabilities. This, too, Parliament surmised, and when shortly after Charles's return to London one of the most terrible of Irish rebellions broke out, all its fears came to a head.

The King asked for money with which to put the rebellion down. So much Parliament, no lover of Catholic Ireland, was willing to grant: but not to the King. It suspected that the Queen was not innocent of complicity with her fellow-papists who were busy, according to rumours flying over the Irish Channel, massacring on a scale and with a ferocity compared to which St. Bartholomew's Night with its ten thousand dead had been little more than a street brawl. It blamed the government's incompetence for the revolt occurring at all; in any event it would not put Charles in control of an army he might more easily turn against them than against the distant rebels. Repeating its tactics of the previous year, it seized the occasion to plunge the King more inextricably than ever into its power. In a paper known as the Grand Remonstrance, it demanded in effect that Charles should freely confess the error of all he had done in the past and submit in the future to do what it required of him while doing nothing without its express approval.

The Grand Remonstrance was no ordinary legislative Act; it was an ultimatum on whose reception, as every intelligent man now knew, hung the issue of peace or civil war. Unlike a common bill, limited in scope and ephemeral in effect, it sweepingly affirmed Parliament's claim to be by right and in fact the supreme authority in the State.

This was no longer reform, it was candid revolution: so obviously so that the Commons themselves split squarely into two over it, and only after a wild debate of twelve hours, in the course of which swords were flourished, did its sponsors, headed by Pym, succeed in forcing its passage by a bare eleven votes; so passionately so in the minds of its partisans that one of the foremost of them, the word-thrifty member for Cambridge, declared that " if the Remonstrance had been rejected I would have sold all I had the next morning and never have seen England any more; and I know there are many other honest men of the same resolution ". It was a more critical moment than even the participants in it guessed, when the change of half a dozen votes—two per cent of the total—would have sent Oliver Cromwell into permanent exile to help in founding the new Connecticut colony. . . . As for Charles, if he accepted the Remonstrance, he would have renounced the essential principle of his being and transformed himself from a responsible plenipotentiary of God into the decorative flunkey of a group of irresponsible demagogues. If he refused, it was clear that his enemies would not hesitate to ruin his realm in order to ruin him.

Charles faltered. A ceremonial reception accorded him by the City merchants on his return from Scotland deluded him into an exaggerated estimate of returning popularity. While rejecting the substance of the Remonstrance, he expressed a readiness to discuss its details. Even then the conditions he laid down made it plain beforehand that the discussions were likely to prove barren. In the meantime he started preparations for active conflict if it had to come. To overawe the unruly London mob he strengthened the garrison of the Tower and placed in command of it an officer on whose lack of squeamishness in dealing with mobs he could count. Such measures naturally aroused the alert distrust of those against whom they were aimed. Collisions in the streets between the citizens and the royal troops occurred with increasing frequency and violence. The former continued to surge to Westminster, audible and terrifying intruders into the debates going on behind its walls. Suspicion rose to fever-heat as the King prepared to raise an army on his own for Ireland, to be officered by his swordsmen in the street fighting. The suspicion was matched on the King's side when the Commons asked for a guard, ostensibly to protect it from the mob, under the command of one of its leading supporters, the Earl of Essex, son of Elizabeth's favourite.

A momentary glimmer of light flickered through the onrushing darkness when on New Year's Day, 1642, Charles offered to take Pym and possibly other leaders of the opposition into the government—one of the major demands of the Remonstrance—but the gesture was so vague and perfunctory that it came to nothing. How perfunctory it was became evident three days later when the King, to head off a rumoured impeachment of the Queen by the Commons for criminal conspiracy with Rome and Ireland, sent the Attorney-General to sue out a warrant in the House of Lords for the arrest of Pym, Hampden, and three of their principal colleagues, on a comprehensive charge of treason and sedition. The Lords refused on grounds of legality; the Commons counter-charged the King with a scandalous breach of its privileges in having sequestered the private papers of the five members, and, when Charles dispatched the serjeant-at-arms to carry out the arrest on his own warrant, sent the royal messenger back with strong words to that effect, in which the Lords joined. Collecting a band of three hundred retainers, the King set off to execute the arrest in person. But there was disloyalty round him; someone had warned the Commons (some said it was one of the Queen's ladies who was also Pym's mistress), and when the King entered the House the five were already on their way to the City by river. Discomfited but with remarkable dignity in the circumstances, Charles withdrew to look for his quarry elsewhere.

The Commons, with the approval of the Lords, at once proceeded to recruit a guard from the City militia to protect themselves from another armed invasion by their sovereign. The local hostility towards him reached such a pitch that he fled with his family from London to Hampton Court and thence presently northward to York. For seven months more he and Parliament kept up a brisk and bitter exchange of propositions,. demands, and ultimatums designed rather to impress the public than out of any real hope of persuading one another . . . both simultaneously racing to impose their authority on ports, arsenals, and fortified points, and the King early on sending the Queen to Holland to pledge the Crown jewels in readiness for the collision. To York meanwhile flocked thousands from all parts of the country who until the last moment desperately hoped for a peaceful solution, but if it was to be by battle had no doubt where their allegiance belonged. On 9th August the King broke off the parleys by proclaiming all who were in arms against him traitors—a compliment which Parliament immediately returned—and on the 22nd, with the King's advance to Nottingham, where he unfurled his standard, the two halves of the nation squared off for war.

CHAPTER XV
The Civil War

IT had long been expected. Yet for most it came like a mysterious visitation of the gods gone suddenly mad. They had seen its portents but refused to believe them with their hearts because unable to grasp them with their understanding. That was the pity, the dreadful puzzle of it . . . humane, enlightened seventeenth-century England, nursery of Harvey, Milton, Purcell, and Newton, visited by a fratricidal war of which not a handful on either side could have told what it was they were fighting for.

A professional incendiary like Edmund Ludlow—author of the Nineteen Propositions whose receipt stung Charles into breaking off the parleys with the not unwarranted comment that they aimed at degrading him to " but the picture, but the sign of a king "—might declaim that

" The question in dispute between us and the King's party was, as I apprehended, whether the King should govern as a god by his will and the nation (be) governed by force like beasts; or whether the people should be governed by laws made by themselves and live under a government derived from their own consent ".

But few even of those who on the delirious eve of the breaking-point voted for the Nineteen Propositions would have endorsed that simple antithesis. Certainly neither Hampden, Pym, nor—though far less tender towards the throne than they—Cromwell himself would have lifted a finger, let alone drawn the sword, had the only alternative to the despotic will of a single sovereign been to entrust the sovereign power to the turgid whims of a fickle and irresponsible multitude. Equally on the other side no one except a fringe of diehard romantics—opposite and perhaps equal numbers to their enemies' fringe of romantic republicans—seriously contended that the King should govern as a god or even that most of what he had had to concede in the past two years ought in practice to be annulled. Hyde, by head and shoulders his party's ablest statesman, had persistently urged him to take the line of a constitutional monarch simply upholding customary rights and established order against disorderly invasion by a selfish, tyrannical minority, and when the parting of the ways came frankly admitted that he followed the King only as the " lesser evil ". Andrew Marvell, far from regarding the Royalist cause as a mandatory summons to crusade, quietly opined, even after he quitted it, that " the cause was too good to have been fought for ". Charles himself was honestly willing to abate the more magniloquent of his pretensions. As for the four or five million on the whole prosperous and contented people being made ready to persuade one another by slaughter, fire, rapine, and pestilence, the great mass of them, as Democracy's foremost spokesman in Parliament, Sir Arthur Haslerigg, testified, " care(d) not what form of government they live under, so they may plough and go to market ".

It was not mere selfishness and indifference on their part. To nearly all save the handful befogged in their cloud-cuckoo theories or blinded by the gloss of their brand-new panaceas, it seemed plain good sense. They had seen the King yield more than the most furious parliamentarian had asked or imagined less than two years earlier. They had heard Pym, most impressive of his critics, state the problem of constitutional revision in words which Strafford might have echoed without the change of a syllable:

" If, instead of interchange of support, one part seeks to uphold an old form of government and the other part introduce a new, they will miserably consume one another. . . . It is nevertheless equally true that time must needs bring about some alterations . . . therefore have these commonwealths been ever the most durable and perpetual which have often reformed and recomposed themselves according to their first institution and ordinance. By this means they repair the breaches and counter-work the ordinary and natural effects of time."

With regard to the vexed question of religion they believed, as implicitly as the Puritan martyr Eliot or the arch-Anglican Laud, in the compulsory inclusion of every subject within a uniform national worship, but until the very end hoped for some tolerable adjustment, either by an agreed compromise or a limited measure of allowance to " tender consciences ", of such comparatively superficial differences as the position of the communion-table, Church organization and discipline, or even the liturgy: indeed, irreconcilable fanaticism was a product of the fighting rather than the other way round.

The popular instinct was right. Like most blood-bought revolutions, this one had in all essentials been achieved before it broke out. But a curse had overtaken England, the old periodic curse of humanity which, like some grisly law of nature, seems to require it to purge its humours every so often by a frantic blood-letting instead of submitting to the medicaments of reason. Reason did not enter in because patience had been cast out. Absolutism had collapsed of its own natural decay, shrouding for a while in its dust the memories and aspirations it had nurtured, and, as always in the interval between the spending of one creative inspiration and the resurging energy of a new, a dangerous emptiness settled on men's spirits, the weary feeling that the world had seen its best days: a mood peculiarly prone to be lashed by equally dangerous enthusiasms. Long belaboured by conflicting exaggerations, tantalized by reforms that always promised but never brought tranquillity, many an otherwise stolid intelligence gave way under the strain. From the dilemma of things and distrust of men they sought escape in a hectic revivalism. Some succumbed to weird religious aberrations, some to the lure of improbable terrestrial Utopias, others to nostalgic yearnings for the recall of bygone dispensations whole and entire. They were no longer in a state to reason causes but, ridden by ecstasies and the morbid suspicions of the fevered, fought because they could no longer think of what else to do.

The futility of the war was thus intrinsic in its origins. The artificial paradox of despotism was not to be solved by plunging it into the elemental paradox of violence: the seven lean kine simply consumed the seven fat and were no fatter than before. For six years the King, embodiment of absolutism, struggled to restore his sway by the promise of the most irreconcilable and impossible liberties to all and sundry. For six years the Parliament, avowed champions of liberty, strove to prevent him by the most odious and licentious devices of tyranny. Both by taking up arms doomed themselves to flounder in contradictions as miserably as they doomed England to wallow in blood. For that reason neither could win. Neither did.

The King had to offer promises because he had little else to offer. The parts of the country that remained obedient to his authority, the north and the west chiefly, were in general the poorest and most sparsely populated, and even there the seaports, as in the rest of the kingdom, were in his enemies' hands. To cherish any hope of victory he had to decrease their following while increasing his own. To do that he had to acknowledge as just and permanent the very reforms Parliament's right in principle to extort which his loyal Cavaliers were denying with their lives; to fortify the natural good disposition of the Catholics towards him with measures of indulgence unpalatable alike to his adherents and his potential converts; and, especially later when things were growing desperate, to solicit with important concessions the Scottish Presbyterians whose aggressive missionizing amongst them Cavalier, Catholic, and most Puritans joined in detesting. Every effort at the advancement of his cause impaired by so much its integrity and augmented the reputation for double-dealing which was his enemies' prime asset.

Yet the Parliament, though materially much better off, was morally in an even worse quandary. It commanded the ports and with them the great sea-borne trade, the navy to protect it and prevent foreign aid reaching the King, the most thickly populated part of the kingdom to draw on for men and money—an overwhelming preponderance of the raw materials for military success. But to transmute those materials into the finished product of victory demanded its resort in an alarming degree to the exact processes for which it reproached the King. To fight a war it had to raise money in quantities of which Charles had never dreamed, and raise it from part only, if the wealthiest part, of the country instead of the whole. It had immédiately to raise and train the army to whose existence it had previously been so opposed; apart from the various local militias, of which the City of London's alone was worth anything as a fighting force, it had to begin at the beginning and extract the necessary numbers from a lethargic and unmilitary populace by the brutal, capricious, and inefficient system of impressment. The lethargy had to be overcome by a ferocious propaganda in press and pulpit, dissent and incipient trouble quelled by an inquisitorial censorship of speech and print, the suppression of civil rights, arbitrary imprisonments, and heedless executions. Because of its greater financial resources and comparative similarity of religious sympathies, Parliament was able to outbid the King for the Scottish alliance; but the direct result of this diplomatic *coup* was to give the direction of its policy to the extreme Calvinist elements and commit it collectively to the establishment in England of a Church copied from the hated Presbyterian model.

There was one thing more, however, an intrinsic strength on the side of the King and a corresponding weakness on the side of Parliament of which all but the most single-minded and stoutest-hearted of its leaders were conscious and afraid. They were fighting not only a mortal man but an immortal idea. " If we beat the King ninety and nine times," remarked the Earl of Manchester, one of the most eminent of their generals, to his subordinate Colonel Oliver Cromwell, " yet he is King still, and so will his posterity be after him; but if the King beat us once, we shall all be hanged and our posterity made slaves." That was the great imponderable weighing the balance against them. Nothing but success, consistent and complete beyond anything they dared envisage, could alter the fact that they were rebels, owning no authority beyond what they could compel, possessing little appeal in themselves to make their followers forgetful of its burden. Whereas to his followers (and not to them alone) the King radiated the glamour of an authority sanctified by the mystery of anointment and a millennium of tradition—something continuous and indivisible in its essence and indestructible even by the chances of war; and his resources, however meagre, not only belonged to him of right but were to an extraordinary extent freely given, in the form of the well-mounted gentry flocking in with their tenants to volunteer and of the plate and jewels consigned to him with their donors' blessings.

So, despite the enormous physical disparity of the contending forces, the struggle was for a while not unequal. Neither side could attain the ultimate object of its strategy, which was on the King's to take London, on Parliament's to take the King, but by the measure of battles won and ground gained the royal armies more than held their own. Superior in the unity if not the quality of their generalship, on the whole better disciplined and distinctly better equipped in the then dominant arm of cavalry, they had little difficulty in outmanœuvring the miscellaneous drafts opposed to them. Only, each time they cleared one such obstacle out of their path Parliament was able out of its brimming human reservoir to interpose another; an advantage which even its fatuous interference with its commanders in the field—inveterate habit of every civilian assembly self-constituted into a Committee of Public Safety—was unable entirely to dissipate. The King advanced to Turnham Green, on the very outskirts of London, could advance no farther, fell back. Successes elsewhere made him master again towards the end of the second year in two-thirds of his kingdom—but with no more prospect than ever of mastering the other third. The war which had begun in a spirit of forbearance, even of chivalry, the impulse to hatred tempered by the knowledge on the part of each of the combatants that the other numbered not only men of their own race and breed but brothers, fathers, sons, friends, soon degenerated through haphazard cruelty into surly ferocity. The spreading anxiety of those who wished they were well out of it led to frequent attempts at negotiation, which invariably broke down on the contracting obstinacy of those for whom disappointment and sacrifice merely raised the price of peace. The fighting dragged on, now languishing, now swaying to and fro, now flaring up in new and previously tranquil areas, until the wretched victims tiredly supposed that it was destined to drag on so for ever.

Then quite abruptly, within the space of a few months, the picture changed — not the deepening boredom and misery and barbarity in the background, but by the introduction of clarity and direction into the churning indecision

of the foreground. Suddenly and unmistakably it was the
Parliament that was winning. Its cavalry outrode and out-
fought as well as outnumbered the best that the King could
send or his dashing nephew Prince Rupert lead against it.
Its military effort took on a unity and resolution all the
more startling by contrast with its infirmity and disintegration in every other respect. Never again did the King
win a major battle. The tale of that transformation was
largely the record of the rise of Oliver Cromwell.

The imminent prospect of war had sent him, like a
great many others of his class, home to put his own neigh-
bourhood in a state of defence and raise what troops he
could for the service of his side. When contributions to the
Parliamentary war-chest were called for in June, 1642, he
had subscribed the not inconsiderable sum, for him, of
£500 and given another hundred to supply arms to his
constituents, amongst whom he helped to improvise three
volunteer companies. By prompt action he had prevented
the King's officials from carrying off £20,000 worth of
plate at Cambridge University and enforcing the King's commissions of array in that Royalist oasis. With the rank of
Lieutenant-Colonel he led his own picked troop of sixty to
join the main Parliamentary force under the Earl of Essex
and took part in the first important engagement at Edgehill
on 23rd October, where he attracted the favourable notice
of his superior as a steady and resourceful cavalry leader
amidst the crazy vacillations of a battle in which Essex's
army was only saved from a shattering defeat by the total
disappearance of the enemy's horse from the field on the
momentum of a too-successful charge. His superior's praise
was the first modest intimation, as the occasion of it was
the exciting revelation to himself, that the greatest soldier
yet born on English soil had discovered his calling.

He was then forty-three, rather late in life to take up a
new career of which he had no experience or knowledge

except what he had derived from his reading, and no apparent qualifications for it except a strong body, a cool head, the habit of command appropriate to his station, and—for the particular sort of warfare ahead of him—a profound understanding of horseflesh. Of his sort both sides numbered thousands, good potential officers of troops and companies raised by themselves, or, particularly as the fiery elimination by fitness and death set in, possibly of regiments. Beyond that it would have seemed vain for these amateur soldiers to have aspired even had their inclinations and abilities pointed that way. The higher commands awaited either the great nobles whose historic perquisites they were or the many eminent veterans not long returned from service with the continental armies in the Thirty Years' War. Even the eruptive combination of hidden genius and unusual circumstances might not have availed to thrust the mature novice through those resistant layers of dutiful mediocrity and professional seniority, at least at so dizzy a speed to so prodigious a height, had it not been abetted by the soaring conviction, born in him during the din and smoke of his first battle, that he had at last found his vocation.

For as a vocation it came to him in the literal sense, the sense, that is, of having been called. Like Joan of Arc starting out to fight another King of England, he might have exclaimed, " For this thing was I born!" The external Voices in obedience to which she also exchanged husbandry for arms were not similarly present to him, but otherwise the parallel was (as in many purely military respects it continued to be) curiously exact. He had gone forth to fight what conscience told him to be God's cause: because it was God's he enjoyed fighting it; and because he enjoyed fighting it, it was indubitably God's. That the argument ran in a circle would not have trouble him, but would rather have seemed to him a confirmation. A circle is a thing complete and he knew himself to be a man completed. As he had through long inner turmoil reached his experience of faith, so in the mighty stresses of battle he reached instantaneous fulfilment of himself, of his functional being—the one process rounded off the other. In violent action he could release every craving, give outlet to every faculty, allay every doubt that faith was unable to provide for: yet a battle was an act of faith, " an appeal to God ", in his own words, each victory " the seal of God's approbation " for having done what he thoroughly enjoyed doing for its own sake. By being most completely himself, he might thus have the satisfaction of knowing that he was most completely serving God.

His genius, being no less intensely practical than visionary, proceeded to consider the tangible means by which the immediate object, the King's defeat, might be accomplished. Objectively meditating visible cause and effect amidst the bedlam of Edgehill, he had come to the conclusion that the equipment, training, tactics, and, above all, the composition of Parliament's forces stood in need of drastic revision. " Your troops," he wrote to his cousin John Hampden, " are most of them decayed serving-men, tapsters and such kind of fellows; do you think that the spirits of such mean, base fellows will ever be able to encounter gentlemen that have honour, courage and resolution in them? You must get men of a spirit that is likely to go as far as a gentleman will go, or you will be beaten still." Obtaining leave of absence, he went back home to secure the co-operation of his neighbours for what he had in mind.

Luckily the ground was fertile: not only was enthusiasm for the Parliamentary cause high in East Anglia, but the will to support it was strong enough for five (later increased to seven) adjacent counties to sink the selfish local jealousies which were obstructing efficiency elsewhere and pool their efforts in an Eastern Association, with headquarters at

Cambridge, for the vigorous prosecution of the war. Of this Association Cromwell was the instigating as he later became the dominant spirit. Under its ægis, after careful personal selection of " such men as had the fear of God in them and made some conscience of what they did ", he increased his own command to five times its original strength (presently to be doubled and doubled again). Though for officers he would have preferred " men of honour and birth ", of that class too many of those who had not gone with the King failed to measure up to his criterion, so, " seeing it was necessary the work go on, better plain men than none ", he decided; ". . . a plain russet-coated captain that knows what he fights for and loves what he knows than that which you call a gentleman and is nothing else ".

" My troops increase; I have a lovely company . . . they are no Anabaptists but sober, honest Christians." What sort of Christians may be deduced from a Royalist lampoon which described him as

" one that hath beate up his Drummes cleane through the Old Testament; you may learn the genealogy of our Saviour by the names in his Regiment; the Mustermaster uses no other than the first chapter of Matthew."

To distinguish them from the ordinary motley, nondescript rabble of soldiery, and at the same time foster their self-respect and *esprit de corps*, he put them into the fine, new red coats which were for centuries to set the style for the crack units of the British army. Their mounts he chose with his own expert eye, obtaining them either by gift from sympathizers or confiscations from the stables of Royalist " Malignants ", and saw to it that they were properly cared for. Mobility rather than weight being his tactical ideal and the unwieldy pike or heavy carbine being unsuited to it, he cut his troopers' arms down to a pair of pistols and a sword, and their armour to a light helmet (familiarly known as a

" pot ") and a simple iron " back " and " breast ". He drilled them thoroughly, by his own unorthodox lights, to the end that he might rely upon them for an unquestioning obedience and a hardy initiative which should be equally proof against all vicissitudes of battle.

He burned his impress not only on their bodies and minds but on their very souls. They were made to feel that they were dedicated to a cause for which it was necessary not alone to fight well and die bravely, but also to live exemplarily. Determined to keep them immune from the general wantonness that was rendering the ill-fed, haphazardly recruited armies an increasing scourge to the populace, he repressed every manifestation of it with terrifying severity while so far as possible attacking temptation at its source. " No man swears but he pays his twelvepence, if he be drunk he is set in the stocks or worse "; looting was punishable by death; yet the men—already aware of being a band apart, sworn to fight for a cause rather than for money—could count upon their pay, thanks to their Colonel and his indefatigable Eastern Association, when the rest of Parliament's forces often went without. They also knew his pride in them and returned it by trying to deserve it and by an answering pride in him. Nor, despite his formidable exterior—the fierce discipline, the strict piety— did he seem in the least inhuman to them. His piety was their language, his humour of their kind: the rough humour of homely quips, pillow-fights, and face-inkings with eminent Parliamentary colleagues, the loud roar of laughter when an inquisitive trooper got his head stuck in a butter-churn. " Ironsides " they called him, and, as if to mark their oneness with him, achieved the same nickname collectively by popular acclaim after showing their mettle in action.

He led them out first to repel an attempted invasion of East Anglia by detachments of one of the Royalist armies.

It was a fortunate beginning; not only because they were defending their homes, but because they had an opportunity of experimenting upon comparatively feeble contingents of the enemy before trying themselves out against his main body. Then they skirmished their way to help Sir Thomas Fairfax, their future generalissimo, to hold Yorkshire. The ribald laughter that had greeted their inception died away in a startled recognition that they brought something new to the art of war as currently taught and practised. The difference, recorded Clarendon (no friend of theirs) in his *History of the Great Rebellion*, was " that though the King's troops prevailed in the charge, they never rallied themselves again on order, nor could they be brought to make a second charge that same day, whereas Cromwell's troops if they prevailed, or though they were beaten and routed, presently rallied again and stood in good order until they received new orders ". In other words, they had been drilled to win battles, not to bring off showy feats of arms: the same principle which was to inspire their leader, when he came to command larger units, to seek out the enemy's armies instead of his innumerable individual castles for destruction.

The idea caught on, at least with the Eastern Association, which reorganized its forces in January, 1644, with Cromwell as Lieutenant-General in command of the horse under the Earl of Manchester, " a sweet, weak man, who permitted his Lieutenant-General to guide all the army at his pleasure ". The following June, in the decisive battle for the control of the North at Marston Moor, it was the cavalry of the Eastern Association on the left of the Parliamentary line which, when the right had been broken and the infantry in the centre driven back, charged in supported by the Scots to retrieve the day in the most murderous fighting, hand-to-hand, of the whole war. As the result of it, Cromwell received a bullet in the neck from so close a range that the flash temporarily blinded him, and his own " lovely company ", the spearhead of the victorious charge, won their brevet of Ironsides from their gallant enemy Prince Rupert himself.

But elsewhere the war was not going so well for Parliament. The same month the King defeated its hitherto most successful general, Waller, at Cropredy Bridge in Oxfordshire, and later in the summer crushed its commander-in-chief, Essex, at Lostwithiel in Cornwall. The root of the trouble was with Parliament itself, which was steadily losing both the power of coherent decision and the confidence of its troops. Hampden and Pym were dead, the one in action, the other of cancer, and with the further loss of some of its most stable elements to the King, it was nothing like the same purposeful yet balanced assembly it had been. It was trying, with the obstinacy of feebleness, to set up the Presbyterian establishment to which it was pledged and which represented the wish of its now dominant faction. The rank and file of the army were independent Puritans, out-and-out dissenters, sectaries of one sort or another: by whatever name, having rebelled against the forms of a Church of England which they found intolerable, they had no mind to fight for compulsory inclusion in a Church of Scotland. They accused Parliament of giving preference in promotion and pay to Presbyterians—a partiality which only the Eastern Association had been strong enough to resist; they more than suspected it of readiness to patch up a peace with the King which would leave their own desires and grievances untouched if he would agree to ratify the Presbyterian settlement. Instinctively they turned to Cromwell, himself an independent in religion, a soldier, and by way of being the current popular hero.

He, too, was dissatisfied, though as yet chiefly on the grounds of his colleagues' military incapacity: the conditions of peace seemed to him a futile topic of discussion until the King was beaten into surrender. Having proved himself as a soldier, he felt himself in a position to do something towards victory as a politician. His prestige, particularly in the eastern counties, was enormous: already in 1643 a Royalist newspaper had irritably referred to him as the Lord of the Fens. So far as campaigning had permitted, he had remained an active member of Parliament, which had appointed him the previous February to a Committee of Both Kingdoms charged with the conduct of the war. In this capacity he took upon himself the burden of inducing his weary and distracted colleagues to put their backs into the war rather than yield to the allurement of a premature and unsatisfactory compromise.

It was not an easy task. Parliament by now distrusted all of its generals who showed eagerness to fight, suspecting them of a conspiracy to prolong the war for their own honour and profit. It morbidly distrusted the erratic engine of force it had called into being, the army which it had begun openly to consider " only fit for a gallows here and a hell hereafter ". Most of all it distrusted the Eastern Association and its most conspicuous military ornament. The sort of Commonwealth which the unruly theocrats of the Association aspired to set up as a result of the war seemed to the ruling clique in the Commons more detestable by far than the state of affairs the war had grown out of. Most of them regarded Cromwell, " the darling of the sectaries ", as a sort of renegade from the parliamentary to the military gospel, many of them as a hypocrite and self-seeking intriguer. There was even a movement started to impeach him as a subversive incendiary.

He retorted vigorously, and with success. He exposed the incompetence of Parliament's chosen commanders, not hesitating to name his own direct superiors like the Earls of Essex and Manchester, but for whose undeniable incapacity the victory might already have been achieved. He taunted them with preferring in their hearts not to beat the King, a challenge which placed their sympathizers in the House in an awkward dilemma, since they could hardly afford, by the very reason of being then engaged in driving a bargain for peace at Uxbridge, to acknowledge that they did not even *want* to win the war. Events came to his assistance. Irritation with the King's obstinacy in the negotiations and the partisan excitement caused by the long-deferred trial and execution of Archbishop Laud produced a revulsion in favour of having the quarrel out once and for all. Parliament agreed to the complete overhaul of its military establishment on Cromwell's lines.

Instead of various armies raised here, there, and everywhere by all manner of contrivances and supported anyhow or nohow, there was henceforth to be one army supported by equitable monthly assessments on the various counties, uniform in pay, equipment, and training, of predetermined strength and proportion between its several arms, and with definite provision for its recruitment and expansion, its maintenance to be the direct responsibility of the central government, and its direction to be placed under a commander-in-chief responsible only to the central government's executive organ, the Committee of Both Kingdoms. For this post the choice fell with scarcely any opposition on Sir Thomas Fairfax, an able and extraordinarily attractive young aristocrat of thirty-three, popular with everybody and adored by his men, to whom he was known from the swarthiness of his Roman beauty as " Black Tom ". To avert the reproach of seeking to prolong the war for their own benefit, and also as a way of letting down lightly various of the half-hearted and incapable, a Self-Denying Ordinance required such other generals as were in Parliament to resign their commissions within forty days. That this device was not intended to apply to the prime mover of the New Model, as the reconstituted army was designated, was made plain by the fact that the office of Lieutenant-General was tacitly left unfilled until Cromwell should be eligible to fill it. Neither the public nor Fairfax would have had it otherwise.

The spring of 1645, while the New Model was preparing, began badly for the Parliamentary cause. While Fairfax besieged Oxford, the Royalist capital, Rupert swept up the Severn valley and the King capped an advance along a parallel line by the capture of Leicester in May. The efforts of various separate detachments, including Cromwell and his 600 troopers, to prevent their junction failed. Abandoning the siege of Oxford, Fairfax hurried north to offer battle before the whole of the midlands should be lost. On 13th June, as the two hosts converged on the village of Naseby in Northamptonshire, " a mighty shout " of " Ironsides is come to head us " announced the arrival of Cromwell to take up his new command. Next day the Cavaliers, as usual, gained the initial advantage; but after the Roundhead cavalry on the left had been sent reeling back before Rupert's impetuous charge and the infantry in the centre driven from their first line, they re-formed farther back to renew the fight, and Cromwell on the right, hurling the Royalist horse out of his way, smashed in the left flank of the Royalist infantry while still deeply engaged on their front. For a moment he and the King nearly came face to face as Charles prepared to lead a desperate counter-charge in person, but he was dissuaded by his staff from so forlorn a hope and led off to safety. Of his army nothing was left except scattered knots of hunted fugitives. Not only were all his guns and stores taken, but his private correspondence revealing his supplications for foreign intervention, which his jubilant enemies hastened to publish with devastating effect on his subjects' minds. In one battle the New Model had irretrievably broken the King's power, and—a corollary ominously evident to the politicians who had half doubted and half dreaded its success—from it emerged the potential receiver for the escheated sovereignty of England. It had also given a demonstration of its essential temper in another, non-military respect by murdering for righteousness' sake the papist and mutilating the Protestant trollops discovered amongst the Cavalier baggage-train.

There were still Royalist forces large and small to over-come, isolated Royalist strongholds to batter down. So long as Charles remained alive, a King wronged in the eyes of a considerable portion of his subjects, there always would be. But with the flower of his army destroyed and himself virtually a fugitive, there was nothing round which desire for further resistance could effectively rally, while in the bulk of the country was nothing but an aching desire for peace. The former emotion Fairfax and Cromwell repressed with firmness, often with brutality, in the south-west where it still chiefly smouldered, the latter they en-couraged by moderation to the civilian population in the conquered areas. Meanwhile Charles, beaten from pillar to post, disappointed of expected assistance from the Con-tinent and from Ireland, frustrated no less by his past double-dealing than by his present helplessness from colla-borating in Montrose's sublime and tragic adventure to bring him salvation out of the Highlands, had finally to choose between his pursuers and flight abroad, and in May, 1646, elected to put himself in the hands of Parlia-ment's Scottish allies as the least unpromising alternative. With the surrender of Oxford in June he formally laid down his arms.

CHAPTER XVI

The End of the King

BUT the struggle was not yet at an end. The bitterness had grown too great, the issues too complicated, for an enduring settlement to be reached by the mere victory of one of the original antagonists over the other. Private hates had to be avenged before they could be appeased, suffering partisans had to be recompensed, families disrupted by murderous passions had to grope their way to reconciliation: all of which was impossible until some new framework of order had been created in place of that which had been destroyed.

There was still the King, and there was still Parliament, and the difficulty was that the one had come through the conflict too little changed while the other had changed almost beyond recognition. On what terms, if any, was the defeated monarch to be reintegrated into the government of the kingdom? More important still, what sort of kingdom, if any, was it to be? A great many powerful voices had many loud and discordant answers to those questions. The King, believing as profoundly as ever that his prerogative and his religion had been instituted by God, knew that he must yield something, but was determined to yield only as much as he should be constrained to by main force, and even that he hoped to circumvent by cunningly setting against one another those who at present wielded it. His late followers implored him, as soon as the fearful penalties and proscriptions decreed by Parliament fell upon the clergy, gentry, and yeomen identified with his cause, to yield as little as possible even if it meant their having to fight all over again. Such schemes and counsels would have been merely foolish had the victors been united, but once the object which had drawn them together, namely the King's defeat, had been accomplished, they quickly discovered antipathies towards one another quite as serious as their several antipathies towards the King.

On one point only were they substantially agreed, that Charles's restoration must be accompanied by juridical restrictions which he should for ever find it impossible to break or evade. Beyond that all was confusion. Parliament construed the victory as a transfer to itself of the ultimate rights over State and Church to which the King had hitherto pretended; and it at once asserted these rights in the form of bills to punish a denial of the Trinity and of Predestination by death and of Infant Baptism by life imprisonment. The Army, the new power called into being by the war, considered the result less a mandate for a redistribution of the secular authority than for liberty of conscience; its members were no more prepared to allow an elective assembly to dictate their religion than a hereditary monarch capriciously to interfere with their lives and property. There were elements in Parliament which sided with the Army and elements in the Army which sided with Parliament, but they were minorities and by no means constant minorities. The Scots, with the enormous advantage of holding the King in their possession, were altogether with Parliament on the religious issue but on not much else: quite ready to treat separately with Charles—for whom, as their native-born King, they had a stronger natural sympathy than for his English rebels—and even to assist him in regaining his throne on favourable terms if he would bind himself to maintain the Presbyterian worship in England. Though also with them there was a strong Puritan minority in noisy support of the point of view of the English army.

The Scots withdrew from the immediate controversy first. With a stubbornness that did more credit to his purity of heart than to his tactical acumen, Charles refused to compromise his faith even to buy the joint goodwill of the political rulers of the two kingdoms, and the Scots, not sorry to be rid of a prisoner capable of stirring up as much strife in their midst as his grandmother had in England's sixty years earlier, handed him over to Parliament and quitted English soil on payment of a round sum for their services. Parliament now had the King where they wanted him; all that remained was to get rid of the Army. This it attempted to do by sending part of it, under trustworthy Presbyterian generals, over to Ireland, where the original revolt against the Crown had evolved into a Catholic last stand for the King, and demobilizing the rest. But the Army declined either to go to Ireland or to be demobilized, at least until it was sure of the pay which had been allowed to fall into arrears on the cessation of hostilities, an immunity from being called to account when the King was restored, and its full liberty of worship. Instead it set up a committee consisting of the chief agitators in each regiment to place its demands before Parliament. The latter sent a delegation headed by Cromwell to mediate, with power to promise the arrears and the immunity. It was not enough, particularly when the King at last gave in to a proposal for his restoration on the basis of the Presbyterian settlement. A formal order from Parliament to disband by regiments was met by a blunt refusal and a counter-order from Fairfax, on the persuasion of the soldiers' delegates, for a general concentration on Newmarket Heath. Meanwhile Cromwell, who had after intense communion with himself thrown in his lot with the Army—one of the most momentous decisions of his whole life—called a meeting of officers at his house in London, where it was resolved that a troop of horse should be sent under Cornet Joyce to " secure " the King's person.

Possibly nothing more was meant than to prevent Parliament from removing him into its own closer custody, but Joyce, putting the most liberal gloss on his instructions, on 2nd June, 1647, coolly carried him off to Newmarket.

Parliament fumed; the Scots threatened; the King, trying to make the best of both worlds, cordially accepted the protection of the Army against Parliament while exhorting Parliament by liberating him to vindicate its own dignity and the outraged majesty of the law. But the Army was neither to be cozened nor bullied. It knew what it wanted and meant to get it. If the King, as the recent conflict had determined, was nothing without Parliament, so long as England called herself a monarchy Parliament was equally nothing without the King; if his possession did not vest the government in his possessors, it at least required their consent to any plausible government at all. Of Parliament it demanded that, having outlived both its mandate from the people and its usefulness, it should, after redressing certain urgent grievances and giving certain obvious guarantees, dissolve and let the voice of the country be heard in a new and more representative body. To the King it offered a restoration based on a limitation of his prerogative, with reference especially to his choice of ministers and his control of the armed forces, a wide amnesty and complete abolition of restraint on conscience. Parliament hesitated, then started to give in. Charles, playing for time, gave a soft answer to the Army's proposals while still dealing on the quiet with Parliament and planning to give the slip to both. King and Parliament thus deluded one another, each counting on using the other, to their ultimate cost. Stiffened by his apparent tractability, by offers of armed help from the Scots and the clamour of the London mob, Parliament reversed itself, invited the King to return to London, and again attempted to disband the Army. The latter, then at Reading, thereupon struck camp, marched on the capital, leaving the King at Hampton Court on the way, and took military possession of it for the first time since the Wars of the Roses.

Before the consequences could be assessed, the general anarchy exploded into a second civil war. It was shorter and sharper, even more confused in its bearings but far more decisive in its results, than the first. In November Charles fled from Hampton Court to the South Coast. His escape gave the preconcerted signal for a Royalist rising already concocted by the Queen and the Prince of Wales from abroad. It also gave the signal to the partisans in the Army of a group of extreme republicans known as Levellers to vent their anger at the long and to them suspicious forbearance towards the King by breaking into mutiny. Various other detached units, none of them of the New Model, revolted as well. The Scots, incurably hostile to the heretics of the Army and exasperated by Parliament's inability to cope with them as they deserved—more than exasperated when Parliament to propitiate them announced that it would have no more dealings with the King—entered into a pact with him and in July, 1648, invaded England on his behalf. Encompassed on both sides, Army and Parliament joined again to make war. The mutinies were quelled, the King was soon recaptured and more strictly confined. Fairfax harried the Royalists out of Kent and into Colchester, where he held them closely besieged. Cromwell, who had been putting down revolt in the Welsh marches, sped north to intercept the Scots, defeated them at Preston in Lancashire on 17th August, though outnumbered nearly three to one, annihilated them in a fortnight's campaign, and continued on to dictate peace beyond the border. In the South the war ended with the surrender of Colchester on 27th August.

It was the end, or practically so, of other things as well: of the truce between Parliament and the Army, of Parliament itself save as the servile client of the Army, and of the King. Going back on its word, Parliament again took up direct negotiations with Charles as the last resource against final and utter subservience to the Frankenstein monster it had created. The Army had had enough: somehow the Gordian knot of deceit, shuffling, disappointment, and recurrent strife of which it bore the consequences in poverty, suffering, and death had to be cut. Though it had helped to put down the Levellers, their ideas—as so often with violent minorities repressed for speaking out of their turn, and as indeed was to happen with the Army itself and its principle of religious toleration—had begun to permeate their repressers. Henry Ireton, the Commissary-General and Cromwell's son-in-law, prepared a Remonstrance incorporating their declared resolution " if the Lord ever brought us back to peace, to call Charles Stuart, that man of blood, to account for the blood he has shed ". For a moment the responsible leaders of the Army shrank from so stark a step as trying and executing an anointed King. But Cromwell, now their recognized chief, more influential even than Fairfax, who could not make up his mind to these strange and revolutionary proceedings, procured its adoption and submission to Parliament. The lawmakers rejected it with the declaration that all differences between themselves and the King were at last on the point of being happily solved. The Army's answer—there was no other—was to get a Parliament that would do as it was told.

The paradox of liberty stood exposed in all its leering contradictions. The King's claim to rule as a benevolent despot by divine right had been successfully contested by Parliament in the name of Law, construed as historic and traditional rights. The Army now accused it, with at least equal justice, of twisting the very Law from which it derived its existence to set up a despotism of its own. That despotism

the Army proposed to overturn on the explicit ground of
offence to the self-evident truth " that the people are, under
God, the original of all just power ". Yet to the people the
Army dared not refer, knowing only too well that the people,
yearning for peace and quiet far more than for a religious
freedom they did not want and a political sovereignty they
would not know what to do with, would express an over-
whelming preference for the King—for which reason the
proposal of the previous year for a new general election
had been quietly and firmly forgotten. The only solution
for the Army, then, if the liberties and security for which it
had fought were to be achieved, was to compel Parliament
by brute force so to manipulate the Law as to render the
popular desire for ever impossible of realization by destroying not only the monarch but the monarchy. In the early
morning of 6th December, 1648; a cordon of troops was
drawn round the palace of Westminster of whom some,
holding the doors, turned away ninety-six hostile members
while the rest followed their leader, Colonel Pride, into the
House of Commons and arrested forty-six others. The
Rump, as the remnant of the Parliament was known after
" Pride's Purge "—for the process went by the same name
then as long, long afterwards—three weeks later dutifully
ordered the King to trial for having, amongst other cruel
and tyrannical acts, " subverted the ancient and fundamental laws and levied and maintained war against the
Parliament and the Kingdom "

Three weeks after that, on 20th January, 1649, he faced
the special commission of peers, members of the Commons,
and judges set up to try him in Westminster Hall. He ˙
refused to answer to the indictment or recognize the com-
petency of the court. How could the giver and interpreter
of the Law under God break it? Who save God could judge
if he had? As for offending against the people, " Do you
pretend what you will," he told them, " I stand more for

their liberties (than you). For if power without law may make the laws, may alter the fundamental laws of the kingdom, I do not know what subject he is in England that can be sure of his life or anything that he calls his own." Later, on the scaffold—for the verdict was, of course, a foregone conclusion—he still persisted that " for the people, I desire their liberty as much as anybody whomsoever; but I must tell you their liberty consists in having government in those laws by which their life and goods may be most their own. It is not their having a share in government, that is nothing pertaining to them." Nor did the people altogether repudiate his right to speak for them, to judge by their tears and prayers as he stepped to the block from the window of his exquisite Banqueting Hall, or by the words shouted earlier from the gallery of the court as Bradshaw, its president, condemned him in the name of the people of England: " It is a lie! Not a half, nor a quarter of the people of England."

It turned out to be the voice of Lady Fairfax, who, on the absence of her husband from the court being noted, called out, " He has more wit than to be here ". In both gallant interruptions—for the temper was such that the court all but ordered the troops to fire into the applauding spectators as a signal for their silence—she spoke for a countless multitude, high and low, shocked at the incongruity of subjects calling a king to account, at the blatant rule of sheer, vengeful might, at the unheard of blasphemy of cutting off a crowned head. But the last word lay with men like Bradshaw, who brushed aside uncomfortable scruples about legality with the dictum that " the will of the people is superior to the law ", and like Algernon Sidney, the fanatical Republican himself one day to perish in the same manner as Charles for the opposite cause, who waived the troubling difficulty of distinguishing between the Crown and its wearer with an easy " I tell you we will cut off his head with the crown upon it ". For behind the Bradshaws and the Sidneys, sitting inconspicuously in the back of the court, loomed the overshadowing presence of Oliver Cromwell, executive director of the court's conscience by virtue of the personal idolatry and iron resolution of nearly fifty thousand unbeaten and unbeatable armed men.

Yet though he dominated the cabal which formulated the King's death, inwardly he was not of it. He participated neither in the sentiments which motivated nor the argumentation which justified it. For him the motive and justification lay elsewhere. " I verily think," he told Fairfax when the latter hung back, " they are things which God puts into our hearts." The " fleshly reasonings " by which the divine inspiration was recognized and articulated, being superfluous, left him cold. It was God who had hardened Charles's heart to frustrate the Army's last effort at a settlement made as recently as 23rd December. To have wishfully plotted the King's deposition or disinheritance—let alone his death —would, he confessed, have made him " the greatest traitor and rebel in the world, but since the Providence of God hath cast this upon us, I cannot but submit to Providence ". For what he did he needed no other authority than the divine will, nor would any other have satisfied him— exactly like Charles whom he was destroying, except that to the one it manifested itself by direct revelation, to the other through the sacrament of his ordination. The exception contained the vital difference between their respective Puritan and Catholic creeds, but the resemblance between them was, as presently appeared, equally important and profound.

There were no two men in England more tranquil about the rights and wrongs of the matter on that icy afternoon of 29th January when the sentence was carried out. Completely serene, Charles took leave of his children the evening before in St. James's Palace—one of the most moving scenes ever recorded of real people—distributing his few remaining precious trinkets, chiefly old stars of the Garter, among his younger children, and begging his elder daughter Elizabeth " not to grieve and torment thyself, for it will be a glorious death that I shall die, it being for the laws and liberties of this land and for the true Protestant religion ". To his wife he sent a last loving message and comforted them all with the assurance " that the Lord will settle his throne upon his son, and that they would all be happier than they could have expected to have been had he lived ". He felt no sense of injury: " for all this, God's judgements are just; an unjust sentence that I suffered to take effect (Strafford's) is now punished by an unjust sentence upon me ". With almost his last breath he affirmed that " if I would have given way to have all changed by the power of the sword, I need not have come here; and therefore I tell you (and I pray God it may not be laid to your charge) that I am the martyr of the people ". Apparently many of the people believed so, and his enemies feared so, for it took a cavalry charge to disperse the weeping, frightened, re-morseful concourse in Whitehall, many of whom dipped their kerchiefs in his blood or cut off locks of his hair, and some of whom presently sold these relics to eager buyers.

CHAPTER XVII

The Man on Horseback

WHETHER or not it was a crime, as most people believed, to cut off the King's head, to cut it off with the Crown still upon it soon proved to have been a thoughtless blunder. Kings of England had been killed before, but only to the lasting advantage of such successors as had taken the precaution, like Henry VII, Henry IV, and the Conqueror, to envelop the nakedness of usurped power in the regalia of consecrated authority. That precaution the present regicides had in the nature of the case been neither able nor willing to emulate, nor had they in their preoccupation with the actual capture of power made any other provision for arraying it acceptably: it was theirs simply by the crude fact of possession, and the authority which could alone render it seemly and stable lay buried with Charles at Windsor. For thirty generations and more men had marked the beats in the mighty diapason of change and continuity by the reassuring shout of " The King is dead! Long live the King!" No one felt any disposition to shout " Long live Parliament ". In the general opinion it had already lived far too long. It could neither relax upon the past which it had repudiated nor upon the living who had repudiated it. It could not even look forward to a quiet termination of its own existence lest everything it had struggled to gain should be swept away in the reaction it had provoked. All it could do was to hang on mulishly: very like a mule in lacking any valid pride of ancestry or reasonable hope of posterity.

Ninety only were left of the original four hundred and ninety when the Commons resumed business after Charles's execution. About a third of the missing had seceded to the Royalist Parliament at Oxford, an approximately equal number had been eliminated in Pride's Purge, the rest were ejected for permitting themselves a doubt whether the House had in the last instance acted altogether rightly towards the King. The survivors then officially abolished the monarchy and the House of Lords, whose membership had dwindled to some bare half-dozen, and for an executive body set up a Council of State of forty-one, all but ten of whom were chosen from amongst themselves, renewable annually and with powers restricted to certain defined spheres like the military administration and foreign affairs. A new lot of judges was appointed by test of political allegiance, a new Great Seal struck showing on one side the Commons in session and on the other the inscription " In the First Year of Freedom by God's blessing restored, 1648 ",[1] and in May " the representatives of the people in Parliament " formally gave their improvised creation the name of " Commonwealth, or Free State ".

They might call it what they liked, but they still had to get it to work and make people satisfied with it. For nearly four years they tried without coming within sight of either object. Seldom can a revolutionary government have lasted so long with so few well-wishers. The beaten Royalists of course hated and despised it. The remainder of the nation regarded it with feelings ranging between critical toleration and exasperated disillusion, which were reflected on its own sparsely filled benches. The most powerful and active of these internal enemies were the Levellers, out-and-out democrats who demanded its summary liquidation and a fresh start under a written constitution resting upon universal manhood suffrage; their

[1] By the Old Style reckoning the new year began on 25th March.

leader, an eccentric demagogue known to his admirers as " Honest John " Lilburne, a late victim of the Star Chamber and an ex-soldier, enjoyed a delirious popularity with a certain section of the lower ranks of the army, and the sea-green ribbons they wore as their party emblem were the flaunting banners of mutiny and riot against the ruling oligarchy. After them in number but not far behind in turbulence came the Fifth Monarchists, who, taking their stand on the second chapter of Daniel, held that, since three of the four kingdoms there (by popular consensus) alluded to—Assyria, Persia, and Macedonia—had already perished and the fourth, the Holy Roman Empire, was for its iniquities about to do so, the time was plainly come to set up the fifth, the Kingdom of Christ: and since this form of state would require for its instrument of government only the Word of God and be ruled exclusively by the godly, its advocates naturally had no earthly use for the Levellers with their profane machinery for the indiscriminate count-ing of noses whereby the sinners would be assured of a clear majority over the saints every time. There were also, *inter alia*, the Communist Levellers, distinct from and dis-owned by their larger namesakes, who planned to " restore the ancient community of the fruits of the earth ", and made a beginning that spring by digging up a tract of unoccupied land in Surrey, to the alarm and annoyance of the authorities. Only the reluctance of the representatives of these groups either to combine or to precipitate a fresh crisis which might end in a Royalist restoration enabled the Government's supporters—puritan republicans, chiefly, who accepted it as a faulty but necessary medium of transition towards something radically superior in more settled times —to maintain a precarious parliamentary balance.

With the problem of keeping alive were bound up others sufficient to have tested the most anciently solid of governments. It was spending, in money extracted from a war-stricken people, three times the amount available to Charles in his palmiest days. There was no help for it. On top of the ordinary charges on the exchequer, inevitably swollen by the wastefulness and enlarged commitments inseparable from a strange regime, lay the huge expense— five-sixths of the total—of the largest armed establishment in English history, a burden neither to be discharged nor appreciably reduced. For Parliament to disband it was to remove the one sure prop of its own existence, while to disband it without meeting in full its considerable arrears of pay was to convert forty-four thousand well-organized and politically sensitive retainers into instant and deadly enemies. To go on paying them was to keep them quiet at the cost of constantly exasperating the public with an odious military domination, yet any attempt to extort from the public the sum needed to wipe off the arrears would have been, to say the least, inadvisable.

And even had the internal conditions somehow permitted Parliament to dismiss its dangerous servants, the external situation rendered such a course impossible. The execution of the King, which had unspeakably horrified opinion everywhere, had made the infant Republic a pariah amongst the nations. The Catholic peoples of Europe felt towards it as they had towards Henry VIII; with England's old ally Holland, the rising Protestant power of the Continent, disapproval was inflaming commercial and colonial jealousies to the mood of war. In Ireland the friends of the Crown enthusiastically joined the hereditary foes of English dominion; while in Scotland, again simply a foreign country by the sundering of the dynastic tie, indignation at the treatment of the Stuart king lashed the fury already excited by the repudiation of the Presbyterian Covenant into a popular outcry for intervention. On the other hand, those very dangers provided the Government with a justification for keeping the army together and, because of the army's magnificent response to them, did more than anything else to keep the Government going as long as it did.

In the same month that the Commonwealth was proclaimed Cromwell was relieved of the duty of suppressing Levellers' mutinies and ordered to Ireland as Lord-Lieutenant, with 12,000 troops of his own choice and unlimited powers at his own insistence, to stamp out the ten-year-old revolt. What followed was not pretty, but it was thorough. Into no task of his life did he throw himself with such complete conviction. To Cromwell as to his favourite historian Raleigh the Irish were an inferior race, papists by natural bestiality as well as by profession, who had " unprovoked " put those thousands of the master race " to the most barbarous massacre . . . that ever the sun beheld ". Landing in Dublin in August, four weeks later he stormed the fortified town of Drogheda at the mouth of the Boyne because he dared not wait to besiege it—his first grand operation of the kind—and delivered the inhabitants over to " the righteous judgment of God ". He was never quite sure whether he regretted the ghastly business or not; at one time he defended it on the ground of policy, " that it will tend to prevent the effusion of blood in the future ", at another on the plea of " being in heat of action "; like so many mystics with a genius for doing, he was seldom troubled by the frequent inconsistencies in his conduct or mental processes. Other butcheries followed, though not again at his order. In the course of the next nine months he suffered some stinging reverses from adversaries fighting also for their God and race, but on the whole carried out his commission with such effect as to leave them, in the words of their most eminent leader, " stupefied ", unable " to act anything like men towards their own preservation ". His ultimate object—to dispossess the Irish and then incorporate Ireland as a Protestant English province with " equal justice ", free trade, and Parliamentary representation like any other province of England—he was unable to attain because recalled by events nearer home with the conquest only half completed. The remaining half took his successors six years, in the course of which the Irish lost a third of their population and two-thirds of their land.

All the principal personages of the Government met him at Hounslow Heath on his return and escorted him into London to receive the honours due the first citizen of the State. But there was no time to bask in glory or even to nurse the malaria which had all but prostrated him in Ireland and which he was never to shake off completely. The Scottish Parliament, delayed in his absence by Montrose's last fling at reviving the Cavalier cause on behalf of the Prince of Wales, had, after affixing Montrose's head to the Tolbooth in Edinburgh, itself succeeded in drafting the helpless young heir into the quite different cause of importing a Presbyterian monarchy into England. With a great army assembling round Edinburgh and the Scots deaf to overtures, the English Government decided on a prophylactic invasion. Fairfax, who disapproved of the policy, refused the command, and Cromwell received it with the rank of Captain-General of all the forces of the Commonwealth. On 22nd July, 1650, he led an army of 10,500 foot and 5500 horse over the border, and on 3rd September fought the most astonishing yet most characteristic battle of his career at Dunbar; outmanœuvred as well as far outnumbered by his old partner in the charge at Marston Moor, David Leslie, he wriggled out of a sea-and-ravine-bound trap by a flank march which was the one move no one dreamed he would dare to make, attacked at five in the morning by moonlight, called to his men as the sun came out of the sea, " Let God arise, let his enemies be scattered ", and by six was ordering the 117th Psalm to be sung in celebration of a victory which cost the enemy, when the pursuit was over, 13,000 dead and prisoners and himself approximately twenty.

But the danger, instead of being over, merely took another and more serious form. The Scottish Government fell; Charles II, delivered from its Calvinist bondage, became much more truly King of all Scotland and was crowned as such on 1st January; and the Royalists of both kingdoms prepared to throw themselves into a supreme effort on his behalf. Under cover of an exceptionally long and fearful winter, two new Scottish armies were raised. One, entrusted to Leslie, held Cromwell fast before Stirling throughout the spring, while the other presently moved southward, twenty thousand strong, to escort Charles to his throne. It was a moment of life or death for the Commonwealth. If the unhappy lovers of the monarchy rose in their unknown strength, it was doubtful whether there remained sufficient will in disgruntled England to resist him. Leaving a small force to watch Leslie, Cromwell raced south-west to head off the invaders. He caught up with them at Worcester, where on the anniversary of Dunbar he inflicted on them the defeat that flung Charles II into one of the most romantic of flights and a nine years' exile. Scotland, exhausted by the loss of three armies in three years, became by the terms of the ensuing peace a virtual dependency of England. Cromwell returned to London to receive the ovation of a Cæsar, Wolsey's palace of Hampton Court for his country residence, and an income amounting with previous grants to the equivalent of £30,000 a year: a royal welcome which inspired in many a king-hungry mind the thought that in the saviour of a Commonwealth not worth saving might be found a worthy successor to the Crown relinquished by a dynasty seemingly past restoring.

For, like the French Convention of a hundred and fifty years later or the moribund Roman Republic, the Commonwealth was no nearer to solving its domestic difficulties by the brilliance of its achievements abroad. It skilfully secured the American colonies against all Royalist efforts to estrange them; it boldly asserted English prestige by insisting that the Dutch dip their flag on sighting an English man-of-war in the Narrow Seas, as under the monarchy, and when they refused embarked on a war (unluckily neither useful nor popular) in which their fleet under Colonel Robert Blake, late of the army for Ireland, fought the reputedly invincible Dutch navy to a standstill; but at home it could do nothing right. Its enforced religious toleration affected the great majority like a novel form of persecution—as from the orthodox Anglican, Presbyterian, or Catholic point of view it was—while it had frankly to persecute minor sects like Quakers, Socinians, and Ranters because their unorthodoxy was too eccentric even for official nonconformity to tolerate. Foreign conquests neither repaired the damage to trade of a decade of civil strife, nor restored the thousands of ruined estates, nor put the tens of thousands of vagrant beggars back into employment, nor decongested the prisons of their debtors. On the contrary, the taxes required to furnish conquests tended to amplify those evils. But when the Government, freed from its more pressing external concerns in Ireland and Scotland, would as a start towards alleviating them have disengaged itself from its military thraldom, it found itself fairly caught between the hammer and the anvil.

The returning troops had not the slightest intention of being made scapegoats for evils which afflicted them equally with their civilian compatriots and which, like them, they were inclined to blame on a reigning clique's too narrow preoccupation with remaining in power. Nor was their respect for Parliament increased by the discovery—invariable phenomenon of social upheaval—that many of its friends were quietly fattening on Cavalier property expropriated not only outside the law but against solemn engage-

ments of amnesty. Sore and suspicious, they needed only
the slightest pretext for turning on it. The occasion came
when it repudiated a promise to General Lambert, most
conspicuous of Cromwell's lieutenants, of the succession to
the office of Lord Deputy for Ireland at the expiration of
the latter's term in 1652. Reading into the act a deliberate
insult, the leaders of the Army decided that the preservation
of the Commonwealth demanded the dissolution of Parliament. The demand was met, after the immemorial manner
of Parliaments, by referring it to a select committee. A
petition urging the provision of work for the poor and a
decent honouring of pledges given to Royalists who had laid
down their arms went the same way. Under threats the
House notified the petitioning council of officers in January,
1653, that it was ready to grant a general election; in April
it informed them that instead of holding an election it would
fill its depleted ranks by co-opting new members nominated
by the old. The dodge of " one Parliament stepping into the
seat of another just left warm for them " snapped the Army's
patience. The council of officers appealed to the commander-
in-chief to make the tenacious Rump do by force what it
would not do of itself.

Cromwell did not want to, or at least so he said, and
there is no fair reason to doubt his sincerity. What there
was in it for him was obvious, almost too obvious, to anyone. If he, the Army's chosen master, chose to assert its
mastery over the Government . . . it was the most glittering opportunity ever presented to a subject in England.
But that he had prepared it, or was even prepared for it,
seems contrary to his whole psychology. He was an opportunist, not a maker of opportunities: one (Queen Elizabeth
was another) temperamentally disposed rather to act by
intuition when emergencies arose—" to await God's leisure ",
as he called it—than to contemplate them purposefully
in advance. He might have served for an apt, an almost

unbelievably apt, illustration of his own apothegm that
no one goes so far as he who knows not where he is
going.

The Commonwealth Parliament was to a large extent
his creation and under his protection by sworn oath. On
the other hand, so was the Army. If he was disappointed
in the one, he was equally disturbed by the other's poten-
tiality for violence. In his heart he was a man of order into
whom experience had bitten, deeply and unforgettably,
the truth that successive doses of violence, far from reducing
the causes of disorder, incited them fatally to multiply. He
had done inconsistent things and pursued irreconcilable
ends, but his vision of the England that should emerge from
the turmoil remained precisely the same as the one he had
carried into it: a social order based upon property yoked
to responsibility and dedicated to the furthering of the
felt truths of abstract justice—God's justice, as he would
have put it. In a moment of impatience with the whole
monarchical hierarchy he once remarked that he did not
care if he never saw another nobleman in England, but his
deeper, essentially conservative instinct—as well as his later
actions—spoke in the dictum " A nobleman, a gentleman
and a yeoman is a good interest in the land, and a great
one ".

It was for differences of emphasis leading to abuses of
application rather than any vital conflict of principle that
he had taken arms against the King. It was for a really
far more fundamental difference that he had turned against
the Long Parliament. For that body had, after passing
under the control of the Presbyterian wing of the Puritans,
too largely identified itself with the City of London, where
the Presbyterian interest was dominant—so much so that
after Pride's Purge the Metropolis was left with but a
single member—and thus came to represent the irresponsible power of money. Its original objection to the State's

meddling with private conscience had expanded into a resentment at its interfering with private business, that is, the right of unlimited acquisition; and in place of the mystic state of the Tudors—beloved by Cromwell no less than by Charles I, Strafford, and Laud—in which each man was told to his place, desired to substitute the " convenient " state where each man would be free to scramble for whatever place his industry, cunning, thrift, and other such symptoms of the divine grace enabled him to reach. The cropping out of similar tendencies in the Rump had drawn from Cromwell, after Dunbar, the admonishment that " if there be any one that makes many poor to make a few rich, that suits not a Commonwealth "

As well as an orderly he was a practical man. The Fenland grazier had never been swallowed up in the crusading visionary. They lived on side by side: a duality which has always made any understanding of him so difficult. He had no more use for the tyranny of ideas than of money, of rule by lawyers and theologians than of financiers or firearms. States evolved, he would have argued, according to their own organic nature, subject only to such modification as was plainly dictated by moral necessity; they could not be redesigned entire by logic or inspiration. Since England had not yet been governed either by the masses, as the Levellers argued it ought to be, or by the saints, as the Fifth Monarchists proclaimed it must be, he deprecated the preachings of both. That of the Levellers he in particular abhorred, considering their doctrine of a classless society to be a shoddy and pernicious sophistry, " a pleasing voice to all poor men and truly not unwelcome to all bad men ". His son-in-law Ireton's answer to the levelling argument in the Commons echoed his exact sentiment: " If every man has a right to political power, every man must have a right to property." As for the Fifth Monarchists, while sympathizing with their ideal, he thought them addled for expecting to pluck a perfect society ready-made out of Heaven instead of working to perfect one which would give pleasure to Heaven.

The acuteness of his dilemma when finally the quarrel between Parliament and the Army strained to its climax lay in the fact that it was these two turbulent elements in both which were pressing hardest for a drastic solution. If he tried to restrain the Army, he ran the grave risk of losing its affection; but if he did not, he was only too likely to be turning the country over to the mercies—and subsequent strife—of two lunacies. " Pushed on," as he complained, " by two factions to do that the consideration of which makes my hair to stand on end," he toyed with strange alternatives. " What," he asked a friend, " if a man should take upon him to be a king?" He quickly put the thought aside, if he really entertained it, but only to transpose himself in imagination from king to king-maker, with Charles I's youngest son and sole remaining child in England as beneficiary. That idea also was too glaringly incongruous, as well as too impracticable. There was nothing for it but to face the situation as it existed: either to justify the Army's faith in him, to hold it back at the peril of forfeiting its allegiance to the extremists—the Levellers, who hated him as much as he did them, were already shriek-ing that he meant to betray it for his own advantage—or to do nothing. Duty, the solemn sense of indispensability peculiar to men of great powers and ambition at fateful moments, ruled the third course out. Those two major components of a man's destiny, his previous history and innate character, more obscurely but with equal certainty ruled out the second.

Working to the last possible instant for an accommo-dation, he arranged a meeting between the council of officers and the leaders of the Commons at his house in Whitehall on 19th April, 1653. The representatives of the

Army proposed that Parliament should drop the bill for perpetuating its own existence but be empowered to appoint from its own number a committee of " well-affected men . . . to settle the nation " between the time of dissolving and the election of its successor. Though on the whole hostile to the suggestion, the parliamentary delegates promised to consider it and meantime to put off the bill's final reading. Next morning word was brought to Cromwell while dressing that the House had already taken up the third reading, which was to be followed after the bill's passage by immediate adjournment till November and his own subsequent removal from his command by the Council of State.

Unable at first to believe that old comrades like Vane and Haslerigg could be guilty of such treachery, he sent for confirmation. Receiving it, he strolled over to the House " clad in plain black clothes with grey worsted stockings ", took his usual place on the back benches, and listened to the debate in silence for fifteen minutes until the Speaker put the question. Then he murmured to General Harrison, leader of the Fifth Monarchists, " This is the time I must do it "—to the dismay even of that stern man of righteousness, who implored him " seriously to consider of it "—stood up, took off his hat, and addressed the Speaker. He began by praising the House for its work in the past. He went on to curse it fluently for its selfishness, futility, and encouragement of evil in the present. Growing angry, he shoved his hat back on his head and strode up and down the floor delineating with acid strokes the sins, public and private, of various prominent members, though without naming them. One of them, Sir Peter Wentworth, angrily interrupted to point out that such speech was hardly fitting from a servant whom they had so highly trusted and correspondingly honoured. " Perhaps," came back the caustic retort, " you think this is not parliamentary language. I confess it is not. Neither are you to expect any such of me. You are no Parliament. I say you are no Parliament."

Amidst an uproar of astonished unbelief he called to Harrison, " Let them in." Harrison opened the door to admit some twenty or thirty of Cromwell's own regiment posted outside. Sir Henry Vane leaped to his feet crying shrilly, " This is not honest! It is against morality and common honesty." The central figure in the pandemonium turned upon the fiery little tribune the celebrated ice-blue stare and shook his head: " Oh, Sir Henry Vane! Sir Henry Vane! The Lord deliver me from Sir Henry Vane!" Returning his attention to the Speaker—William Lenthall, elected in that remote autumn of 1640 to signify Parliament's independence of the King and forcibly restored to his post by the Army after fleeing from the Presbyterian wrath seven years later—he directed Harrison to " Fetch him down!" While Harrison obliged with the ironic offer of an assisting hand, Cromwell's eye fell on the mace, ancient symbol of the Commons' proud immunity from trespass even by Majesty itself. " What shall we do with this bauble?" he asked aloud, and then commanded the nearest soldier, " Here, take it away."

For a few moments he watched the House being cleared amidst a brisk exchange of epithets with his ex-colleagues as they departed, designating one a thief, another a drunkard, a third a whore-master, Wentworth an adulterer, Vane a liar and juggler with words—the charge of dishonesty from one he thought had just betrayed him had plainly hurt. As the last of them straggled out he flung after them, " It is you that have forced me to do this, for I have sought the Lord night and day, that he would rather slay me than put upon me the doing this work." It may or may not have been true; but to deny that it could have been true is to misunderstand not only him, but his whole Bible-soaked, God-intoxicated generation. When no one was left but the clerk, he took from him the bill that had been the occasion of the scene, put it in his pocket, ordered the doors to be locked, and went home.

On the locked doors a wag hung a sign " This House to be let unfurnished ". The notice, though not literally, was metaphorically quite true. So-called Parliaments sat there again during his period of power, but for all the use they were they might have been conducted parties of sightseers. The government of England for the next five years resided elsewhere—in Oliver Cromwell's pocket.

CHAPTER XVIII

The First Protectorate

THE country's first feeling was of immense relief and gratitude. The episode of the Rump's discomfiture supplied the theme for endless street ballads; a lustre almost of semi-divinity surrounded its hero's name; many expected, and not a few hoped, that he would make himself King.

Had he been so disposed, there was nothing to prevent him. The chiefs of the Army, anxious to incorporate the objects of their struggle into the permanent constitution of the State, urged him on. Even a certain proportion of the Royalists were ready, in their glee at the discomfiture of the regicide Parliament, to approve on the basis of some arrangement, such as the marriage of one of his younger daughters to Charles II, which would not leave the lawful dynasty for ever in the cold. Most fervently of all, perhaps, did the inarticulate, long-suffering masses long to see the crown reappear on the head of the titanic figure by whom their enemies, domestic and foreign, whether Irish papist or Covenanting Scot, Cavalier or politician, had been impartially prostrated. For them it was a solution to satisfy two of their deepest instincts, monarchy-worship and hero-worship; the only solution that promised deliverance from the insatiable factions and the exorbitant soldiery alike.

But, like Cæsar, he did not dare—at least not yet. It was not, as with Cæsar, desire wrestling directly with fear and yielding to it. His desire was certainly less and his fear of another, less tangible sort. The Republic had never been sacred in England as it had been in Rome: far from it. But the monarchy was, and Oliver Cromwell, as " mere English " as Elizabeth, with the incurable reverence for kingship derived from his blood and his well-thumbed Old Testament, had himself to persuade before he could be persuaded. No subject had ever attained, or even aspired to, the throne without some prior hereditary claim. Should he, without the least shadow of such right, accept it, men might applaud him out of momentary relief and the expectation aroused by the sheer drama of the act. But later, when his will crossed theirs, when they grew dissatisfied or merely indifferent, the emotion on which his title solely rested would depart and he stand for nothing more than the desecration by force of the ideals for which both parties in the late struggle had sacrificed and died: the renegade to liberty, the sham king. The fusion of the old and the new, of present power with traditional authority, could never take place in his person, he was shrewd enough to perceive, until it had been achieved in their minds by the slow alchemy of time.

The monarchy apart, three other courses were open to him, representing the three different schools of thought in the Army. For the fundamental factor in the situation was still the Army, both by reason of its physical strength and the fact that his commission from the late government as its commander-in-chief was the only legal warrant he or anyone else could show for exercising the functions of the State. One group, headed by Lambert, second in military influence to Cromwell alone, wanted a Parliament selected by a limited franchise and a small executive Council with a written constitution which should strictly define their respective powers. The Levellers wanted as before a " free ", that is sovereign, Parliament chosen by universal suffrage regardless of the consequences. The Fifth Monarchists, who thought the whole matter of but passing importance, since they knew that in seven years a great change would come when " the saints shall take the kingdom and possess it " (they were right about the date but wrong about the saints), wished to institute for the interval a Sanhedrin after the model of ancient Israel, its seventy members to be appointed by the temporary Council of seven officers and two civilians Cromwell had invited to assist him after the dismissal of Parliament.

The Levellers' solution he threw out altogether. Combining certain features of the other two, he decided for a small Parliament of 140—129 from England, six from Ireland, five from Scotland—to be chosen by himself and his officers from the lists " of men fearing God and hating covetousness " submitted by the various independent congregational churches. The writs were issued in the name of " Oliver the Lord General ".

The " Little " Parliament, as it became known, otherwise the Barebone's Parliament from the name of one of its not least characteristic members, Praise-God Barebone, a London leather-dealer, met in Whitehall on 4th July, 1653. Cromwell had high hopes of it. In his inaugural address he told it that it was manifestly called by God as no other assembly had ever been: " You are at the edge of the promises and prophecies . . . indeed, I do think somewhat is at the door." He had soon to change his mind. Taking him too literally, his hearers rushed to the door, as it were, to drag in the promises and prophecies without more ado. In their enthusiasm for perfecting the machinery of the law they started out as if they meant to dismantle it altogether, and in their zeal for purifying religion threatened to purify the churches out of all visible means of support. When Cromwell tried to calm them, the House shouted him down with the query of the two Israelites to Moses: " Who made thee a prince or a judge over us?" Soon growing jealous, like its predecessor, of the military power that had created it, it incautiously offended that power while rendering itself an object of contempt to the rest of the country as well. The Levellers of course disowned it; the Fifth Monarchists, whose membership the artful " scrutiny of the lists " had kept to a minimum, damned it as an obscene caricature of their proposed Sanhedrin. Appointed for sixteen months with power to choose its successor, its credit had sunk so low at the end of five that Lambert and his clique (known as " the Colonels ") decided to put an end to its existence. By discreet pressure all but thirty of the members were induced to place their resignations in the hands of the Lord General. The thirty, refusing to budge from the House, were visited by two of the Colonels, who demanded what they thought they were doing there. " Seeking the Lord," they replied. " Come out of this place, then," advised one of the Colonels, " for to my knowledge the Lord has not been here these twelve years past." They took the hint, and the Parliament was deemed to have dissolved itself by its own petition.

How much Cromwell knew beforehand of Lambert's scheme or its immediate sequel is unknown. He himself said later that he knew nothing, and though the plea of ignorance was useful when he made it, he may have been telling the truth: it was important for the Colonels to keep him above any suspicion of violence or illegality, since they had again in mind to make him King, this time under a written constitution which they had previously prepared ready to thrust before him. The Crown he once more refused, but the constitution, known as the Instrument of Government, after brief reflection he accepted on their earnest plea that otherwise " blood and confusion " would surely follow.

The document was candidly reactionary, a bold attempt to reconcile the old and the new at some expense to the latter. Repudiating the doctrine of the absolute supremacy of Parliament which had seemed a permanent legacy of the Civil War, it provided for a division of the sovereign power between a single person called the Lord Protector, assisted by a Council of fifteen, and a representative assembly. Cromwell was named Protector for life, with many of the former royal prerogatives, including the right to pardon and bestow honours. In larger matters, however, such as the control of the armed forces and foreign affairs, he could exercise his powers only with the advice and consent of the Council or Parliament as expressly stipulated in the Instrument, which also appointed his original councillors and left him only a limited voice in filling vacancies amongst them. The Parliament was to be elective, but voting was restricted to the higher levels of income. With little faith in democracy and none whatever in the rule of the godly, the authors of the new constitution had resorted to the old ideal of authority and property. Without a great deal of faith in their Parliament, they postponed its first meeting till the following September.

On 16th December, 1653, " Oliver the Protector ", symbolically discarding the red tunic of a soldier for the plain black coat of a civilian, was inducted into his new office in a simple ceremony at Westminster: a simplicity all the more impressive by contrast with the quasi-coronational rejoicings in London. And indeed, save for the absence of the crown with its association of durability and continuity, the event had much of the significance of a coronation. The State possessed once more a Chief Magistrate independent of party will and irremovable except by death. Until Parliament met, his word was law, and even after it met it could not call his actions to account since he derived his powers from a source beyond its competence. The eight and a half months he had been given in which to govern as he liked and consolidate his own position without previous or subsequent reference to Parliament was a privilege no king had enjoyed since remotest times. For him that brief interval of constitutional dictatorship was, politically, the most fruitful of his life.

It produced social laws so enlightened that they emerged again two hundred years after being snuffed out in the Restoration; grafted religious toleration on to the national genius so shrewdly that even the violence of reaction never quite ejected it; gave a fresh impulse to England's imperial growth which was to continue almost unabated for centuries. It also introduced novel oppressions and cruelties and unheard-of trespasses into people's private lives. Suffusing it and interfused with each other, like a blended emanation of its two primary energies, were the harsh, apocalyptic, in some respects apocryphal, illumination of a new dawn and a rich after-glow of the reign of Elizabeth whom the Protector so greatly admired.

His ideas of social legislation, though advanced for his time, he took over in large part from the two Commonwealth Parliaments. The difference was—as with other of their ideas—that he also had definite views on how to make them work. They were humanitarian, Puritan, and paternalistic: at once extraordinarily large-minded and small-minded, like himself. In those eight and a half months he placed no less than eighty-two laws on the statute books, an almost unparalleled number for the period, covering an astonishing variety of subjects and often requiring an intensive preliminary study. They provided relief for the hordes of imprisoned debtors, a better and more humane administration of the poor laws, work for the unemployed (in large part through much needed public improvements like the extension and maintenance of the highways), fairer general conditions of labour. The Court of Chancery, which the Little Parliament would have abolished because of its cumbersomeness and corruption, leaving nothing to

take its place, he overhauled so as to enable it to dispense
justice more swiftly and cheaply. He mitigated the horrible
rigours of the criminal law both by enactment and the
liberal use of the pardoning power because he thought it
abominable " to hang a man for a sixpence and I know not
what ". He was dead nearly two hundred years before
society caught up with him in so thinking. To help him in
the technical work of framing his ordinances he employed a
Royalist lawyer named Matthew Hale, whom he elevated
to the bench—one of the greatest judges ever to adorn it.

But in addition to ameliorating the earthly lot of his
fellow-men, he thought it possible by legislation to render
them fitter for heaven. That idea, too, was an inheritance
from the preceding republican governments, which he
proceeded to carry out with greater vigour though, to judge
by the aftermath, problematical success. He decreed a
stricter observance of the Sabbath, increased the previous
penalties for profanity, gambling, and drunkenness, raised
adultery and duelling to the dignity of capital crimes. Yet
in all this he actually lagged behind the wishes of his immediate supporters. When Parliament met—a more " moderate " Parliament, at that, than they relished—it confirmed
all of these decrees and added others more stringent, like its
savage edict to punish " those playing and making music in
taverns " as vagabonds and rogues. Towards what he
considered innocent enjoyments, " lawful and laudable
creations ", he felt not only no disapproval, but actively
encouraged them: he himself hunted, hawked, played
bowls, drank wine and small beer. The principle underlying
his moral laws was not the perfection of human nature by
depriving men of their proper pleasures, but to prevent
their jeopardizing their souls or the public order, both
equally the concern of the State as he conceived it. " It will
be found an unjust and unwise jealousy," he declared, " to
deprive a man of his natural liberty on the supposition that

he may abuse it. When he doth abuse it, judge." Thus he prohibited cock-fighting because of its incitement to other vices like gambling, drinking, and quarrelling, and horse-racing once for six months because discontented Royalists met there to plot.

Nevertheless, even his comparatively temperate inter-pretation of what constituted abuse sorely irritated the country. Adulterers went unscathed because their fellow-sinners refused to hang them. Men insisted on having their fun, illicit as well as licit, while he lived, and blew off their suppressed steam in the celebrated orgy of the Restoration after he died, to the scandal of the laws and the law-abid-ing, both of which survived in surprising degree.

It seems a somewhat odd inconsistency, in view of the Puritan doctrine that the secular power should keep its hands off matters spiritual, that Puritan ascendancy should have resulted in the head of the State becoming the intimate guardian of private morals. But it was nothing compared with the inconsistency involved in his reform of the Church. For with the aid of his censorious minority, and against the seething opposition of the lax majority who were loudly damning them for meddling busybodies and blue-nosed spoil-sports, he reconstituted the religious system of Eng-land on a foundation of tolerance. It was not so wide as would be meant by true toleration now, or was meant even then by radical spirits like John Milton, but it was fully as wide as it could be stretched in his time, and perceptibly wider than his comparatively unbigoted race stretched it again for a long time afterward. Even so, his accomplish-ment was not up to his desire, which reached nearly to Milton's own. What that desire was he stated to the Scots in Edinburgh in 1648 when, after defeating them, he imposed a magnanimous peace instead of pillaging them:

" I desire from my heart—I have prayed for—I have. waited for the day to see—union and right understanding between the godly people—Scots, English, Jews, Gentiles, presbyterians, anabaptists . . ."

And of the Little Parliament he demanded that

" We should be pitiful and tender towards all thought of different judgements . . . love all, tender all, cherish all and countenance all in all things that are good. . . . And if the poorest Christian, the most mistaken Christian, shall desire to live peaceably and quietly under you—I say, if any shall desire but to lead a life of godliness and honesty, let him be protected."

The two statements indicate the breadth of his toleration and at the same time the limitations placed upon it by the fact that as Protector he was not merely an individual proclaiming an ideal, but a statesman seeking a workable settlement. Public order had to be considered as well as private conscience. Some form of national Church there had to be, ensuring a certain decorum of worship and ensured of adequate financial maintenance, if religion was to be anything more than an arid battlefield of the sects: it had to be Christian and Protestant in order to be in any sense English. That sort of Church, neither more nor less, he attempted to secure. Within it was room for many diverse opinions. Its ministers were required to pass no doctrinal test, merely to satisfy a non-denominational commission of mixed clerics and laymen, known as Triers, of their personal fitness for their calling and their fundamental allegiance to the State. The Triers, instructed to look for " something of the grace of God " in a candidate rather than " pitiful certificates " of Latin and Greek, did their work so honestly and well as greatly to improve the character of the parish clergy.

Yet, elastic as the Cromwellian Church was, no one was required, as in the past, to enter it who preferred to remain outside. The extreme nonconformist creeds, whose early period of exuberance, often characterized even with the gentle Quakers by brawling in the churches and assaults on the preachers, had led to their being outlawed as enemies of religion by the Commonwealth, were granted full liberty for their observances subject to their not disturbing the peace. The old penal laws against the Catholics for abstention from the established rites were abrogated, though they were still not legally allowed to practise their own, their assemblies, as well as those of the orthodox Anglicans, being considered, not without reason, probable centres of sedition. Even them, however, the Government quietly refrained from molesting unless they bred disorder. In an age when religious toleration was regarded as a sin against the Holy Ghost, after many consecutive ages during which no man might escape the rigid profession of whatever faith the law decreed, it was something to have given every man the right, if not to profess exactly what he pleased, at least to refuse any profession which did not harmonize with his conscience. From Elizabeth's shrill protest that she " made no windows into men's souls " to Cromwell's quiet dictum that " Notions will hurt none but those that have them " was a long second stage on the steep and slippery ascent at the bottom of which the spirit of the Inquisition had been tending the fires of Smithfield less than a century earlier.

But if the Protector's religious policy was an unconscious progression from the Elizabethan, his foreign policy was a deliberate, full-blooded emulation of it. This is scarcely surprising, seeing that it was the Puritan influence in her counsels that persuaded her to it. Their aims were three—to prevent the accession of a Stuart; to advance the Protestant cause abroad, the better to forestall foreign intervention on behalf of Mary Stuart at home; to use the advancement of the Protestant cause for the increase of English power and through it English trade wherever possible. Exactly the same three—substituting for the Queen of Scots her great-grandson Charles II—were para-

mount in Cromwell's mind. Very little distinguished his
methods of carrying them out.

Two serious obstacles stood in the way of his restoring
the Elizabethan alignment. Holland, cornerstone of the
old Protestant alliance, was an active enemy. Spain, its
target, was technically a friend. To go on fighting co-
religionists over trade and prestige when both might be got
in far greater degree by spoiling the idolater seemed to
Cromwell futile and short-sighted. First by energetic
action at sea which convinced the Dutch that they could
not win, then by moderating the Commonwealth's extreme
demands on their dignity and independence, he was able to
induce them to sign a peace, in April, 1654, giving way on
all essential points; after which both delegations adjourned
to celebrate with a banquet at the Guildhall, where they
joined in singing from the 123rd Psalm, " Behold how good
and pleasant it is for brethren to dwell together in amity ".
Though the re-enfolded brethren begged off for the present
the offensive league " for the preservation of freedom and
the outspreading of the Kingdom of Christ " which Cromwell tendered them, the terms which they had accepted
(including a withdrawal of asylum from the Stuarts) were a
triumph so impressive that within the next few days Holland's rival Sweden, and the next few months her ally
Denmark, swung into line with treaties of commerce and
friendship.

England's stock soared to a point untouched since the
decade following the Armada. Spain and France, peren-
nially at war, opened a spirited bidding for her favour.
For a while the Protector kept both in play, partly because
his council was divided between them, partly to see how
much he could get out of each without becoming involved
in their quarrel, though it seems probable that he had
Spain marked down for the enemy from the beginning. She
was the weaker as well as the more papist; she possessed a

larger and more vulnerable colonial empire for English expansion; and like Harrington, the author of *Oceana*, he believed that England, to be safe and strong, must have room to grow: " You cannot plant an oak in a flower-pot . . . she must have earth for her roots and heaven for her branches." From Cardinal Mazarin, ruler of France during the minority of Louis XIV, he secured an offer to expel Charles II and his partisans and many other valuable considerations, but when he insisted on being recognized as official protector of the unhappy French Protestants, Mazarin naturally jibbed. Feeling sure, however, of an understanding in that quarter whenever he wanted one, Cromwell turned on Spain with the demand that English residents in Spanish ports be accorded freedom for their worship, and English traders free access to Spain's colonial markets. When Philip IV refused, as Philip II had refused the same demands from Elizabeth, he ordered Admiral Penn to the West Indies to open up trade no matter how, though with strict instructions not to implicate his country in a European war—in other words, to do as Drake and Hawkins had done, collect the cost of such a war in advance from Spanish shipping in case the process of collection should goad the King of Spain into declaring it. To be further prepared for that eventuality, the Protector closed a most advantageous bargain with Portugal, eager to recover the independence lost to her greater neighbour eighty years earlier, and sent Blake into the Mediterranean for the present purpose of putting the fear of God into the Barbary pirates, and the ultimate purpose of threatening the Spaniards' long suzerainty over those waters.

Before these missions could be carried out the period of grace allotted him by the Instrument of Government was over. The country, or such part of it as had been rendered legally vocal by the Instrument, had in the course of the

summer chosen the Parliament with which he would henceforth have to share his powers. He could have had little
illusion as to the sort he would get. Restricted as the
franchise was, it would have had to be restricted to the
Army for him to have commanded a majority. His arbitrary changes in so many directions had raised new enmities
and discontents, while eight and a half months had been
altogether inadequate for appeasing the old. To the Levellers, who denounced him as a traitor to " his lords the people
of England ", were now added the Fifth Monarchists, to
whom he had become " the man of sin " for having usurped
the Crown of Christ and palmed off his obscene statutes for
the true Mosaic code. They loved him little better for
having brought his fist down hard on their unrulier members for offences against military discipline and having
cashiered Harrison from the Army. The Republicans hated
him for having done down the Republic, the Presbyterians
for having set up the " foul iniquity " of toleration. The
irreconcilable Royalists carried their dislike so far as to hatch
a plot that spring—the first of many—for his assassination,
which miscarried through the excellence of his secret service.
Largely moved by and entangled with one another through
their respective lunatic fringes, all these various groups
joined in the Levellers' cry for a " free " Parliament as the
short way of getting Cromwell out and, in the case of the
Royalists, getting Charles II in. Though none of them
gathered anything like a majority, all obtained a greater or
lesser number of seats from a propertied electorate terrified
equally of the Army's rule and of its cost. The only important body of opinion not represented in the returns was
that of the mass of the people, who would have liked their
King back but, if that were impossible without bloodshed,
still preferred as second choice a Protector whom they
could at least admire and trust to keep order.

From the very beginning of the session it was evident

that the two branches of the Government were in hopeless disagreement. The Protector wanted to get on with the necessary work of government. The Parliament insisted on going back to inquire into the propriety of the Instrument to which it owed its being. The Protector, though agreeing to the Instrument's revision in detail as need arose, refused to allow any alteration in its fundamentals. But it was precisely those fundamentals—the principle of joint sovereignty and liberty of worship—that the majority of the members would not acknowledge. In vain the Protector reminded them that in order to qualify as a Parliament at all " you . . . must own the authority that called you hither "; in vain tried to divert their attention from the seductions of constitutional theory to the practical task of " healing and settling ". Unheeding, they moved to make the office of Protector elective, to gain control of his council and abolish his veto, to establish an obligatory list of twenty " damnable heresies ". Most serious of all, from the Protector's immediate point of view, was their effort to gain control of the Army in order to attenuate it. Admittedly its cost was terrific and its enrolment—57,000—nearly twice that laid down in the Instrument. But with Scotland disaffected and Ireland still in revolt, the Royalists notoriously arming and the Levellers, together with many Republicans, almost openly ready to join them if they rose—and all of them eagerly watching the dissension between the two halves of the Government for their chance to spring—altogether it seemed an ill-chosen moment to weaken the armed strength of the regime or the nation.

Logically there was much to be said on Parliament's side. Assuming its major premise, that it was the accredited spokesman of the will of the people, its case was unanswerable. The case for democracy is in pure logic always unanswerable. The proposition that the will of the one or the few ought to prevail over the will of the many can only be sustained if into the argument is injected some illogical factor either mystical or empirical or both.

But the Protector was no logician. He was a compound of the visionary and the pragmatic—a type not uncommon amongst English statesmen, including the greatest. To him it was no more possible for men to create a living State than for a State to create living men. Both were the work of God, devised for His purposes, serving one another in so far as they helped to serve Him. That being so, he rejected *a priori* the hypothesis that an enduring and successful State could be predicated upon, or its purposes fulfilled through, a mere numerical count: like John Selden, wittiest of literature's deputies to the Parliaments of Charles I, he could not bring himself to identify the odd man with the Holy Ghost. " What's for their good, not what pleases them," he retorted to the parliamentary democrats—a *credo* which might have been a deliberate paraphrase, succinct and emphatic, of the late martyr to Divine Right's valedictory remark that " liberty . . . is not their having a share in government, that is nothing pertaining to them "

Nevertheless he was characteristically ready, in order to avoid futile bickering, to concede his opponents their " free " Parliament in principle, had he seen any hope of their getting it in practice or making it work if they did. " What is it you really want?" he demanded of Ludlow. " That which we fought for, that the nation might be governed by its own consent," replied the Republican leader. " I am as much for government by consent as any man," returned the Protector, " but where shall we find that consent?" The question was no mere dishonest rhetoric. He had tried, and was to continue trying, to keep parliamentary government alive. But to repose it upon consent meant in the first place collectively improvising machinery, totally unfamiliar yet of warranted fairness and accuracy, for ascertaining consent, and in the second accepting the

grave risk of its registering an unmistakable desire for a
Stuart restoration: in which event either the Civil War
would have to be regarded as cancelled or, more probably,
fought all over again. As things stood, " free " and " Parliament " were terms hardly compatible. Nor could the
Protector accept the premise that the present Parliament
was the authorized spokesman of the people. Whom
exactly did it represent, after all, except the comparatively
minute electorate enfranchised by the very Instrument
which it disdained?

Indeed, rightly or wrongly, he believed that he was
much nearer being the representative of the true popular
will. " The people will prefer their safety to their passions,"
he affirmed with confidence, and, regarding himself as that
most indispensable pillar of the common safety, " a good
constable set to keep the peace of the parish ", irresistibly
moved towards the conclusion that the passions being
released by the prolonged fractiousness of the Commons
brought it within the definition of a lawless assembly. In
Lambeth a madman collected a hysterical crowd by starting
a bonfire into which he flung a Bible, a saddle, and a sword,
proclaiming that these were now the gods of England.
When the Protector's horse bolted, dragging him out of
his carriage and painfully injuring him, there was a stir of
rejoicing in various quarters that looked dangerously like
organized incitement. Signs of political unrest shook the
discipline of both the army and the navy; the London
mob looked like breaking loose as it had against Charles I
in similar conditions. Meanwhile the Protector fretted to
get on with his various tasks at home and abroad. A fortnight before the expiration of the five months fixed by the
Instrument as Parliament's minimum term, he abruptly
summoned it to the Painted Chamber to learn that it was
" not for the profit of these nations, nor fit for the common
and public good, for you to continue here any longer ".

He had no need this time to use force. A slight juggle with dates, reckoning a month as four weeks, the basis of the Army's pay, enabled him to exercise his constitutional right of dissolution before the rising tension might have made force necessary. But in extricating himself from an impossible position he plunged into a curiously anomalous one. His power of making laws by decree had lapsed with Parliament's meeting. Henceforth, unless he convoked another or brazenly disregarded the Instrument, he could only administer, not legislate: a limitation which, by checking the creative, opened up the full coercive energy of his despotism. Not to introduce new reforms but to assimilate the old ones, not to perfect the regime but to preserve it, became the prime object of his endeavours—the policy to which he had tried vainly to win Parliament because he believed that what the country most urgently needed after all those years of turmoil was a respite from disorderly change . . . " healing and settling ", as he called it.

CHAPTER XIX

The Second Protectorate

THAT *would* require force. He knew it and did not shrink from it. To a protest that what he was doing was "against the will of the nation, there will be nine in ten against you", he coolly responded, "Very well; but what if I should disarm the nine and put a sword in the tenth man's hands? Would not that do the business?" Under one of his own ordinances of the previous year empowering him to prosecute as treason conspiracy or evil-speaking against his person and government—a law hitherto not very whole-heartedly enforced, to judge by the picturesque scurrility of his adversaries' language and the acts it provoked—he set up a machinery of repression and espionage at which Henry VIII would have marvelled. In his secretary, an Essex lawyer named Thurloe, he found a director of secret police worthy to stand by the side of Walsingham. With £70,000 a year to spend, the secretary planted his spies in every European court, every Royalist group in Britain or on the Continent, every gathering of disaffected radicals. Risings and assassinations were nipped almost as soon as they had been meditated; a press reduced to one official semi-weekly deprived sedition of all the resources of print. The activities of the Royalists, whom the Protector had tried without success to conciliate, of the Levellers, whom he had long vowed to crush for tampering with the loyalty of the Army, of the Fifth Monarchists, from whom he had parted company with regret, dwindled noticeably under the systematic and inexorable pressure of executions, imprisonments, and transportations, often without trial, to the West Indies. Even Sir Henry Vane, most honoured of Commonwealth republicans, whom Cromwell had tried to entice over with a seat in his Council, went to prison for publishing a forbidden pamphlet. The judges and lawyers sometimes resisted on the ground that the ordinances designating the offences (and thus implicitly the Instrument which authorized them) were invalid, but dismissals and punishments and subsequent references to fresh tribunals generally ended in the sentences being upheld.

To see that the law was administered uniformly and effectively everywhere, the Protector divided the country into twelve military districts over each of which he placed a Major-General. Nominally they were only to command the troops in their jurisdictions, but actually they wielded the powers of a secret police, the ordinary civil police, unofficial tax-collectors and official censors of morals. Thus they served to kill two birds with one stone—the maintenance of the regime and the enforcement of its ethical programme. These duties they performed to the complete satisfaction of their superior, who thought them " more effectual towards the discountenancing of vice and the settling of religion than anything done these fifty years ". The people over whom they ruled felt otherwise. To them the major-generals represented military arrogance at its worst: bullying their former social superiors, breeding distrust of neighbour by neighbour, casting a dismal gloom over the whole land by their interference with popular pleasures, some at least becoming grossly rich through their opportunity for graft at the expense of the wretched Cavaliers. Nevertheless, these Puritan satraps brought order of a sort, not only political but to the brigand-infested highways, and the fact that when local insurrections did break

out the common men composing the militia took up arms
for instead of turning them against the Protectorate, seems
to indicate that on the whole they considered it worth the
price.

All this could be contrived within the law and without a
Parliament. But one thing could not beyond a certain point
—money, though the Protector resorted for it to the same
methods as Charles I. A London merchant named George
Cony, imprisoned for failing to pay a fine imposed on him
by executive order for having previously failed to pay the
customs duty on silk, swore out a writ of *habeas corpus*, at
the hearing of which his counsel urged, like Hampden's in
the ship-money case, that the duty was illegal since it had
not been voted by Parliament: they lost, and being up
against an even more inflexible absolutism than Charles
I's, all three of the appellant's lawyers went to prison until
they retracted, while the Chief Justice who had entertained
their argument was persuaded to resign. But the most
stringent collection of all the revenues to which the Government had any colour of pretence could not meet the expanded obligations which its paternal domestic and aggressive foreign policy imposed upon it. The Protector tried to
woo the tax-payers by reducing—another Elizabethan device
—by a third Parliament's monthly grant towards the military
establishment: that merely left him with the prospect of
an enormous debt to fund. He then, in agreement with the
council of officers, took steps to diminish the cost of the
Army by an all-round decrease in pay and a gradual decrease in numbers through the substitution of a territorial
militia under the major-generals—a reform which en-
hanced his popularity without seriously impairing the
military bulwark of his regime. But it was a process that
could not be carried too far. Penn's expedition to the
West Indies and Blake's to the Mediterranean had turned
out dazzlingly successful—so successful that they defeated

his resolution—as similar exploits had defeated Elizabeth's
—to keep out of a war in Europe. Spain broke off relations;
Cromwell, learning to his regret that the Protestant nations
when summoned to a holy crusade against " Pope, Spaniard
and Devil " preferred " gain to godliness ", turned to France,
with whom he negotiated a highly advantageous offensive
alliance, and girded himself to the necessity of summoning
another Parliament to vote supplies for the navy and for
an expeditionary force for the Spanish Netherlands.

He hoped through the active participation of the major-
generals in the election this time to secure a tractable
majority. He was disappointed: the major-generals antago-
nized more than they intimidated, and the voters, rallying
to the cry of " no courtiers, no swordsmen ", returned a
large proportion of hostile Republicans. By placing guards
at the door and refusing certificates of election, the Government managed one way or another to exclude a hundred
and fifty of them, about a third of the whole. The rest,
with a certain amount of grumbling at so flagrant a breach
of privilege, voted a substantial sum for carrying on the
war.

In other respects, however, they were not so amenable.
They opened a furious attack on the major-generals, concentrating in particular on an extraordinary tax of ten per
cent, known as " the decimation ", on the property of
Royalists. When the Government presented a bill to enact
the tax into a law, they opposed it so vigorously, enlisting
even the support of the Protector's friends and his son-in-
law, that he was compelled to withdraw it. They also
returned to the old theme of heresy tests: on their own
initiative they brought to trial before them and sentenced
to scourging, branding, and hard labour a poor insane
Quaker who fancied himself to have some vague identi-
fication with Christ. In vain the Protector interceded—
he could do nothing since he had consented in the last

Parliament to a limitation on his veto. He tried to stop the proceedings by reminding the House that under the Instrument of Government it possessed no judicial powers, but it ignored him on the tacit assumption that it had inherited all the powers of preceding Parliaments, including the judicial which had belonged to the Lords.

So again there had bobbed up the fundamental enigma which, unless it were satisfactorily answered, threatened the stability of the regime and the peace of England. Was Parliament's authority ultimate or only co-ordinate? Since the Protector, backed by the Army, would not allow it to be ultimate and it would not allow itself to become merely co-ordinate, it was patent that the system set up by the Instrument of Government was unworkable. But was it impossible for human wisdom to devise no system other than a perpetual military despotism or the supremacy of a talking body without an acting head? Obviously it was not. The greater part of English history proved, the original doctrine of the Great Rebellion presupposed, that it was not. The ordinary unlettered peasant could have explained that the enigma was fictitious, that it could be made to disappear simply by invoking the tried and ancient principle of government embodied in a king and a parliament acting together as the King in Parliament. For that solution, however, two conditions were indispensable which had been lacking these many years—the King, and Parliament's voluntary consent. At the beginning of 1657 a determined group in the Commons maintained that the time had come when both could and must be obtained.

The suggestion had already been raised in October of making the Protectorship hereditary. Though it had strong support because of the fear of a Stuart restoration if Cromwell died—and overwork combined with much illness had made an old man of him at fifty-seven—he himself frowned on it, in part owing to the opposition of the Army's

leaders, in part to his belief that surely *this* Parliament
would work out. But the intervening months had again
conjured up the spectre of an ignominious dissolution,
with further discredit to the regime and corresponding
comfort to the Royalists. Their hopes were already taking
the form of incipient revolts on the one hand and a positive
fusillade of attempts on the Protector's life on the other.
Rebellion the Government was well able to cope with, but
a lucky bullet was another matter—if the office were made
hereditary there would no longer exist so high a premium
on procuring the death of its holder. But even that was no
longer a sufficient answer. The office itself had, it was now
abundantly clear, to be transformed into something more
solid than a hasty veneer of respectability for armed usurpation, to rest on something deeper and more rugged than
a paper constitution to which but a tiny fraction of those
whom it affected to govern had given the allegiance of
their minds and hearts. It had somehow to identify itself
with that transcendent constitution composed of a nation's
common memories, habits, and inmost beliefs, and also for
practical purposes to receive a solemn recognition of that
identity from the Parliament with which it would have to
establish an organic harmony if the future was to be spared
the grisly dilemmas of the recent past.

So on 23rd February the Protector's friends and admirers
tabled in the House an " Address and Remonstrance " calling
upon him to accept the Crown according to the ancient
constitution of the realm. The resolution was appended,
for greater popular effect, to a vote of congratulation on
the stunning successes accruing in the war with Spain.

> " With ermine clad and purple let him hold
> A royal sceptre made of Spanish gold,"

exhorted Edmund Waller. The City of London, formerly
so hostile to Cromwell, echoed him: the mercantile middle

classes because they welcomed a return to stability (even though they disliked the war), the lawyers to a true and recognizable constitutional authority. From the country there rolled in a swelling chorus of approval, broken only by the voices of his sworn enemies—but numbering now some of his hitherto staunchest partisans. Those of the Levellers and the Fifth Monarchists, who were almost literally frothing at the mouth, in themselves hardly counted, had they not gone to swell the volume of the Army's, which did.

Not that the Army, speaking through its leaders, objected directly, like the others, to Oliver being King—they had long wanted him to be. But now that it was confronted with all the implications of a final settlement along those lines, it felt a sinking dread. For when the Parliamentarians spoke of the " ancient constitution ", they meant what they said. Their proposal called not only for a king but a House of Lords, consisting of from forty to seventy nominated members, to resume its old function of a judicial and legislative balance-wheel on the House of Commons. Though it left the immediate direction of the armed forces to the Crown, it gave Parliament the ultimate control over them, as well as over policy in general, through its discretionary financial powers and its conceded right to approve or disapprove the Crown's choice and dismissal of ministers. Moreover, in order to command the support of the majority, it set up a uniform test of faith which, though altering little in practice, since it admitted all who believed in the Trinity and the truth of Scripture and excluded only upholders of papistry, prelacy, and the more disorderly forms of originality, was nevertheless in principle a backsliding from the pure dogma of toleration.

The ensuing struggle, inside and outside Parliament, was bitter, the outcome inscrutable: nowhere more so than in Cromwell's own soul. When the council of officers waited upon him on 27th February with their objections,

he rated them angrily for putting their own interests above
those of the country. The Crown, he protested, mattered
to him not at all—it was " a mere feather in the hat ", but
he was tired of the eternal friction and uncertainty; he felt
himself getting old and no longer up to them; the one
thing on earth he craved was a final, peaceful settlement
that would not be called into question over and over again
and require a precarious preservation with all his energies
and the constant putting forth of the Army's strength;
such a settlement the Address and Remonstrance seemed
to offer the best, perhaps the last, hope of attaining in the
circumstances. " You might," he stormed at the Army's
representatives, " have given me a kick in the breech and
turned me going." Instead, he reminded them, they had
used him to ride roughshod over three Parliaments, to try
out a constitution of their own devising, etc., etc. The
Instrument of Government had not worked; that was
unarguable. They were sore, he told them bluntly, because,
having brought this Parliament into being, it had not
turned out to their liking, even though he had expelled the
members they objected to. If they fancied that he would
consent to be their " puppet " in order to destroy it as he
had its predecessors, they were much mistaken. . . . " I
never courted you nor ever will." The scolding had its
effect. After consulting, the officers sent a delegation to say
that the Army was ready to " acquiesce in what he should
think to be for the good of these nations ". On 24th March
the Remonstrance, its name changed to the " Humble
Petition and Advice ", was adopted as an Act of Parliament
by 123 votes to 62. A week later the House, led by the
Speaker, old Lenthall of the Long Parliament, solemnly
laid it before the Protector in the Banqueting House at
Whitehall from whose windows Charles I had stepped to
the scaffold eight years earlier.

Even then his mind was not made up. In a voice trembling with emotion he asked for time to think it over. Reluctantly the members agreed, though several times they pressed him and introduced various changes in the Act to meet his wishes. For weeks he brooded and prayed apart while even his intently watching family and friends knew nothing more than the rumours which ebbed and flowed through an anxiously waiting nation. At times the argument crystallized by Thurloe, that the people "knew their duty to a king and his to them" whereas all else was new and obscure and therefore subject to change, seemed to carry decisive weight, as did the corollary expressed by himself that "Protector" must always signify "sword". At other times he reflected aloud upon the offence that the title of king must give to so many sincere followers who had loved and trusted him; upon how that title, sacred when worn even by a mediocre Stuart, might become a profanity when worn by a Cromwell, simply because in the one was the strain, however diluted, of Plantagenet, Lancaster, and Tudor, and in the other there was not; upon the melancholy and inescapable truth that if, on the contrary, the sanctity adhered, it would separate him for ever from the comrades-in-arms (who had given their consent with their lips but withheld it, as their attitude showed, in their hearts) for the reason stated by the last King, that "a subject and a sovereign are clean different things". On 6th May his intimates reported that he would accept. On 8th May he informed Parliament, assembled in the Banqueting House to hear his answer, that though he approved the Humble Petition and Advice as the basis of a constitutional settlement, including its hereditary clause, "I cannot undertake this government with the title of king". On 25th May the House, with widespread regret and some reproaches, amended the Petition accordingly, with power to name his own heir. What it came to was that he had decided it was wisest to rule as a king without being one.

And it was as a king, with the significant exception that there was no Archbishop of Canterbury to perform the ritual offices of the Apostolic Church, that he was reinstalled in office on 26th June at Westminster Hall. The Speaker draped him in the purple, ermine-lined velvet robe, " being the habit anciently used at the investiture of princes ", laid a Bible on his knees, girt a sword at his side, and placed a golden sceptre in his hands. Enthroned in the Chair of State, he took a solemn oath to defend the Protestant faith and the rights of the three nations under his rule. The trumpets sounded and the people shouted " God Save the Lord Protector ", after which the heralds made their proclamation in the old royal style. Nor was the ceremony the only indication that the practice and magnificence of royalty had been renewed. The Ambassadors of France and Holland, standing on either side of the throne, witnessed that the Powers recognized the advent of a monarch. Embassies came from abroad in all the old massive pageantry to congratulate and to court him. When his son-in-law went on a mission to Louis XIV, he was received not only with the honours due to the envoy of an allied State, but on the footing of a near kinsman to the mightiest king in Europe. His Master of Ceremonies, a former diplomat, reinstated the ancient protocols, his new House of Lords, sixty-odd, including some of the former peers, the ancient hierarchical precedences.

This ceremonial ostentation penetrated little, however, into his private and serious working life. His interviews with ambassadors and other high personages were notably informal, and he remained easy of access to every sort of petitioner, even to slightly unhinged visitors from the wilder religious sects whom he allowed extraordinary licence in addressing and arguing with him. Three times a month he sat in full Council, but for the most part transacted business with small committees or his secretary Thurloe alone. " He would," records the latter, " sometimes be very cheerful with us, and laying aside his greatness he would be exceedingly familiar with us, and by way of diversion would make verses with us, and every one must try his fancy. He commonly called for tobacco, pipes, and a candle, and would now and then take tobacco himself; then he would fall again to his serious and great business."

His household combined regal display with pious simplicity; of the £100,000 a year allotted him for its upkeep, more than a third went in charity. His gentlemen-in-waiting wore for livery grey cloth coats with black velvet collars and silver lace, to which comparative sobriety the red coats and polished metal trappings of his retinue added a bright splash of colour when he rode abroad in state. Many Puritans objected even to this mild grandeur, but the public approved of it " as necessary for the honour of the English nation ". His own clothes as a rule were plain, " rather affecting a negligent than a genteel garb ", except when he had to dress up in all the pomp of the Lord Protector. Though his hospitality was generally reputed to be excellent, he himself kept a very simple diet, " no French quelquechoses ", no fancier drinks than " a very small ale " known as Morning Dew and a light wine prescribed by his physicians.

Until his strength completely failed, he clung to his hunting and hawking, with an occasional change to bowls at Hampton Court. Apart from his sport, his favourite diversion, whether as listener, patron, or practitioner, was music, especially for voice and organ. Once his enthusiasm for a bass singer with a voice " very strong and exceeding trolling " was so great that he caused him to be restored to a post he had lost at Oxford after having " liquored him with sack ". Most of all he enjoyed his music, apparently, in the bosom of his family, where he indulged in glee-singing with lively gusto if not the most perfect sonority.

Through all the varied and strenuous activities of his life he remained very much a family man. His mother, who died in Whitehall Palace in 1554 in her 95th year, he visited daily, no matter what other calls there might be on his time, because the poor old lady, who adored and admired him equally, could, like Napoleon's mother, not believe that all this could last and shivered in terror every time she heard a sound resembling a shot outside until she had seen him again well and whole. Her last known words were, " Dear son, I leave my heart with thee: good-night ". His wife, " Her Highness the Protectress ", was little known to the public. A simple soul, several years older than he, she remained to the last disconcerted by the demands of the station to which God had seen fit to call her, perpetrated social blunders in trying to transform the domestic habits of a lifetime to the requirements of keeping house for the master of three kingdoms, and thereby gained, together with his undiminished if undemonstrative affection, the derision of the Royalists and the jibes of the climbers. Like a very different style of woman, Catherine de Medici, she made a hobby of collecting likenesses of the great of the earth by solicitation, either in person or, in the case of her foreign examples, through the diplomatic corps, of voluntary contributions from the originals.

Of her six surviving children, four daughters and two sons (two other sons had died in early manhood), the girls were admittedly handsome, with fine eyes and upper heads but a trifle heavy in the jaws. All four had a flair for biblical language which usually pleased their father, and for gay clothes and sprightly conversation which occasionally did not. Bridget, or Biddy, the eldest, married first to Henry Ireton and after his death to Charles Fleetwood, two of Cromwell's ablest generals who succeeded him in turn in Ireland, was the most serious, so engrossed with the state of her soul that the Lord Protector himself felt constrained

" to bid her be cheerful and rejoice in the Lord ". Elizabeth, the second and his favourite, was, except for her
unquenchable vitality, almost platitudinously unlike him.
Married to a " debauched ungodly Cavalier ", John, Lord
Claypole, with whom she got on badly, she came very near,
with her flashing curls and " naughty " eyes and chin, her
quick and fearless tongue, her impetuous kindness for the
oppressed and unhappy, to the popular ideal of a princess:
too near in some respects for her adoring father, who for
her benefit once remarked (with a shade of ambiguity),
when asked at a wedding where the wives of the Major-
Generals might be, " I'll warrant you washing their dishes
at home as they used to do ". Though Puritan society disapproved and some of its female members frankly detested
her, there were poets and not a few Royalists who all but
worshipped her: a reason, perhaps, why the latter left her
body in Westminster Abbey when they dug up her father's
and hung it on the gallows at Tyburn. The two younger
daughters, Mary and Frances, were married respectively
to Thomas Bellasyze, Lord Fauconberg, and Robert Rich,
grandson of the Earl of Warwick; their weddings, the one
celebrated at Hampton Court, with a masque by Andrew
Marvell presenting the bride as Cynthia, the groom as
Endymion, and the Protector as Jove, the other at Whitehall
with " 48 violins and much mirth with frolics besides mixt
dancing till 5 of the clock " in the morning, caused grave
offence and consternation amongst the godly. Both women
lived on until well into the eighteenth century, as did their
elder brother Richard, whom his father long distrustfully
suspected of making " pleasure the main business of his
life ", but whom, after the Protectorship became hereditary,
he sensibly apprenticed to the serious tasks of an heir-
apparent, which he performed with dignity and charm.
Equally cautious, though for a different reason, namely a
reluctance to any display of nepotism, was the Protector's

advancement of his younger son Henry, a more gifted and forceful though somewhat unstable character, who, when he finally went to Ireland as Lord Deputy at the end of 1657 as successor to his brother-in-law Fleetwood, exhibited gifts which won him the esteem even of many of the Irish as well as of the Royalists, who permitted him quietly to resign after Richard's abdication in the year after their father's death. He himself died in 1674, and with the death of his great-grandson Oliver in 1821 the male line of the Cromwells ended.

Fourteen months only remained to the Protector after his second installation, to see if this time, at least, he had hit on the right formula for " healing and settling ". By almost every visible criterion it seemed that he had. Those fourteen months were his apotheosis—a troubled apotheosis, draining his energies without respite, but with his power and prestige next thing to superhuman. The Army, purged of its troublesome elements, particularly in the higher ranks, had been reduced from an unruly state within a State into a disciplined and magnificently specialized instrument of the State's will. While at sea the Protector's fleets continued to emulate the Elizabethan tradition, on the Continent his expeditionary force surpassed it. His successes did not, unluckily, bring peace, since in the high sphere of policy his conception was as essentially false as his military execution of it was formidable. His practical aims were too moral, it turned out, for his moral aims to be practical. There was no chance of forming a solid Protestant front, since Protestantism was no longer in any real danger; its exponents were moved rather by considerations of trade than of religion; they feared one another and England's redoubtable ally France more than they did her ailing and factitious enemy Spain; and so, although he gained considerable of the world, the Protector could not arrive at the decisive victory he craved on behalf of its soul.

Nevertheless, by the commonplace and somewhat sordid irony of things, though the crusade he had intrigued for missfired, the purely nationalistic war he had tried to avoid abundantly supplied, despite its terrific cost, its own kind of justification, and its triumphs promised peace always just over the horizon. The second session of Parliament (the first had ended by adjournment after his re-inauguration) provided no more than a fretful little interlude to emphasize his Olympian unassailability. It began on 20th January, 1658, with the hostile members previously excluded again in their places and many of the Protector's supporters withdrawn to the new Upper Chamber. The composition of the House thus adversely altered, it opened a furious attack on the settlement embodied in the Humble Petition and Advice, with particular animosity towards what the Republicans contemptuously called the " other House ". After five days the Protector intervened with a stern warning to drop constitutional controversies and get down to business. Its response was a public agitation in conjunction with the Levellers and the Fifth Monarchists to reduce his powers and a secret intrigue to replace him with Fairfax in command of the Army. At the end of a fortnight he called it before him and dismissed it with the valediction " And let God judge between you and me "—to which the opposition could offer no more effective retort than a loud " Amen ".

He himself did not despair of striking the elusive harmonious balance with another Parliament, but his time was too nearly over to make the trial. A series of family bereavements that spring and summer exhausted his already waning strength. First his daughter Frances lost her young husband after three months of marriage; then Elizabeth her son, his favourite grandchild; and then, after watching at her bedside at Hampton Court through the long-drawn agony of cancer, on 6th August he lost Elizabeth herself.

He collapsed, and though on recovering he told his wife
" I shall not die this bout, I am sure on it ", the reprieve
was short. The very elements seemed to be announcing, as
the ancients would have fancied, an event as prodigious as
the death of a Cæsar. A violent summer reached its climax
on 30th August with the worst storm in a hundred years,
which carried away roofs and steeples, tore up forests by
the roots, and overwhelmed ships at sea. By then, back at
Whitehall, he knew that he was dying. After a moment of
sombre awe—" It is a fearful thing," he told his chaplain,
" to fall into the hands of the living God "—he passed into
the clear serenity of a man weary but reconciled and un-
afraid. " The Lord hath filled me," he said three days
later, " with as much assurance of His pardon and His
love as my soul can hold." Of England, and his work for
it, he seemed to acquire the same growing confidence. On
the day of the great storm he prayed that its people might
be granted " consistency of judgement, one heart and
mutual love . . . and make the name of Christ glorious
in the world ". At the very end, on 3rd September, the
day of Dunbar and Worcester, he murmured almost with
his last breath, " My work is done. God will be with this
people."

Less than two years later a Stuart again reigned at
Westminster. The affable, easy-going Richard proved
inadequate to the task of keeping his Parliament and the
Army from flying at one another's throats as his father had
done; he abdicated, the Army split in two, the stronger
half, under General George Monk, restored the Long
Parliament, expelled it again, resummoned it, dissolved it
for good; finally, with the country on the brink of another
civil war, the young Charles II, conducted by Monk amid
the frantic acclamation of the people, was called back from
exile to his throne. Thus in nineteen months were roughly
recapitulated in reverse order the events of nineteen years,

and all that the man whose corpse they hastened to swing from Tyburn gallows had striven for and accomplished was seemingly undone.

In one, a very important sense, that was true and inevitable. He had tried to erect by force something inaccessible to force—a Commonwealth of God which by its very nature pertains to men's inward hearts alone: like King David—surely one of the aptest parables ever spoken—he found that to the man of violence could not be accorded the building of the Temple. But in another, and by no means trivial sense, he had not failed. One has but to ponder what would have happened had he not been there. For over a hundred and fifty years the governance of England had rested almost constantly, and on the whole in increasing degree, upon the king-post of dictatorship. It had rotted; rebellion pulled it heedlessly away, putting nothing in its place of sufficient strength to support the tottering political structure of the nation, which must surely have collapsed into chaos, with unspeakable consequences, had not the victorious soldier of the rebellion taken the weight on his own shoulders. If often wrong-headed and cruelly hard-handed in defending the threatened fabric, he did at least cherish much of what was historically valuable and lovely in it, and protected it from perhaps fatal damage by bigotry and the ferocity of rival idealisms. He introduced into it some of the beauty of toleration and preserved for it the indispensable coherence of authority: and passed it on certainly not less worthy than he had received it to point his friend Milton's exhortation, " Let not England forget her precedence of teaching the nations how to live ".